Copyr

M000044980

Adobe Acrobat, Kindle, Apple Books, Kobo, B&N, and eBook
Reader January 2021

ISBN 978-0-9898042-9-5

10 9 8 7 6 5 4 3 2 1

Clarke Publishing Group

About the Publisher
500 West 5th Street
Winston Salem, NC 27105
Website: www.clarkepublish.com
Email: hello@clarkepublish.com

GEORGE WEAH

THE DREAM

THE LEGEND

THE RISE TO POWER

The Amazing Journey of an
Enigmatic Leader

Emmanuel Clarke   &

Isaac Vah Tukpah Jr.

Clarke
WE PUBLISH YOUR DREAMS

Emmanuel Clarke

To my family, thank you for making the ultimate sacrifice, especially for time not spent with you all. This book would not have been possible without your support. I love you all!

Isaac Vah Tukpah Jr.

Special thanks to my wife, Natalie, for her total support in this and all endeavors. To my kids, I say thanks for bearing with me and sharing me with this projects. Without your support, the journey to complete this book would not have been possible. THANK YOU!

CONTENTS

7

Acknowledgment

For this book, there are several people and institutions that we would like to thank. Without their timeless efforts and support, it would not have been possible for us to complete this journey.

We would like to thank George Oppong Manneh Weah for the extraordinary and incredible life he has lived thus far. Without your exploits this book would not have been written. The truth is, George Weah already wrote this book by the life he lived. All that we did was to compile it by piecing his life's story together one chapter at a time. Thank you, George!

We would also like to thank a few of the Weah family, relatives, and friends who were generous with their time in sharing information with us about the life of George Weah.

We do not want to forget the following persons and institutions that give us resources through hours of interviews and other means: William Weah Jr., D. Zeogar Wilson, Jerry Massaquoi, Franklin Duodo, Omari Jackson, G. Alvin Jones, Dru Wellington Banna, Wallace Octavius Obey, George Ggodeayee Solo, Joseph F. Robertson, Aaron Davis, Momolu "Monk" Massaquoi, Rodney Scere, J. Emmanuel Z. Bowier, Wortoh Anderson, various coaches, the Daily Observer Newspaper, Inquirer Newspaper, FIFA Magazine, and other print and electronic media in Liberia and worldwide. Thank you for providing us with the treasure trove of information that helped us complete this book by cross checking and piecing together all the facts we gathered.

Authors' Note

The writing contained in this book is based on thorough research from various sources that include, local and international newspapers, FIFA Magazine, football magazines from around the world, hundreds of online media and video footages containing interviews with George Weah, various coaches, family members, teammates, friends, fans, and supporters. Significant information also came from direct authors' interviews with more than 30 close friends and family members of Mr. Weah.

Introduction

George Oppong Manneh Weah is not angry for being raised in the ghetto of Gibraltar, in Clara Town. Weah who is the greatest living African football player; having made a name for himself on football fields around the world and for the country he holds so dearly to his heart, has lived an extraordinary life. Having conquered the football world and scoring one of the biggest goals of his life by winning the presidency of the Republic of Liberia, George Weah's life is fulfilled. Though he is loved by millions of fans and supporters, he's often misunderstood by some of his political critics for fitting as well as failing to fit into their perceptions. There is no doubt that he has come a long way and his story of life which is mixed with pains of poverty, hope and joy, needs to be told. Being a man of lowly birth from a humble background, Weah has carved his name forever in history and on the sands of time. He can humbly tell the world that he is a happy and accomplished man, because he had the support of so many people who helped him reach where he is today. It is because of his football achievements that he has achieved all he has up to this point in his life. Every goal he scored as a player, every football victory he celebrated by running around the full length of a football field and throwing wild hands toward the sky, every coast-to-coast run he ever made during his golden days, was intensely felt at home and around the football world—whether it was his first goal or his one hundredth goal. Football fans worldwide will speak George Oppong Weah's name forever with love because of what he brought to the game of football and to the continent of Africa. He has forever changed the game of African politics. The political establishment on the African Continent will forever weep on his name in their secret corners for having changed the political game—especially the way modern political campaigns are run using celebrity star-power.

Without a shred of doubt, it can be said that King George, as he's widely known by fans of all ages, is happy because he hails from the most beautiful country in the world, Liberia. George Oppong Manneh Weah is a very happy soul because he has shared football pitches, shots, goals, and matches during his blissful sojourn with players like Phillip Kamoh Sayon, James Salinsa Debbah, Marcel Desailly, Roberto Baggio, Pewu Bestman, Abedi Pele of Ghana, Dejan Savicevic, Roger Milla, of Cameroon, and so many other talented football players across the globe. Oppong has lived through the golden years of Liberian football—the Samuel Kanyon Doe era when football unified a divided nation and foot-ballers were seen as national heroes or perhaps, modern day glad-iators. George Weah broke the negative stereotype in Liberia that said, *"Football players were poor street kids that had no future in the development and politics of their country."* In fact, he made many Liberians fall in love with the game. Oppong's passion and his joyful way of playing the game gave the rest of Africa's youth a taste of this wonderful sport that would later make warring factions that were engaged in endless battle during Liberia's wars in the 1990s to lay down their weapons and cheer for their national team, the Lone Star.

This skinny boy who once played with homemade plas-tic bags balled up together while being barefooted on concrete pavements and in fleas infested dirt and muds with determination, moved on to play on the national stage, and with professional ball on some of the most unimaginable and exotic pitches around the world. George Weah has traveled the world, he has met a lot of great and wonderful people from all walks of life— old and young, rich, and poor, prince and kings. Most times, his name opened doors that other people could not open. He is a man who has tran-scended stereotypes and a hereditarily predisposed condition like poverty. George Oppong Weah knows the taste of victory and the agony of defeat; and that is why he keeps his eyes trained on his goals. It was his mindset and his can-do attitude that helped him to conquer poverty. Like a lion that represents strength and fear to its prey and enemies, and with poverty that seemed mighty like an elephant, George Weah used his inner strength and his ingenuity to beat the giant (poverty) at its own game.

He can never forget where he comes from, the slum of Gibraltar, or the teams he played for and many of his teammates on those teams. Oppong's time on the football pitch was very pure and innocent, rough-and-ready in terms of simplicity which was within his grasp without the interference of today's modern technology like Facebook Live, Twitter, Youtube, Instagram all of which have changed everything for us, and the beautiful game of football which will never die in Liberia and in many places around the world. This is the only game besides politics, and singing Mr. Weah will live and die for.

George Weah has more than beat the odds. Rising from the hopeless ghetto of Gibraltar where poverty reigns supreme, he was able to use his raw talents which he'd developed over the years in Vai Town, Clara Town, West Point, the Walker Cinema's football field, the Antoinette Tubman Stadium, the Samuel Kanyon Doe Sports Stadium, and Ahmadou Ahidjo Stadium in Yaounde Cameroon to win international accolades from princes and world leaders for his unsurpassed performances on the lush turf of Stade Louis II in Monaco, Parc des Prince in Paris, San Siro Stadium in Italy, and on many patches around the world. George Weah has come to cherish many of the moments he had shared with coaches, managers, especially Arsene Wenger, the man whom he calls his father away from home.

While many critics of George Weah contend that it was a misstep for the football maestro to have entered politics upon retirement, those who know Mr. Weah believed that he may one day prove his critics wrong when he becomes president of Liberia. Weah on the other hand argues that he did not go to politics; rather, it was politics that came to him so he could stand up for the down-trodden across Liberia as well as make his country what it should be. For the most part, he has never been a student of politics or political science. It happened when he realized that the people of Liberia needed a different kind of leader who was from the young generation that can bring a breath of fresh air into the Executive Mansion on Capitol Hill in Monrovia. Weah understands that to comprehend the nature of the presidency, he had to become one of the people who has been the victim of Liberia's failed political system. Also, he knows that to truly know the nature of the Liberian people's problem, he had to become the president of Liberia who will give his people a listening ear and fight hard to solve the country's many problems. Against those backdrops, he made the bold move by taking a stab at the presidency of his beloved country, Liberia—this didn't turnout the way he had expected in 2005.

Since taking full-time residency in Liberia in 2005 in pursuit of his political agenda, George Weah has been saddened to see his country that has so much potential continually be steered in the wrong and opposite direction by unpatriotic politicians, many of whom preached *"the brown envelope politics of anything goes—withering away the country's resources in different forms and shapes"*. With that revelation, Weah decided in 2005 that he was no longer going to stand on the sideline and allow the only country he knows as his true home to remain what it is. Instead, it is his hope to make his country what it should be because he believes that the Liberian people deserve far better than what they were being given. He didn't want his fellow citizens to continuously struggle by scratching for a living while the country's wealth is exploited by global corporations and corrupt politicians who rather amass wealth for themselves than to seek the country and its people's welfare.

Whether he is successful as a senator or as president, history will judge and remember George in so many ways; it could be for the good, the bad, and the ugly. After the dust of history and time have settled and Liberia and African history are told in its fullness, the name, George Oppong Manneh Weah will be mentioned on the lips of historians and folklorists forever. For those generation who may be around during that time, they will say, *"we walked in the days of King George Oppong Weah, the black diamond of Africa who put Liberia on the map of the football world. I celebrated impossible goals during the golden days of Oppong who brought excitement to the game of football. I was made proud by the great talents and deeds of our greatest football hero when Liberians were labeled as killers and cannibals during the country's civil wars in the 1990s."* Others will say, *"I lived in the days of George Manneh Weah; the only man who introduced disruptive political campaigns in Liberian's body politics by using his celebratory power to change minds and change people's perception of leaders and leadership within a country."* This seemingly quintessential gentleman who openly acquiesces to his many flaws and limitations, will live forever in the hearts of his millions of football fans and supporters locally and across the globe. One indelible mark he has left on the residents of his beloved Clara Town and the larger Liberian society is his audacity to succeed by not allowing poverty to cheat him of his prosperity like it had done to millions of Liberians and billions of people around the world. His name will forever ring on the lips of millions across Liberia and around the world long after he's gone. Whether he is successful as president of Liberia, his rise to political power has forever changed the political landscape in Africa and around the world. Hundreds of celebrities, artists, and athletes around the world will now veer into politics as a new art or sport, just as George Weah has done in his beloved Liberia.

Part I
The Dream

Chapter 1

Early Childhood and Family History

The man known today as George Oppong Forky Klon Jlaleh Gbaku Gbeh Tarpeh Tanyonoh Manneh Weah was born on October 1, 1966, as simply George Weah in Ganta Nimba County, northern Liberia, and not Gibraltar or in Gbi & Doru in Nimba County, as has been asserted by so many people and media outlets. His paternal grand aunty, Emma Klonjlaleh Brown named him 'Manneh' which means "First to come" in his native Kru language. The name "Manneh" was the name of his great, great grandfather who was a Kru Chief in Grand Cess Territory in Southeastern Liberia. Growing up he named himself 'Gbaku Gbeh Manneh'. In fact, George Weah didn't follow the proper traditional Kru naming convention when he adopted his paternal grandmother, Agnes "Gbaku Gbeh Weah's" name. According to the Kru, Bassa, Mano, and Gio tradition, a male child is called by his mother's name before his given name. Therefore, his proper name should have been, "Gbaku Gbeh Tarpeh ne Saywon Monnie Manneh". Using this form of naming standard, it would have reflected the following, Tarpeh which was his father's given name, and Monnie which was his mother's given name both being combined to form his unique name. The "ne" between the two names means "and" in Kru. In English, one would say Gbaku Gbeh Tarpeh and Saywon Monnie's Manneh. But again, George was not the first child for both William Tarpeh Weah Sr., and Hannah Monnie Quiawhea (Quiwey) to have been given the "Manneh" name. Their first child together was Wil-

1

liam T. Weah Jr. His nickname "Oppong" was what young George Weah chose when he played for his community team, Young Brazil. He chose the name because he liked the playing style of former Ghana Black Star defender, Charles Oppong. Charles Oppong also played for Ghanaian first division club Asante Kotoko. The rest of his middle names were given to him by family members and friends at some points in his life. George Weah cherishes these names as was evidenced by his self-references in his inaugural speech of January 22, 2018.

Young George was born through the courtship of William Tarpeh Weah Sr., and his common law wife, Hannah Monnie Quiawhea. Mr. Weah Sr. hailed from the Kru ethnic group from Southeastern Liberia. He was born in 1943 in Sasstown Territory, now Grand Kru County. William T. Weah was humble, quiet, and a loving father to his children. At an early age, young William came down to Monrovia from Sasstown to live with his aunt Emma Klonjlaleh Brown. Emma B or Ma Emma as she was affectionately called by family members and friends. Madam Brown would later go on to raise William's two boys, George Weah, and William Weah Jr. While living with his aunty in Monrovia, William Tarpeh Weah learned auto mechanic as a trade through apprenticeship by hanging around local garages and mechanics. His learned skills would eventually lead him to become one of the few heavy-duty mechanics in the city. After working at various low-level mechanic shops around the city, he later found employment opportunities with prestigious companies like AGROMECO, and LIBTRACO. During those days, it was difficult for Liberians that were not well connected politically to find gainful employment with international companies. Fortunately for Mr. Weah Sr., he found himself lucky to have found work with the Israelite based AGROMECO and Senegalese based LIBTRACO during various times in his career. William Tarpeh Weah passed away on October 7, 1983, just one week after George Weah's 17th birthday.

On the other hand, George Weah's mother, Hannah Monnie Quiawhea the matriarch of the family was born in Gbi & Doru, Nimba County on April 14, 1949. Though she was born "Hannah",

2

over the years, family and friends have always referred to her as "Anna". After many years of trying to correct people of the real pronunciation of her name, she accepted the "Anna" name up until her death on March 18, 2013, in Accra, Ghana. Annah Quiawhea was a homemaker and a businesswoman or petit trader of agricultural products. Ms. Quawhea after dropping out of school and getting pregnant at the age of 13, spent most of her time traveling between Nimba County, Cesto Territory, and Grand Bassa in search of agriculture products to buy and sell to residents of Monrovia.

On many occasions, there has been a lot of misinformation about George Weah's place of birth and his early formative years growing up in Gibraltar, Sasstown, and in other places around Monrovia, and around Liberia. Often, a person's place of birth may not necessarily define or limit them from achieving greatness; this is the case with Georg Weah. While young George may have been born in Ganta Nimba County in northern Liberia and was raised in the ghetto of Gibraltar in the slum community of Clara Town on Bushrod Island in Monrovia, he was able to transcend the odds that were lined up against him—he somehow defeated poverty by using his football talents for the betterment of his children and himself. Though Nimba County is the birthplace of one of the greatest Liberian footballers and political heroes, growing up George Weah knew little to nothing about his place of birth—for he only had a brief stay in Nimba as an infant. Thanks to his young and business focused and adventurous mother who had gone on a family visit in Gbi & Doru during her pregnancy.

According to Weah's birth story, When Anna was in her sixth months with baby George in July of 1966, she took a trip to Gbi & Doru to visit her family. Upon seeing her condition after arriving, her mother advised that she stays with them until she gives birth before returning to Monrovia. Anna reluctantly accepted the suggestion. The days soon turned into weeks, and the weeks turned into months. In the early morning of October 1, 1966, Anna went into labor and was taken in by nurses at Ganta United Methodist Hospital. Following several hours in the hands of doctors, nurses, and midwives, she finally gave birth to her second male child for

William Tarpeh Weah Sr. When news of George's birth reached Weah Sr. in Monrovia, he immediately left Monrovia and rushed to Gbi & Doru to see Anna and the newborn. After spending several days with Anna and the newborn, he had to leave Anna in the hands of her parents and returned to Monrovia for work and to prepare for Anna and the baby's arrival. When Anna and the rest of her family believed that the baby was strong enough for the long journey to Monrovia, she packed up her belongings and the few markets she had bought and headed back home a few weeks before Christmas so they could begin a new chapter in their children's lives.

Up to the time of George's birth, William, and Anna's first child, William Weah Jr or Junior Boy, had been living with Willian Tarpeh Weah's aunt, Madam Emma Klonjlaleh Brown, commonly called Emma B or Ma Emma in Gibraltar due to his poor health condition. Since Anna travelled quite often to conduct business transactions in the various rural counties and territories around Liberia, this was a brilliant idea to have some structure for Junior Boy. She would often take the young baby, Junior along with her on many of these trips. According to family accounts, this brought friction between William Weah Sr. and Anna. Prior to conceiving Junior, Anna had already had a daughter named Margaret Mayoupeh Pennoh at the age of 14 years old. According to a family source, Mr. Jimmy Pennoh who was a thirty-something year-old medical practitioner in Gbi & Doru, had taken advantage of Anna who had gone to seek medical treatment in his place of practice. He sexually manipulated and raped her against her will and got her pregnant. At the time of the rape, she was just 13 years of age. The incident infuriated Anna's parents to the point that they insisted that Mr. Pennoh must marry their daughter for what he had done to her. The issues of statutory rape are highly pervasive in Liberia and in many places across Africa and the world. Often in Liberia, wealthy people in authority, and other well-placed individuals usually use their social status to sexually abuse poor boys and girls in their community. Shamefully, the incident between Anna and Mr. Pennoh is still a common practice in Liberia. While there may be a law against this immoral act against minors, sometimes bringing

4

some of the powerful perpetrators to justice is impossible. The victims' families are often coerced and bribed with little cash or other favors and are asked to remain silenced forever. As for Anna, she was disgusted by the idea of marrying the man who had raped her and impregnated her against her will. Young, innocent, and not being in love with an older man who raped her, Anna ran away from Gbi & Doru to Monrovia with the help of her sister Teetee Konah. It was in Monrovia that she met young and handsome William Tarpeh Weah, who she thought was a Ghanaian and fell in love with. According to a family source, Anna was attracted to Ghanaian men. That union that lasted for less than ten years produced two handsome and outstanding men, William Tarpeh Weah Jr. and George Manneh Weah. William and Anna had a total of 11 children with only George and Jr. (Junior Boy) as the two they both produced. George Weah siblings are as follows (beginning with the male), William Weah Jr. George Weah, Boye (deceased), Clarence, Moses, and Wallo. The female siblings are as follows, Margaret (Maryupleh), Agnes (Gbaku Gbeh), Regina (Wlongbe or Nyon-nohweah), Miatta, Wanita (Dehkewlueh), and Kamah (Youkpeh).

Working as a mechanic in Monrovia during the 1960s and 1970s was like working a minimum job in today's job market in Liberia. Back then the pay was not that good, but it was manageable, especially when high paying auto mechanic jobs were not plentiful in Monrovia. Sadly, street mechanics hardly made $50 a month, but the well-established and well-trained ones working for internationally connected companies made more than $100 a month. Back in the 1960s and 70s, the population in Monrovia was way below two hundred thousand. Back then, few people owned vehicles in Monrovia and across Liberia. Therefore, mechanic jobs were limited—only performed by Mandingoes and other foreigners. William and other mechanics had to compete regularly for these scarce short-term, part-time jobs. At the time of William Weah Jr's birth, his father, William Weah Sr. financial situation was not great, but he could afford to support his child and his girlfriend, who was a very serious-minded businesswoman who was constantly hustling in the interior to make ends meet through subsistence marketing in agricultural products.

In Monrovia, the new baby brought a mixture of joy and tension between William Tarpeh Weah Sr. and his common law wife, Anna Monnie Quiawhea. According family sources, everybody loved the new baby who was warm and welcoming to anyone who wanted to hold him. It is said that, baby George smiled and laughed most of the time, but his beautiful smile would be replaced by frowns and anger. At that time, his presence warmed the one bed-room apartment home William rented in Central Monrovia. Anna's love for William was unquestionable, but there were constant arguments and occasional physical fight over money and infidelity. While Anna accused him of having affairs with other women, William also accused her of having affairs with other men in Monrovia and in those places, she traveled to conduct business transactions. These two love birds were very different from each other in so many ways. For example, Anna was seen by many as a loving, caring, honest in how she dealt with situations, but she was also seen as an arrogant and aggressive woman due to the direct and no-nonsense attitude she had in addressing issues that affected her relationship with her children and others. She was never afraid to express her feelings to anyone who got under her skin and more. On the other hand, William was always seen as a cool, calm, and easy going. He had the look of a movie star and was loved by women because of his handsomeness and his gentlemanly attitude toward people he encountered. Like Anna, he loved his children and wanted to give them those things he never had while growing up as a kid, but his economic situation could not allow him to. The tension that persisted between the couple was way beyond William's dissatisfaction with Anna tagging along baby George everywhere she went just as she had done with Junior when he was still a baby.

When George was still a child, his father, or sometimes Ma Emma would take him and the family on vacation to the land of his ancestors in Sasstown, southeastern Liberia to visit the Weah's clans and other extended family members. Since his first vacation up to the time he became a teenager, George Weah always went to his father's hometown for vacation. He loved the place because of his historical ties to the land, and its beauty. Now as an adult, he can never stop talking about his childhood experience in Sasstown and Kru Coast when he swam in the nearby river or the Atlantic Ocean. George was the favorite child of their father.

Barely five years old, young George Manneh Oppong Weah's world came crumbling down when his parents decided to split and go their separate ways. Too young to understand a man and a woman's relationship, George was permanently placed in the care of his paternal grand aunt in Gibraltar within the Clara Town community on Bushrod Island. Prior to his relocation to Gibraltar, William's aunt, Ma Emma had suggested that young George be placed in her care since his older brother was already living with her due to his constant illness—William Weah Jr. was always ill as a child. According to a family source, whenever George was taken to Gibraltar for a visit to his brother and his grand aunt, he would never want to leave to go back home with his parents. He would often cry to stay with his brother. William too would cry for his little brother to stay with him whenever it was time for them to leave. This back and forth crying between the brothers led Emma B to suggest that the two boys be united to live together. It can therefore be assumed that his relocation and his adjustment within his new home in Gibraltar was very smooth.

Ma Emma, being the kind-hearted soul who had suggested for the boys to be united months earlier, embraced her grandnephews like she had done with Junior Boy years earlier. She soon took over from where Anna left by filling the void in young George's life. George was still a breastfeeding toddler when he was taken to Gibraltar to live. Like most young adults during those days in Liberia, often relying on family support in raising ones' children was a common practice. This ward system helped a lot of families in Liberia. In fact, it is still a common practice in 21st Century Liberia. The pervasive extended family system that is found in many third world countries is a bedrock in the Liberian family system. Often, if a family member could not afford to provide the basic needs of their child, they would send that child to their grandparents or a more established relative to care for the child. While this system worked in Liberia during the early 19th and 20th Centuries, it is being exploited by some unscrupulous family and non-family members. Children are now being used in Liberia as bread winners or sex slaves by their caregivers in many quarters in Monrovia and other places around the country without a flicker of tension from the central government in Monrovia. This form of caregiving is nothing short of child trafficking.

While young George was still being breastfed at the age of two years old and developing many cognitive abilities when he went to live with Ma Emma, he quickly acclimated to his new environment. Family sources said that young George naturally preferred breast milk to any kind of solid food. To accommodate for the breast milk, Ma Emma arranged for few of the trusted women in the community to breast feed her crying grandnephew whenever he craved for breast milk. Growing up in the slums of Clara Town is a challenge all by itself and this adjustment was just the beginning of young George's long way to defying the odds that were stacked up against him. He used adaptation as an inner positive force to transform his life amidst the many negative environmental forces around him in his formative and adult life.

Gibraltar, the neighborhood of Oppong, as George was affectionately called by people while growing up within his community back then, is a community located between Vai Town on the south and Clara Town in the north, on Bushrod Island about two miles outside the capital city of Monrovia. To be more specific, Gibraltar is just an eyeshot away from Downtown Monrovia. The community was built on a reclaimed swampland which is a breeding ground for mosquitoes and other parasitic insects and fleas like jiggers and lice. It is a microcosm within a larger microcosm when one comes to think of it. In Gibraltar, all of Liberia is represented with a speckle of smaller representations of West Africa which includes Ghana, Sierra Leone, Guinea, Nigeria, Ivory Coast, and the list goes on. The community is littered with cluttered shanty tin roof shacks. One can easily say there are more than twenty thousand inhabitants living within the Gibraltar community. Majority of the residents are between the ages of one to sixty-five with more young adults than the elderly.

Gibraltar is a congested ghetto community that is densely populated with thousands of poor people that have big dreams for a better tomorrow. This community was the only place that George Weah knew growing up, and he loved every bit of it. He made quite a few friends and was one of the most hated boys within the community by the time he turned 10 years of age. His grandaunt's home was a shelter for everyone. At Ma Emma's often overcrowded house in Gibraltar, George Manneh Weah was surrounded by loving and joyful people that did not allow their impoverished living conditions to hold them back from smiling and striving to rise out of poverty. Tapping into his grand aunt's positive energy and not allowing the negative energy from some members of the community who saw him as "Good for nothing child" to hold him back, little George had a big dream of his own. To prove his critics wrong, he needed to work extra hard in bringing his dream to reality. But he had no positive role model or a mentor who could guide him to realize that dream that constantly flash before his face. In life, a person cannot aspire to become what they do not see; this was the case with young Oppong Weah. A person's environment has a lot to do with their growth and development. Back then, his only positive role model was the hawkish, but loving woman who he only knew as Ma Emma or Emma B, his paternal grandaunt who possessively watched over his furthering steps like a lioness protecting her young.

Weah's Ma Emma was an illiterate who once sold smoked or jerk fish (also known as dry fish) and vegetable peddler who did not have the financial means to support the dozens of children that lived under her roof. According to family history, Ma Emma moved into the Gibraltar community back in the late 1950s when the place was still occupied by some of its original inhabitants, mainly Kru tribesmen. She moved there from Kru Coast Territory when she was still a teenager. As one of his grand aunt's favorite grandsons, Little George was her tag along child, usually called handbag in Liberia. She carried her "handbag" to many of the tribal and formal functions she attended. He was the apple of Ma Emma's eyes. She did everything she could to protect her little Manneh from some of the vices that were taking place in the community. She kept him grounded in the things of God—taking him to church every Sunday and making sure he attended prayer service at her mini chapel in her overcrowded home. Ma Emma always had special prayers for George's success. Her commitment to God and having service at home had a major impact on young George and it is a practice that he would replicate in his own life as will be seen in later chapters.

George Weah, like most children that are raised by their grandparents, still cherishes the fond memories of the woman who made the difference in his young and adult life. He considers Ma Emma his personal heroine. Besides God, she was the solid rock upon which his foundation was built. She guided him every step of the way during his life from childhood up to his departure from Liberia to Cameroon where his talent on the field took him and provided him the opportunity to conquer the football world. Tough love from Ma Emma helped shape George Weah's discipline and destiny. She would often give him an old-fashioned butt whipping whenever it was necessary because he was a tough cookie to deal with in that rough part of the city. Though he was one of Emma B's favorite children, he was hated in the community because of his hot temper. People openly told him that he would amount to nothing because he misbehaved outside of Ma Emma's home.

At the time of young George's transition to Gibraltar, he was quick to adapt to his environment at that young age; this is something that has continued throughout his life. According to a family source, several weeks and months went by before his mother, Anna made her first visit to her children. To Anna's utmost surprise during her visit, young George had adjusted himself to his new environment. He was now becoming his own person and quickly developing his own resilient personality that would help him defeat the negativities that would show up in his adult life. His adaptive attitude made him to seamlessly blend in with his new environment: getting used to the smell of the overcrowded home, the smell of the community, its unsanitary conditions, the polluted river, the occasional flooding of his neighborhood, and many other tough conditions that modern day slum dwellers in Liberia are faced with. He has always been a product of his environment, constantly adjusting and adapting as things changed.

The astounding thing about young George is that he embraced his community and accepted the way of life with grace and passion, though he was considered a nuisance by some people within the neighborhood. However, he had something deep inside of him that set him apart from the rest of his friends and those living in Ma Emma's home. He had a natural born talent and a natural born leadership ability to motivate others. He also had a burning desire to compete with his older brother, William Weah, Jr. and to be the best at whatever he did. At an early age, he would tell his young friends that there was life beyond Clara Town and the borders of Liberia. With the nurturing of his beloved Emma B, he would turn out to be one of the greatest sons, the slums and ghettos of Clara Town ever produced.

In Gibraltar, Ma Emma's home was the home for everybody that entered her doors. The little house was occupied by at least 18 family members including relatives and strangers who were taken in by Ma Emma. It beats the imagination as to where this throng slept at night. From the outside, the house appeared small, but it contained more than five bedrooms. The older boys had their own rooms while the girls and the younger boys shared rooms at times. There were other renters in the house; especially the shop that was being rented by a Fulani merchant. Whenever the house was crowded with relatives from the village, there were not enough beds for everyone. Many of George's other siblings and relatives like Tarpeh, Teah or Boye (deceased), William Jr. (older brother), Atlas, and sometimes Theresa Wehleh slept on the concrete floor or anywhere they could find on the concrete floor to sleep whenever the house was overcrowded with visitors. Like the rest of the children, George sometimes slept on the hard-concrete floor, usually next to his young aunt, Rebecca Tehpahboe Nagbe who came from the village in 1978 to live with Ma Emma. When he became a professional football player, he invested some money in the home by adding an extension at the back of the house to make it bigger for the ever-growing family members and constant stream of friends and visitors. He also invested in several business-es that he could not sustain. Without any business acumen, George Weah invested in sport apparel store in Liberia, boutique in the Ivory Coast and in other places in West Africa.

Other than Ma Emma, Rebecca was the primary caretak-er in the home and for young George Weah. Since she wasn't in school at the time, she did the cooking and was responsible for fair and equal division of each meal she cooked. Back in the day in Liberia, it was traditional for each person in a home to have their own specific bowl or pan that their share of food was placed in. Rebecca had to walk a tightrope daily trying to ensure that she shared the meals evenly. Feeding the group was a constant struggle for Ma Emma, but she was able to at least put food on the table thrice a day. With about nine boys living in the house, along with some of their friends living with them, feeding such a group was sometimes challenging, but Ma Emma did it without hesitation.

For little George, his share of food was sometimes never enough, but he would always share his grand aunty's food when-ever he came home in the evening from playing football on the local field. Back then, he had a huge appetite when he was growing up—his close friends and family source also confirmed that Weah still has a huge appetite for good food. His favorite food was rice and palm butter. Palm butter is a popular traditional Liberian dish made from the strained juice of palm nuts cooked with beef, fish, chicken, shrimp, crab, pig feet, dried fish, spices, garnishes, and anything else the cook chooses to put in. Palm butter goes well with rice, fufu, dumboy, and other starchy sides. It is also rumored that palm butter is good for lactation.

Whenever he came home from playing football and he had no food to eat or if his little leftover food was insufficient, George would eat a portion of whomever food he found available on the table. For such behavior, young George Weah received a series of personal butt whippings from Ma Emma or any older adult that was available to aid her in disciplining her troop.

As a young boy growing up in Gibraltar, Clara Town,

George was heavily influenced by his immediate surroundings other than Ma Emma who was everything to him. Unbeknown to young George, he went to bed in poverty and woke up in poverty. Like George, many of the people in Gibraltar didn't know that they were very poor. For many of them, as long as they could afford to eat a meal or two daily, they were satisfied with their living conditions. The only time some of the kids, including George and his brother William knew that they were poor was when they met a rich kid from the other side of town, or when they ventured out to the Sinkor, Congo Town and the Paynesville suburbs of Monrovia. Though food at home was not always plentiful due to the large household, they ate every day—sometimes at a friend's house, and other times off the streets from food peddlers that marketed their food in some of the most unhygienic places within the community. As a child growing up, Emma B sternly warned him and members of her household against eating at other people's homes. As for George, he often did not heed this warning because his active lifestyle constantly kept him hungry. He would eat at friends' homes.

In Gibraltar, poverty reigned supreme, and people accepted the life that was created for them. On the contrary, George Weah knew that something was wrong with the life he found he and many of the people living in. This was not the life he dreamt of for himself and his children—he didn't want to live poor and die poor like many of the residents. This circle of life in his Clara Town community took a mental toll on him as a child growing up, especially when his mother and father didn't frequent him as much as he wanted them to. While some of his young friends accepted their living conditions as a fate bestowed upon them due to societal predisposition or family history, he looked at life differently because his grandaunt had already given him the secret recipe for success—hard work, honesty, determination, and good attitude. A secret that set him apart from his older brother and many of his peers in Gibraltar and those he would later play football with at home and overseas.

At the age of ten, George Weah's second favorite pastime was the game of Blay. This is a game that many young boys and girls still play in Monrovia and in many places around the country. In this game, all the players take turns to hide a circular object, "Blay", which is often a thin wire, or a bamboo thread woven into a circle, in a sand mound the players make on the ground. Once the Blay has been secured under the sand mound, the group of players take turns finding it by using a piece of stick or metal and poking into the mound and dragging it outward in whatever direction the player chooses. If no one finds it, and the player who hid the object retrieves it, he or she withdraws from the game. The game continues until the last two players are left and one can successfully hide the blade from his opponent and retrieve it himself. The other players take turns smashing the loser's hand which is laid flat on the top of the sand mound or elevated as the winner chooses. The choice spots on the hand were usually in the very middle of the palm or the fleshy part of the palm near the thumb. Hitting on that fleshy part of the thumb was called "Eating my chicken bone." For the lesser of heart, this usually resulted in tears. The game starts again and continues up to the number of rounds that was agreed upon by the players. The round number is usually the number of hits each player unloads on the losing player's palm. The game usually went ten rounds.

As a young teen, George Oppong Weah also played marble but was never good at it. There were various games of marble, but two popular marble games were usually played by George and his friends—Triangle and Hole in the Ground. He didn't like marble as much as he loved the game of football and singing. The reason why it was not his liking is that Ma Emma never liked it. She always felt that it was a form of gambling because many of the boys who played marble would fight each other at the end of the game like many of the men did on gambling board in the community. George was always in a fight with the other boys whenever he lost to the other players. Marble and Blay both got George's clothes dirty because they were played in the sand, dirt, or on the hard concrete. In combination with football, George always got his pants' bottom ripped in the seat. His grandaunt hated seeing him dirty or with ripped off and tattered clothes. These games were the prime cause of him contracting jiggers in his hands and toes because he was always playing in the dirt, sand, or mud where the jiggers live and hatched their eggs. At times though, he would come home with his pants torn in the rear end after playing in the dirt with his friends in the neighborhood. In Liberia, a kid with busted pants is often referred to as "Johnny Tear Butt". Of course, young George would get an old-school butt whipping whenever Ma Emma caught him with torn pants, torn up shirt or if he was dirty like a "French Cowboy" as she would often say. Ma Emma was a firm disciplinarian—she disciplined everyone and anyone who lived under her roof whenever her house rules were broken.

Chapter 2

Teenage Years

Growing up as a young teen, George Weah was no angel. He made all of the mistakes teens his age living in his community and in many slums areas of Liberia made. He broke many of the rules of his grand aunty, Emma Brown commonly known as Ma Emma by neighbors and Emma B by the children in her house. Young George spent most of his time learning manhood from a few of the men in the neighborhood. He especially spent hundreds of hours learning football skills in Clara Town and on the streets of Monrovia. He was what is described in Liberia as a "Grona Boy" or a "Gbana Pekin" street kid. He was what many westerners would call a street urchin. Being raised in a Christian home by a God's fearing woman, one would think that George Oppong Weah would have turned out to be an easygoing Christian boy. On the contrary, during his teenage years, he never turned out the way Ma Emma wanted him to be—Bible loving, church going, conflict avoiding, and forgiving. He was mostly shaped and hardened by his environment and by the disaffection, ill will and enmity of some of the people within the community.

In his early teenage years, young George never ran away from a fight. He was never afraid to express his views on issues concerning him—this is an inherent trait he got from his mother, Anna. Due to his self-expressiveness and his defensive attitude,

16

many people within the slums of Clara Town labeled him disre-spectful and rude, belligerent, hardheaded, angry, and a youth who was challenging to both young and adults within the area. Whether it was on the football field or at home, he never backed down from a fight even if it was evident that he would not win. On the other hand, his older brother, William Weah Jr., was seen by many com-munity dwellers as easygoing, intelligent, humble, and prone to be more successful than George. These views brought a form of ten-sion and competition between the two brothers. This made young George hungry to be successful. He didn't want the label that had been placed on him to become his reality—he had to prove his critics wrong. At a point during those teenage years, he came to the realization that he either had to be like his older brother William or become better than him. In hounding his own path, young George chose the latter—he chose to be better than his older brother, Wil-liam. He vowed to become better than everyone he would play the game of football within Clara Town and beyond. His competitive attitudes continued into his adulthood.

In his late teenage years while he felt somehow lost due to the lack of positive role models within the community other than his brother, George began to develop his own sense of purpose using football as a vehicle to succeed, remove the label placed on him by people within the community, and to defeat poverty. He saw firsthand the glamorous lifestyle of some of the local players. He witnessed how local women threw themselves at players, and how their names reverberated on local radio stations as well as in newspapers around Monrovia. In beating his own path, he spent more time outside of Ma Emma's ever growing home playing football and hustling for money by collecting scraps metals, empty bottles, and cans from local dump sites to sell to local merchants. He would also collect soda bottles from trash bags and dump piles, wash it clean, and sell it to the neighborhood Fula shopkeepers. To make a lot of money, he would sometimes follow his older brother, William Weah, and some of his friends to the Freeport of Monrovia to hustle (perform Day Boy tasks) by offloading and loading con-tainers and trucks that came into the country by ships from around the world. During those tough times in Gibraltar, George developed the taste of material things that Ma Emma could no longer afford with the limited financial support coming in from his father who was now married and his mother whose petit business could not sustain her own growing family. He used the money from his many hustles to buy clothes, footwear for football and for dressing himself up. He shared some of this little money with some of his family members and with close friends within the neighborhood.

On the other hand, William being the elder brother did not see football as a way out of Gibraltar. Rather, he saw education as a means of escaping the poor conditions he saw all around him. Though God had given him the desire to play football, but he felt that God denied him the skills and talent that he endowed his brother George with. He was never a good football player. His view was totally different from that of his younger brother. In fact, William Weah Jr. and George Weah were the only two children that Hannah and William Tarpeh Weah Sr. had together. Growing up, both boys had divergent views on the path to success. William was the dressy and more flamboyant kind while George was closely watching him, but he kept beating his own path to success on the football fields around Monrovia and Liberia.

To support himself, young George sometimes sold frozen Kool Aid, yogurt (sour milk), popcorn, and doughnut, puff puff (kala) for the Aido family that were among some of the successful merchants within the community. George also washed dishes for businesspeople in the Gibraltar community in exchange for food or sometimes for cash. Outside of the home, he spent more time constantly hustling for money to support himself since he was neither getting regular financial support from his mother nor his father. While some family members referred to him as being greedy and lazy because of his unwillingness to actively participate in doing household chores due to his constant involvement with football and the street, he never stopped doing what he believed was his destiny, even if he got butt whippings. He dedicated his life to the game of football. No matter what was said to Ma Emma about her favorite grandnephew, Manneh, he was her beloved. She believed that no matter how recalcitrant he was, he would one day change and be a good boy—she never stopped praying for him. It was her belief that he would not always be this rude and frisky child most people in the neighborhood know him to be. She was of the belief that he would one day change her life and the lives of others.

Growing up, Gibraltar had an enormous impact on the life of George Oppong Weah as a teenager and as a footballer. It was a place that taught him everything he needed to learn about life, love, humility, football, intuition, long suffering, leadership, honesty, cheating, fighting, how to dream big, and a hope for a better tomorrow for himself and for his country and its people. Gibraltar is a place where George saw poverty wreaking havoc—robbing many people of their dignity and ambition. As a teenager, he sat in the front-row seat and watched the invisible and powerful hands of poverty drain the life out of many of the people within his community, and sometimes himself. Though George had three course meals a day, slept in a warm house that was filled with love, but he was still considered poor by elite Liberians' standards. He saw a neighborhood where grown men and women still lived at home with their elderly parents with no desire or ambition to explore the outside world. He saw men struggling to feed their families. As a teen, he vowed not to grow up and be that way. He was resilient and enduring from an early age all the way into adulthood.

During the days of George Oppong Weah in Clara Town and up to present, many of the dwellers in Gibraltar believed in the superstitious power of witchcraft and wizardry, and African Voodoo and black magic. As is the case with many uneducated people in Liberia and in other places on the African continent, the belief in the paranormal is an open secret. While still a teenager living in the slums of Gibraltar, George Weah and many of his young compatriots were told that nothing out of the ordinary happened without a cause. Everything that ever happened is attributed to the power of black magic or witchcraft. Most times, the religious dimensions were removed from every likely and unlikely event that occurred in Clara Town and Vai Town. For example, if a child who did not know how to swim well went into the nearby Mesurado River and drowned, that incident would be attributed to African

Voodoo or Neegee (underwater ritualists or witches and wizards that are believed to live under many of the rivers in Liberia. The belief of Neegee is found predominantly among the Bassa ethnic group in Liberia). Many dwellers in the Gibraltar community still believe in mystiques that may have rational or scientific explanations in today's modern word. In fact, if a child dies of a very high fever caused by Malaria or Typhoid Fever, the death of that child may be seen as an act of the dark world. Someone within the community would somehow be accused of being the perpetrator for the death of that child. For the accused, a shaman or a witch or a hunter would be brought into the community to investigate the incident. Often, the accused would be found guilty and would subsequently be turned over to the Government of Liberia through the Ministry of Internal Affairs or the Liberian National Police. The system within George Weah's community was quite different from the Salem Witch trials of the late 1600s in Massachusetts where a series of hearings and prosecutions of people accused of witchcraft in colonial Massachusetts between February 1692 and May 1693 were held. More than two hundred people were accused. Thirty were found guilty, nineteen of whom were executed by hanging. But the Gibraltar version was different because it had a long-lasting stigma on the family within the close-knit community.

In Gibraltar, there is an explanation for everything and anything that happens—if a vehicle kills a dog or a cat, if a person stumps their foot while going to visit a neighbor, or if a person is caught cheating on their significant other, those are all the signs of bad luck or evil working against that person who is affected. Due to his religious upbringing, George didn't believe in some of the superstitious things that existed within his community. His grand aunt, Ma Emma had always told him to, "Trust and believe in God no matter what he was going through." Though he was brought up in a Christian home and was taught to believe and trust God the Creator, young George Weah was not a fool; he always avoided things that he believed would jeopardize his safety within the community. He would not swim in the nearby river when the river overflowed its banks. He didn't climb coconut or mango trees like most boys did during the rainy season. While other young boys went out to challenge the government and to loot people's properties during riots, George Weah would not go out on the street when people were protesting the government that had neglected the people in the slums and ghettos of Liberia. He was often afraid of getting in trouble with Emma B for putting himself into harm's way. At age 13, he witnessed massive looting and killing for the first time in Liberia's history. That violent incident which will be elaborated on in the next chapter had a lasting impact on him.

While his God-fearing grand aunty was a well-respected person within the community, she was not shielded from rumors of being a witch herself. Some people within the community believed that she was using the power of the Devil to make her favorite nephew to play well and to be popular on the football fields. There were several incidents in the area when Ma Emma was accused by members of the community for orchestrating the death of family members for George's fame. One of such incidents was when one of George Weah's brothers, Boye, died of a common curable illness in 1987 in Monrovia. A few months later his cousin, Teah (who was popularly called Teah Fokofo due to his footballing skills) got seriously ill and was taken to the village where he died of his illness. This was a time in Gibraltar when George had just become a semi-professional football player and was on his way to France when this incident occurred. The deaths hit Clara Town and several communities very hard as the cause of the illnesses and subsequent deaths were all attributed to witchcraft, Voodoo, or juju attack by some envious people within the community. Others saw the deaths as human sacrifices made by Ma Emma and the Weah family to ensure success for George's football career. This wild-flying rumor was untrue because the Weah family, especially Emma B, was a God-fearing woman who would never hurt a fly. While there exists such a strong belief in the supernatural or paranormal dark power in Liberia and probably all over the world, not every misfortune such as death or accidental drowning and other naturally occurring phenomenon that cannot be explained by science should be attributed to the dark world. Fate should sometimes be blamed for things beyond humans' comprehensions. The situation of believing in the dark world or the paranormal that still exists in

Gibraltar is not an isolated one, the existence of the dark world is a belief common all over Liberia and in most African countries and other underdeveloped countries around the world. Often, an entire generation or a community is unjustly ostracized by people in society for an incident that is easily explainable from the perspective of science or a medical practitioner. But due to the high illiteracy rate found in Liberia, people believe what the illiterate "medicine man" or witch doctor tells them. Now with the proliferation of churches in Gibraltar and all across Liberia, it has gotten worse as pastors and other religious figures often accuse innocent people for the misfortune of their church's members.

One would have thought that having been raised by a God fearing and a devout Christian woman who had her own little church or prayer-chapel within her house, young George would not believe in such preposterous fallacy of the act of witchcraft that he now understands modern science can easily explain. Instead, at a point in time as a teenager, he became an ardent believer in the very existence of witchcraft, voodoo and African juju, and the devil whom every living soul blames for all of humanity's misfortune. As a teen, George sustained a burn that caused him to be hospitalized and moved out of the community for a long period of time. Being considered a very bad and rude little boy by some community dwellers, George's absence brought a sense of relief to some residents that didn't like him. People openly thanked God for the incident and for young George not being in the area to torment them. But everything changed when his burn wound healed, and he returned home to Gibraltar after spending several months away from the only place he loved. Those that thought he wouldn't return were surprised to see him back. When he was informed of some of the neighbors' feelings towards him, he became cautiously cautious with many of the older people within the community. He believed that someone was responsible for the accident—he decided to see every unfriendly adult as a possible suspect. In life, sometimes adversity introduces a man to himself—the incident surely introduced George Oppong Weah to himself. He became a self-guarded and an introverted person for the rest of his life. He became untrusting of many of the adults in the community. At the age of thirteen, he became very cautious of his environment and his interaction with certain individuals within the Gibraltar Community. For the latter, no one can blame the young man because everyone is somehow influenced and nurtured by their environment. Gibraltar itself has a way of beguiling its residents in accepting every and anything she feeds them with. A practice which festers and implodes like rotten avocados left unattended to in the hot tropical African sun for weeks.

Besides the game of football, what kept young George grounded in Gibraltar was the word of God from the Holy Bible and the fear of going to hell if he continued to sin against God. As a "Hell" and "Brimstone" believer, Ma Emma put the fear of God in her grandnephews, and everyone who lived under her roof—but it was not effective most of the time. Some of the children, including Manneh deviated from those precepts of hers. In Gibraltar, Ma Emma's house was the house of prayers. She was the true epitome of faith and hope for many of the people who knew her. Women from everywhere in and out of the community came to the small house to pray and be prayed for by Ma Emma. As for George, if he was not out playing football, hustling by selling food or merchandise for other families within the community, he would be a part of the prayer service. It was during those prayer services at home that young George learned to beat drums, sing praise, and worship songs both in his native Kru dialect and English, read the Old and New Testaments, recite Bible verses, and learned to pray at a very young age. It is believed that before he could learn to read any textbook or secular book, young George's grand aunt had someone to teach him to first read the Holy Bible—though she was not well educated at today's standard. Had he not become a successful football player, George Oppong Weah would most likely have become a pastor, or a local boxer as an uncle of his wanted him to become.

George Oppong Weah's teen years in Gibraltar was a tumultuous one—he often mingled with some of the bad boys within the community to break the laws. He was considered by many of the adults living within the community as a thorn in their sides or as they say in the west, 'pain in the ass'. Had it not been for his stern grand aunty's continuous intervention, George Weah's life would have ended in the ghetto with all the talents he possessed on the football field. George openly acknowledges some of his short-comings like drinking alcohol or smoking Marijuana during his teenage years in the ghetto of Gibraltar. Life in Gibraltar was survival of the fittest for those who did not have any family support or those who were not innovative and adaptable to their environment. Many of the young men in the surrounding areas like the Struggle Community, Terminal Island which is now called Doe Community mostly raised themselves. Many of the teenagers resolved to fishing, street peddling, stealing, and committing other vices as a means of surviving the harsh reality of poverty. Those who could not fight back against the pinches of poverty, died a premature death. But for George, he fought his way out of poverty.

While life was tough back then for many of the residents of Gibraltar, including George, it has gotten harder in present day Monrovia. Between 1960 and 1980 in Gibraltar, the life of many of the residents was marked by extreme poverty and sometimes self-doubts. While growing up in poverty-stricken Gibraltar, George never had any other positive role model besides his grand aunty, Jr. and the football icons' pictures he saw in the magazines he would often tuck in his back pocket and sometimes in his school bag. While his mother Anna continued to be in his life, her financial involvement as a mother was very much inadequate during those years. She never had the financial means of supporting her two children, Junior Boy and George Weah; for she had gone on to mother other children by other men in the country. Conversely, Mr. William Weah Sr. who was a career man, was now married to Mary Gargar (Ma Mary), the daughter of the former Bassa Chief in Sierra Leone. She was the woman who Anna had earlier accused William of cheating on her with. Back then, William provided some financial support for the boys—money to get them in school, buy uniforms, buy food, etc. His growing family also limited his financial support for his two boys living with his grand aunty Emma B. As a good mother and a woman of faith, Ma Emma managed whatever little finance she received from Anna and William Weah Sr. for the support of the children they had taken to her to help raise as well as other children living under her roof. While there have been varieties of media accounts about George Weah's parent's involvement and lack of support in his early and teen-age's life, it should be known that Mr. Weah and Anna remained in the life of George and the other children up to the time George Weah departed Liberia to pursue a semi-professional and professional career in Cameroon and France respectively. William Weah Sr. predeceased Anna, he died on October 7, 1983. According to friends of William Weah Sr., he was one of those fathers who worked behind the scenes for the benefit of his children. Like Anna, he often frequented the Gibraltar community to check on his aunt and the children he had taken into her care. Mr. Weah was so loved by his two boys that he wanted to keep them after he and Anna separated, but could not because he was not fully employed and due to the strong grips of poverty that had entrapped him and many other people in the financially segregated country that only comprised two classes of people, "Rich and Poor".

Like every teenager growing up in the ghetto, George Weah was not shielded from the vices that every boy of his age committed during his days in Clara Town—he was exposed to "The Good, The Bad, and The Ugly. Though he was brought up to do the right things, George oftentimes got in trouble with Ma Emma for following the wrong crowd. To make quick cash he would gamble on joker car boards, play Monrovia's famous three cards gamble game (You take this you win), as well as hang out with the neighborhood street gang at Gibraltar's popular drugs and alcohol joints around Zinc Factory, and Shaolin Temple. Ma Emma hated hearing about George and William or anyone in her household following the neighborhood street boys to swim across the Mesurado River that children from their community and other communities often drowned in. Though he had relatives living in the slums of West Point, Ma Emma didn't like young George going to play football or visiting any of her relatives there without her permission. As a young teen George got various types of punishments including being flogged so many times by Ma Emma or by some other able-bodied relatives with her permission. She most hated hearing about him smoking Marijuana or drinking alcohol. For Ma Emma, her little Manneh was a special boy—she saw him as someone who was pure and uncorrupted no matter how hot tempered, he was to his brother and others at home. Whenever he or any of the other children misbehaved, she would go into her room to pray to God for His intervention into their lives. Whether those prayers worked, only she and God knew.

While these minor infractions were met with swift and firmed disciplinary actions from Ma Emma, she continuously prayed to God for her children and the children under her roof to follow the right path in life and for God to grant them favor before men. As a way of chastising George, Ma Emma would deprive him of the things he loves so dearly—football, leaving the house to go to dancing to neighborhood parties, playing marble, and playing Blay, and Boskini with his friends on their next-door neighbor's unfinished foundation or on the neighborhood football field. All Ma Emma wanted from the children living under in her house was for them to be good citizens and serve the Jehovah God that she worshipped both at home and at Georgia Patten United Methodist Church in on Somali Road in the Johansen community of Monrovia. Unknown to Ma Emma, George was hanging out with Mr. Vamoyan Konneh's children in the Vai Town Community next door. At that time, Mr. Konneh who practiced Islam, was one of the wealthiest Mandingos businessmen in the Vai Town community. His friendship Mr. Konneh's children and his comfort with members of the Mandingo tribe, along with his subsequent education at the Muslim Congress School would eventually lead to George embracing the Islamic faith in 1989 when he was still playing football for AS Monaco in France. Upon his conversion to Islam, he changed his name to Ousmane which was similarly closed to one of his middle names, "Manneh" a name given him by his grandaunt, Emma B. Following the death of his grandaunt during the height of the Liberian Civil War in 1994, he converted back to Christianity having practiced Islam for almost a decade.

Growing up in Gibraltar, Weah was very tall for his young age—from age twelve and up, he towered over most of the boys of his age. His tall and skinny frame caused some of the neighborhood boys and his classmates to nickname him 'Senegalese' while attending C. William Brumskine Elementary School, located on Front Street in Central Monrovia. He was initially home tutored within the community, but Ma Emma wanted the best for her grandnephews and those who lived under her roof. When she thought that he was prepared for regular school, she had his parents enroll him at Daniel E. Howard Elementary School, and later at C. William Brumskine Elementary School was much closer to Gibraltar. At times, George was between both parents, Ma Emma and his grandfather in Sasstown Territory which is now a part of Grand Kru County in Southeastern Liberia. George Weah's migratory behavior caused him to sometimes miss school which caused him to fail and repeat grades. Though she had taken him in as a toddler to raise, Ma Emma was always flexible to allow George and his brother, Junior, to go to any of their parents for school or vacation. In Gibraltar, about a quarter of the boys and girls in the community attended C. William Brumskine Elementary School which was a very good public school in Central Monrovia at the time. Those that did not attend Brumskine went to other public elementary schools like C.D.B. King, Oral M. Horton, Daniel E. Howard, or Monrovia Demonstration Elementary School which was the greatest elementary school in the country at that time.

In the 1970s, life was still a struggle in Gibraltar and in many places around Liberia. There were people living in Gibraltar that could not put their children through school because of the lack of finance, though public schools were said to have been free. Ironically, free education in Liberia at that time was not free because parents had to buy school supplies, uniforms, and pay registration fees to school administrators. If a parent could not afford the basics, their children would stay at home and out of school for that semester or the rest of the school year. For many of the residents of Gibraltar, they are aware of the pitiful reality of slums dwelling— they know that Gibraltar has a very strong hold on many of them. The hard and established fact during the days of George Weah in Gibraltar and up to today is that many of its residents are content with their lives due to several self-inflicted circumstantial beliefs which range from financial curse done to them by witchcraft. Some believe that their economic condition is due to their genetic pre-disposition of poverty—being born in a poor family. While these superstitious beliefs abounded in the community, George never succumbed to the defeatist mindset. His attitude to succeed remained in the game of football, even if he was viewed differently by people within his community or at school.

As a young teen growing up, George was very shy. When in the company of his friends or strangers he often took a backseat, becoming more of a listener than an active participant in their conversations. When other teens discussed girls or sex on the football field, shy George Weah would evade the discussion or walk away from the group to do some self-practice with the football. It was only in his late teens he started warming up to girls and sex. Once he got his first kiss from a community girl who he later fathered a child by, going back to being a shy boy again became irreversibly impossible. He became the girls and women's magnet.

During George's early teen years in elementary school (this will be covered in more details in Chapter 5), he was quite an introvert—he talked only when it was necessary to talk or whenever a teacher asked him a question in class during a class discussion. Even at that, George Weah was never the talking type in school. According to many of his classmates, he was very shy to read out loud in class. Many of his classmates believe that he didn't know how to read well in the fourth, fifth and six grades. He was a quiet teen who made few friends in school and on the football pitch at that time. It was in C. William Brumskine that George Weah's life began to change when he joined some of his schoolmates to play football after school in Central Monrovia or compete in class leagues during the school's annual celebration. Besides playing in many of Monrovia's Around Town Football Tournaments, he also participated in the elementary, junior, and senior high schools' football leagues that took place among schools in the Monrovia Consolidated School Systems, MCSS which was often sponsored by the Ministry of Youth and Sports. It was during the schools' leagues that George Weah who started out as a goalkeeper with his neighborhood teams, began playing as a striker and ultimately became a top goal scorer.

Young George never allowed his early fame to alter his humility. As he played active football within the community and around Monrovia and in other places around Liberia, he still found the time to help Ma Emma by doing his chores at home. He never allowed fame to blind him from staying in contact with his humble beginning—he remained true to himself by remaining a common man. As a rising football star, he always tried to uphold those disciplines that Ma Emma had instilled in him. While sitting at Ma Emma's little market table by the family home selling various types of dry goods, he would sometimes tell her that he would one day build her a better house and buy her a new car. But for Ma Emma, fancy things didn't capture her imagination more than her children, grandnephews, and grandchildren doing the right things. She would often counter young George's future promise of building her a new house or buying her a new car with a statement like, "I don't want a new house or a new car. All I want is for you to have the fear of God within you; and for your life to be blessed." For young George, Emma B, as he sometimes calls her, was the second single most important person in his life with God being the first. He would listen to everything this diminutive loving woman and spiritual giant told him, until the day he decided to embrace the Islamic religion which happened when he was thousands of miles away from Liberia's shore.

According to close friends of his, George Weah didn't see a big difference between Islam and his Christian Religion. The only two key variations he told friends he saw was in their forms of worship and the difference in view about Jesus and the Prophet Mohammed. Other than that, he saw the two religions like fraternal twins that had the same parents and upbringing, but society has come to misunderstand by slicing and dicing them as separate.

As a teenager, George Oppong Weah's life was still constricted by the strong hands of poverty that have robbed many people within his community of their opportunity for prosperity. Often, when a person is poor, they do not recognize it, especially when everyone around them is poor. This was the case with young George, but he incrementally worked his way out of the misery of poverty by using his talent. If one comes to think of it, he was not as poor as many of his friends because his father later had a very good paying job as a heavy-duty auto mechanic. Had his father given him the financial support that he should have, perhaps his life would have been different, and he wouldn't have been that young man in want of so many things. Since opulence was not evidence in his appearance, people only saw him as a poor hungry ghetto boy. But for George, he never saw himself as a poor boy because he grew up among poverty, and ate three times a day. Sometimes the only way he and many of his friends from the ghetto knew that they were poor was when they met a rich person in Central Monrovia or in the suburbs of Monrovia. By the age of thirteen, he began working for people within the community as a means of earning his own money. With his earnings, he bought some of those extra things that neither Ma Emma nor his parents were providing for him—like dress shoes and sneakers, fashionable clothes, sunglasses, colognes, and deodorants. When he was still a teen, he shared clothes with some of his close friends within the community. As a young boy, George Weah loved fashion. In fact, many boys of his age were into fashionable things and some of them wore some of the latest clothes of the era, that is the 1970s and 80s. Sometimes sharing clothes with some of his friends proved very difficult for George Weah because of his tall and slender or skinny frame— the pants were either too short or the shirts were too big for him. Whenever he borrowed pants from a friend who he was taller than, he would alter it to make it fit. To fit the pants, he would remove the hem of the pants and re-hem it to his length. Before returning the pants to its owner, he would then re-hem it in its original form. With shirts, it was difficult to perform the alteration magic and he had to wear them as they were.

In the mid-1980s when a popular Quarter Brogues Shoes that was locally called "College" hit the fashion craze in Monrovia, George Oppong Weah could not afford it initially. He normally borrowed the shoes and clothes from some of his good friends to make his own fashion statement. After being noticed by some of the big football heavyweights and sponsors in Monrovia, young George's life took a positive different turn—he received monetary gifts from many of them. By the end of the early to mid-1980s, he was now able to buy shoes he loved, clothes he wanted, and cologne he desired. In fact, when he became so popular, Lebanese merchants would give him clothes from stores like Elegant which was a popular store on Randall Street in central Monrovia, or La Mode on Broad Street. As his popularity grew, so did the many gifts he received. This became a blessing and a curse because he began to freely give away his clothes and shoes to friends and people he didn't know well. With money he earned from playing football or as stipend for his part time job as a telephone switch-board operator and technician at the Liberia Telecommunications Corporation, LTC, he was able to share with his grand aunt, Ma Emma and used what was left to buy his favorite Giorgio Brutini shoes, and football gear along with fashion sneakers like Nike and British Knight.

Chapter 3

Liberia, the Sweet Land of Liberty

Since independence in 1847, Liberia has attracted many people to her shores. For many of her distance admirers, she had been their envy for so many reasons—the home of freed black slaves, Africa's first independent country, freedom of speech, its abundance in natural resources, its beautiful and peaceful people, its food and cultural diversity, and the birthplace of one of the world's greatest people who has played the game of football, George Oppong Weah. Liberians being considered peaceful people may sound ironic due to a protracted 14 years of civil wars, but the people are peace-loving. Liberia is the oldest independent country in Africa, but she does not often live up to many of the hypes strangers hear or see from afar. Liberia was once referred to as the "Sweet Land of Liberty", and a land of opportunities by many foreigners including Africans, Americans, Arabs, Jews, Asians, and Indians. The small seaport capital city of Monrovia was once the emblem of freedom and hope for black Africa. Today, only grime semblances of her glorious past can be seen from the remnant of what once were. The once beautiful Sweet Land of Liberty is now void of almost everything she once stood for, freedom of speech without fear, honest character of its citizens, prosperity for all, value for human life and for what is right, cleanliness of its capital, love of country and fellow citizens, and enemy of injustice.

No matter how badly the country had been mismanaged, Liberia still has one of the best business environments in the world—a government that is very foreigner-friendly with a low corporate tax rate. For many of the ordinary Liberians, it is a prevalent belief among them that the central government only caters to the social and financial welfare of the rich and powerful, government officials, foreigners and not the common citizens. Prior to George Weah entering politics following a very successful football career, he had always promised to one day create more opportunities for the ordinary Liberians so they too could experience the "Sweet Liberia" that is often talked about, but he went broke upon his retirement from playing professional Football—critics believed he spent it on women, partying and competing with Liberians and Nigerians scammers (Black Money Boys), etc. While the sweetness of Liberia has only been experienced by the privileged few at the very top of the Liberian society due to corruption, kleptocratic and nepotistic governments, the bitter brunt had always been swallowed by the ordinary citizens that make up more than 90% of the country's population. It was by no doubt that George Weah formed a part of that unfortunate demography during his days in Gibraltar, and his days kicking football on jiggles infested sandy fields as a means of survival.

This beautiful country that was founded by former American freed slaves and freed men of color has come a long way since declaring independence on July 26, 1847, which was based on encouragement from the American Colonization Society, ACS. The organization was formed in 1817 by a few philanthropists as well as some racist elements within the U.S. Government for the purpose of forcefully removing freed black slaves from the United States and sending them back to Africa. The ACS began shipping freed slaves and free-born men and women to Liberia in 1820. By 1822, the ACS formed a colony in Liberia, West Africa. Liberia as a nation, has made history around the world and she has had many 'first' moments in her 174 years of statehood. Liberia, commonly called "The Sweet Land of Liberty" was the first nation to declare independence on the African Continent. Liberia was the first country to organize a democratic system of government on the African

Continent. Liberia was the only black founding member of both the League of Nations in 1920 and the United Nations in 1945. Liberia was vehemently opposed to Apartheid which was a system that discriminated against the black race in South Africa. A Liberian woman, Angie Brooks, made history in 1970 as the first African female to be elected as president of the United Nations General Assembly. "King" George Oppong Manneh Weah of Liberia is the only African footballer ever to win three prestigious titles in the game of football: FIFA World Player of the Year (World's Best), BBC African Footballer of the Year (Africa's Best), European Footballer of the Year/Ballon d'Or (Golden Ball), (Europe's Best), all in a single year, 1995. The trifecta, World's Best, Africa's Best, and Europe's Best in the same year will continue to be an honor that Weah will revel in for a while as a replication seems very unlikely.

A country that is rich in natural resources, pristine ecosystem, rich shoreline, and its people, Liberia has so much to offer to the world. Liberia has many beautiful beaches, expansive tropical forest reserves, plant and wildlife diversity, access to deep sea fishing, and a friendly population that is welcoming to foreign guests of all colors and ages. Since the end of the civil war almost two decades ago, hotels, resorts, and adventure tourism have gained a niche in this tiny West African business hub, especially as people are curious to visit areas that were previously inaccessible due to political and social instability in the 1990s and the early 2000s. Hotels and motels have already sprouted up in many parts of Monrovia as well as across the country in order to accommodate the large influx of personnel associated with international organizations and tourists. However, with the exit of the United Nations Military in Liberia (UNMIL), coupled with the Ebola Virus Disease that ravaged Liberia in 2014, the decrease in demand for rubber and iron ore which is Liberia's traditional raw materials of exports, corruption, and mismanagement, the Liberia economy has taken a downturn. Notwithstanding, the country's greatest resource is its youthful population that has the potential to turn the economy around for the better with the advent of technology and the demand of remote workforce from the US.

If you ask any smart or educated demographic of Liberians about the country's greatest asset, you might be told that Liberia's strengths are in its young population that has adopted technology as part of their everyday lives. If these young people think wisely, they will create wealth and power for the next hundred years. What makes Liberia so sweet is its youthful population; about 70% of which are between the ages of 15 to 35, according to the United Nations. With a population of nearly five million people, there is much more to be seen and experienced in this sweet land of freedom that is beloved by George Oppong Weah. Here are some highlights of the beloved things that make Liberia sweet and so beautiful.

Not only is it the home of Africa's greatest footballer, but it is also a country that believes in cultural diversity and religious tolerance. Liberia is one of the few freer countries on the African continent where women are allowed to express their views on social and political issues without fear of retribution from the national or local government. People sometimes openly make fun of the government by saying, "Liberia is so free and sweet to the point that even corrupt officials who embezzled millions of US Dollars in public funds are allowed to walk freely in the streets of Monrovia and are sometimes hailed as national heroes." Most Liberians believe that this culture of impunity brought the Sirleaf's Government under sharp criticism from both international organizations and local rights groups. On the contrary, it is believed that at least few Liberians are honest and have some semblance of moral platitudes.

As a country founded on the premise of liberty, justice, and the pursuit of happiness and religious freedom, Liberians pride themselves on being a group of people that know their basic human rights. Though the justice system in Liberia is currently not the best, but the dual justice systems, traditional and statutory, still deliver the legal needs for all those that seek legal redress from either of those two systems. In Liberia, everyone is equal in the sight of the law, unlike in other African countries where minority rights are trampled upon by those in power and the justice system. While there might not be a perfect system of government in Liberia, the sweet land of liberty, everything is being worked on for now— from education to healthcare, from agriculture to technology, from human rights to, of course, sports.

According to data from the IMF and other international financial institutions, Liberia's economy was one of the best in Africa between 1955 and 1975—making her attractive to foreign investors. The country's friendly business atmosphere saw dozens of direct foreign investments during that period. While the country's economy was thriving, it's middle class was steadily on the decline due to income inequality and political tensions from internal and external forces or stakeholders. These tensions would later escalate into a full-scale carnage in later years with many Liberians including George Weah becoming an indirect victim the stupid of said carnage.

Founded by former American slaves some 174 years ago, Liberia was and is still a foothold of the United States Government in Africa. This is a fact George Oppong Manneh Weah and other Liberian leaders should always remember whether they like it or not. This sweet land of liberty was once used as a place from where the US Government exerted its interests and its sphere of influence in other African countries. While the rest of the countries on the African Continent were feeling the brunt of European colonialism, America's presence or engagement with Liberia helped to bring some credibility to the young and lonely independent nation on the west coast of Africa. Many critics believed that Liberia was a failed experiment of the United States—the country was being used as a dumping ground for freed slaves and other social agitators that were feared by white America in the early to mid-19th Century.

While other countries on the continent struggled for freedom against European colonial powers during the 1950s and 1960s, Liberia enjoyed total freedom from colonialism as she was well over a hundred years old as the only independent state in Africa. Freedom is so prevalent in this tiny state that most Liberians are allowed to express their grievances and constitutional rights without fear of persecution, at least some of the time. Fondly, citizens of neighboring countries and in faraway African nations, often refer to Liberian citizens as self-made lawyers—they can plead their own cases in any court of law. For example, during the 1990 rounds of the country's civil wars, if a Liberian refugee was arrested in the Republic of Guinea or Cote d'Ivoire for an infraction of the law, that person would first be imprisoned without any due process. The stereotypical notion was that nobody could beat a Liberian citizen in a court of law. In Liberia, everyone knows his/her constitutional rights. The curse of Liberians knowing their rights was the price some Liberians paid during their days as war refugees in foreign lands—they were beaten and imprisoned without a due process. On numerous trips in Cote d'Ivoire and Ghana, George Weah had to bail many Liberians out of jails for unjust imprisonment. What many Liberians have come to realize is that people from the "Sweet Land of Liberty" were the envy of some of their neighbors for many reasons—knowing their rights, not being colonized by Europeans, being vocal and expressive, being beautiful and expressing American lifestyle, and among countless other reasons.

When one speaks of Liberia being the "Sweet Land of Liberty", there are other factors that need mentioning other than the people that occupy the land. During the mid-19th Century and the early 20th Century, Liberia was a major producer and exporter of sugar and coffee to the United States and Europe. Some observers think that it is due to the sugar production along the St. Paul River and the large sugar production factor in Maryland County were the reason why the country got its nickname, "Sweet Land of Liberty". Though it was an industry that was controlled by a handful of settlers, it brought tax revenue to the new country—people were employed, and wealth was created from the sugar plantation along the banks of the St. Paul River and later in Maryland County which was formerly known as Maryland in Africa. When the price of sugar fell due to the introduction of beets sugar that was being produced in the Caribbean, plantation owners in Liberia struggled to survive, thereby ending an era of prosperity.

Two major causes that contributed to the collapse of the sugar industry in Liberia were the producers' lack of innovation and their unwillingness to upgrade equipment. These two critical factors sadly brought an end to the sugar economy in the small West African nation. This collapse brought economic hardship to the country in untold numbers of years. While the country was trying to get out of its dire financial nightmare due to the collapse of the once thriving sugar industry, the Firestone Rubber Company in 1925 engaged the government of Liberia through the United States Government for the acquisition of land on the West African shore that would help them compete with their British counterparts that were controlling the world's rubber supply. It was not long after when an agreement was reached in 1926 and the company began operation that year. Firestone was the first international company to have gone to Liberia during the time the country found itself at an historically economic crossroad. Following the entry of Firestone, dozens of other companies came to Liberia. These companies kick-started the Liberian economy in the 20th Century. Some of the companies included the likes of Liberian American Swedish Mining Company (LAMCO), Bong Mining Company, Bomi Hills and many other international companies and banks.

The Liberian government was cheated during the land's negotiation because of a heavy US Government's influence at the signing of the final Firestone Land Purchase Agreement. For many Liberians, the Firestone story is a Cinderella comeback story for the Liberian economy. With the deal, Firestone Rubber Company established the world's largest rubber plantations in Liberia, and it has employed over 10,000 Liberians from all over the country. As previously mentioned, the coming of firestone was heavily influenced by the government of the United States of America in response to the British's rubber monopoly of that era. No matter what or how one may think, the United States Government may sometimes protect her political and commercial interests using multinational corporations as was the case in the Firestone 1 million hectares of land agreement with the government of Liberia back in 1926. In the following decades especially during the 2nd World War, the Government of the United States put in place several military facilities such as the Freeport of Monrovia, and the Roberts International Airport, RIA located a few miles from Firestone Rubber Company. During that same war, the United States Government also set up an ammunition manufacturing plant which later became Exchem in the RIA vicinity. This factory was used to produce munition for US soldiers in their North Africa and the Middle East campaigns against Germany and Italy. For helping the United States of America during the Second World War, many Liberians believe that Liberia should have been a part of the NATO Alliance, though Liberia was in the South Atlantic.

Following the entry of Firestone into the country, various types of companies began pouring in to take their lion share of the sweet-sugar pie from Liberia. Those companies came to Liberia due to an economic growth policy that was initiated by President William V.S. Tubman which he aptly called, "Open Door Policy" (Porte Ouverte) Policy. Companies were very profitable during the first decade of their operations. As a result of this Open-Door Policy which is a period that is often referred to as an era of economic growth and prosperity for the country, Liberia experienced strong economic growth until the price of rubber and iron ore along with other commodities declined worldwide in the mid-1970 to the early 1980s after the 1980 coup that brought Samuel Doe and his PRC junta to power. Throughout the country's times of growth and stability, the Americo-Liberian elites continued controlling the state apparatus tightly, reaping the benefits of the rubber and iron ore contracts and widening the economic and social gaps between wealthy and poor Liberians. This brought a big income disparity between the elites and the majority native population. Between 1931—1980, there was relatively uneasy peace in the country. While the rich elites became richer, the poor became poorer. When one comes to think of the economy and social atmosphere in Liberia at the time, it was President Tubman's Open Door (Porte Ouverte) Policy that created the wide income gaps between rich and poor. During Tubman's era, repressive measures were used to counter any opposition to the Government of Liberia through a comprehensive intelligence network connected to the Central Intelligence Agency.

While this is not a political book, it is noteworthy for some reflection to be made in a book that highlights one of the great sons of Liberia and Africa. As it is a popular belief among older generations of Liberians, and if it is not a known fact to the younger generation that lack the knowledge of the country's history, Liberia has been a beacon of hope and prosperity for many of her sons and daughters, and for many foreigners that had entered her gates. For these reasons, many Liberians who know and understand George Weah's story and struggles do not believe that the story of one of Liberia's trailblazers should be told without mentioning where the country he so loved had been in its 174 plus years of nationhood.

As a synopsis of the country's history, Liberia was first purchased in 1816 by officials of the American Colonization Society, ACS after the abolition of slavery in most northern states in the United States. The ACS was an organization founded by anti-slaves' activists or abolitionists, the U.S. Government, former slaves' owners, religious leaders and other philanthropy organizations. The founding of Liberia was against the backdrop of black-fear in the Americas by former slaves' owners and the United States Government. Many whites feared that the blacks would revolt against them and take over their country which would eventually lead to blacks enslaving whites. With those thoughts in mind, blacks-fearing whites made it their mission to banish formerly enslaved black Africans and those born free from the Americas back to their native Africa. The group, ACS, sent its agents to purchase land in Africa for the relocation or repatriation project. After failing to secure a conducive habitat for its agents in Sierra Leone's Sherbro Island, the ACS's agents sailed down from Sierra Leone to the Grain Coast (which was the name given to Liberia by early Portuguese explorer Pedro de Sintra) and were granted possession of certain parcels of land after an agreement was reached between ACS agents, Robert F. Stockton, Eli Ayres and several local chiefs and kings, King Peter, King George, King Zoda, King Long Peter, King Governor, and King Jimmy. The agreement was mainly for the purchase of Providence Island and areas around Cape Mesurado for the relocation of black Africans from racist America at the time. A few months after the land agreement was concluded, the first batch of African American immigrants were brought into the new settlement on January 1, 1822—it was the second batch of some 16,000 freed slaves and freed born blacks to settle in Liberia. After some 25 years in Liberia along with the establishment of other colonies by American philanthropy organizations like the Mississippi Colonization Society, the Maryland Colonization Society, and many other antislavery groups in the United States, the former slaves that now controlled the various colonies and settlements established by the ACS, united and declared Liberia as an independent republic on July 26, 1847 from the control of the ACS and other impending threats of Europeans' colonization and land grabs on the African Continent. The reason behind the early declaration of independence was primarily to ward off British and French pressures—refusal to pay taxes to the colonial administration and encroachment of Liberia's land—this will be explained in a more vivid detail in the next paragraph.

After declaring itself as an independent nation (which many analysts see as premature), Liberia was predominantly controlled by the former slaves commonly called Americo-Liberian which were a minority group at that time. By the 1850s, Liberia was heavily involved in efforts to end the West African slave trade that had gone on for almost four hundred years. In addition to taking all the necessary steps to protect her territory integrity in the 1870s, the country became heavily indebted to other foreign powers, this included the United States of America which did not recognize Liberia as an independent nation until the mid-1860s. At the time, most of the debts were very difficult to repay as many tax-revenue generating industries had collapsed years early as well as foreign vessels refusing to pay taxes to the young government of Liberia. The debt problem and constitutional issues led to the overthrow of then sitting president, Edward James Roye in 1871. Several years later, conflicts over territorial claims resulted in the loss of large areas of land to the British and French colonial powers in 1885, 1892, and 1919. On the other hand, rivalries between the Europeans that were colonizing West Africa and the interest of the United States helped preserve Liberia's independence during this period of hostile European colonial takeover in Africa and in other places around the world.

By the dawn of the 20th Century, Liberia took a center stage in African political affairs and international politics as it championed Africans' independence and world peace through its participation in organizing the League of Nations in 1920 and the United Nations in 1945. At that time, the country's economy rapidly improved and a selected few indigenous people were integrated into the nation's politics. The period between 1930 and 1975, the income gap between native Liberians and the Americo-Liberians narrowed a little because of the presences of Firestone Rubber Company, Liberia Mining Company, LMC (Bomi Hills Iron Ore), Liberia American-Swedish Minerals Company, LAMCO, and many other companies. While there were significant improvements in the country, there still existed deep-seated tensions or hatred between the natives and descendants of the former slaves. Though native Liberians were integrated into the society through Tubman's Integration and Unification policy, the natives still felt locked out of mainstream Liberian society. Many of them felt discriminated against by the central government in Monrovia due to the lack of opportunities. During this buildup of tension between the two groups, George Weah was born in the Fall of 1966. About a decade later, the tension that existed in the "Sweet Land of Liberty" boiled over into a series of demonstrations and a subsequent U.S. sponsored military takeover by mainly native men of the Armed Forces of Liberia on April 12, 1980. Since that day, the country that was once called "Sweet Land of Liberty" came to be known as the "Bitter Land of Poverty and Anarchy". George Oppong Manneh Weah has glaring memories of some of these eventful things that transformed the country into a hotbed for conflict and brutality within the West African Region.

Chapter 4

Raised by Grand Aunty, Growing Up Poor

From the apex of his success to his entry into Liberia's politics, George Weah never forgot to turn his eyes toward the lower corners of the Liberian society where the downtrodden thrive in poverty and hopelessness—especially having once had a front row seat that allowed him to see and what it means to be poor. When he found success, he remained true to himself and to the words of wisdom from his paternal grandaunt, Emma Forkay Klonjlaleh Brown, who didn't live to see and reap the best fruit of his labor. Being raised by a peace-loving and God-fearing woman can be both a blessing and a curse to both the one being raised and the one doing the raising. It can have its good and bad sides, but it is of no doubt that George Oppong Manneh Weah's grandaunt raised him to be a kindhearted, loving, gentle, hardworking, and a nationalistic man who can represents people from the gutter most and the underserved population of the Liberian society. Though she might not have given as much as she wanted to give back to her country, Liberia, and the people of her hometown in Sasstown, she urged her children and her grandnephews to put Liberia's interests above their individual interests. This philosophy that was instilled in young George would come to be felt by people around him in subsequent years during his adulthood when his country would need him the most.

In the ghetto of Gibraltar with Ma Emma, George Weah grew up in a tin roof shack that was built over a drained mangrove swamp on Bushrod Island a few miles outside of the city center of Monrovia. Life at home for a child and a teenage boy struggling to find his own identity and to survive was nothing compared to what his half dozen children now enjoy today. Growing up in Clara Town, was a constant struggle between illness, hunger, and hopelessness. George Weah has seen what it means to be in abject poverty with no hope for a better future. He knows the quintessential definition of what it means to be a poor ghetto boy or girl. In hindsight, he knows what it means to be denied certain opportunities, to say the least. While his father may have had a good paying job that would have given teen George, his brother Junior Boy, and their only paternal sister a life of less struggle had they all been living with their father, but that was not the case. He was raised amid poverty for a child who would become a household name in Africa, Europe, and the world over. But Ma Emma often told him never to acquiesce to the label that was given to slums dwellers by the urban elites of the Liberian society—once a poor man, always a poor man. Like many poor Liberians, she too had a bigger picture for her children and all the children that live under her roof. Ma Emma wanted her children and family to be good and great members of the Liberian society. She wanted them to do well in life.

When he was still a toddler, Ma Emma soon noticed a peculiar character in the child she named Manneh—he was different from the other children. At a very young age, he loved to kick objects in and around the house. When he learned to walk, George would kick anything his feet came in contact with. He would freely kick cooking utensils, empty milk cans, or homemade football children in the neighborhood played with. He would kick just about anything he felt that looked like football. Unknown to Ma Emma and everyone around him, he was developing his master dribbling and football skills that would one day amaze the entire world. It can never be argued that George Weah learned to play the game of football in the slums of Clara Town while being raised by a stern and loving grandmother figure who made all the difference in the lives of her children, grandchildren, grandnephews, and all the relatives that lived under her roof.

At Ma Emma's house, going to church was a must. From the age of 18 months to his departure from Liberia, George Weah, and his brother, along with all of his cousins, attended church every Sunday whenever he was at home in Gibraltar. As a teenager, he had his shares of chores to perform at home. At Emma B's house, some family members saw young George as a lazy kid. Though he loved to cook when he was a teen, he hated washing dishes and dirty pot. Most times, he would have some of his friends help him do his share of the household chores so he could go out and do what he loved to do—play football. On days when young George wasn't in church or required to help Ma Emma with her home church service, he would gather a few of his neighborhood friends along with his ball and they would run over to Vai Town, Clara Town, LPRC Practice Ground or sometimes they would go to Walker Cinema's Football Field which was a muddy football field in the heart of the capital Monrovia to play football. Many of these fields were about two miles away from Gibraltar where George first learned to play the game.

Raising an army of children, some as young as 24 months while others as old as 25 years and above was not an easy task for a four feet six inches diminutive woman like Ma Emma. She had to play the role of a father and a mother to everyone she was caring for. She was not dissuaded by her living circumstance, but rather believed that what never was, may someday be. She believed that while she was not educated, her children and their children would one day be highly educated. While they were able to eat a three-course meal that may not have been meals fit for kings, queens, or a president, but she believed that her children and their children would one day afford any food that kings, and queens or presidents can afford. There were tough times at Emma B's house. There were times when she could not afford to buy clothes for her grandneph-ews or the grandchildren and the family members that lived with her. Aside from the festive Christmas Holiday when George's par-ents would bring the little money which they had saved the entire year to buy him and his brother, William Weah Jr. clothes and other gifts, George wore the same clothes over and over most times as a kid. He would often wear the same set of school uniform an entire year—but he kept himself clean most of the time. If his school's pants or shirt tore, Ma Emma repaired it herself or would send it off to the local tailor to have it repaired if the tear was beyond her ability. No matter the tough times he went through, George was always determined to do better at what he loved, football.

Ma Emma was not an educated woman, but she was sur-rounded by some schooled relatives. She sometimes sought their help whenever it came to the education of her grandnephews and the children that lived with her. When young George started being homeschooled and up to when he was enrolled at Daniel E How-ard and later, C. William Brumskine Elementary School on Front Street in Central Monrovia, she was involved with his education. She attended most, if not every parent teacher association meeting that was ever held, even if she didn't understand everything that was being said. When he was still young, she would walk him and some of the other children halfway to school at times. She would go over or send one of her educated relatives at the school when young George Weah misbehaved at school and a parent teacher conference was called that needed her presence. Ma Emma was no doubt the positive force and a true heroine in the life of George Oppong Weah.

The Clara Town slum of Gibraltar was somehow a forgot-ten place by the central government situated up on Capitol Hill in Monrovia. But it was people like Ma Emma and thousands of oth-ers like her that kept hope alive in those slums around Monrovia and in many other parts of the country. No wonder King George Oppong Weah, as many of his football supporters call him, gets teary whenever he speaks of her during interviews and speeches. He knows that without his Emma B, he would have never become this larger-than-life figure Liberia and the world have come to know. Ma Emma took her time to train George and all the people living in her household. She was more than a grand aunt to him, and William Weah Jr. also known as Junior Boy. She was like a mother and a grandmother to all the children and everyone who entered her house. It was through her Christian tutelage and firm disciplines that she was able to mold George and the others in one of the worst places in Liberia that was the breeding ground for malaria, jiggers, leprosy, and sometimes raw violence.

Though she's now deceased, Ma Emma will live forever in the hearts of all the children who lived under the roof of her crowded shanty house in Gibraltar. She was always a very prayerful woman who raised her grandnephew to be God-fearing, to have strong moral values and to have good characters. George Weah in his teenage years broke some of these very precepts of Ma Emma. For example, he hung out with the wrong neighborhood boys late at night, he stole rice and other food items from the family house to cook at midnight with the bad boys in the community, he did not wash his dirty clothes on Saturdays as he was instructed to, he constantly got into physical fist fight with his older brother, Jr. when he was told never to fight his brother, he fought other boys in the community, he went to the dump sites to scavenge for empty bottles, cans or other scrap metals to sell in order to buy things he wanted when he was warned by both Ma Emma and his parents against doing such, he swam in the nearby Mesurado River where children often drowned, he played football when he was supposed to be studying his lesson. As a teen, George Weah was a rock-hard-headed young boy. He was a thorn in the side of many of the adults in the community. Beside constantly getting physical with his older brother, both brothers never agreed on anything; even up to this day, both men still argue over little things. In Gibraltar, the more he became recalcitrant, the harder Ma Emma fought back to have him do the right things. For the most part, George's growth and development are a fitting tribute to her teachings by his life's examples people see today, be it good, bad, or ugly. On the contrary, commanding large followers was not what Ma Emma anticipated for her Manneh. She wanted George to be a good and God's fearing boy—he departed from those paths most of the time. When football gave him fame, that part of her training went out of the windows of his life. He became the most famous son of Gibraltar and the only good name the world would attribute to Liberia during her troubled years from the 1990s to the early 2000s.

One profound thing that George Weah has never forgotten while still a teenager living in the slums of Clara Town was Ma Emma's words to him—never forget where you come from, and always learn how to be able not to be a bad person even if people around you are not good. This learned attribute sparked George's humanitarian character he exhibited during his football career in Europe and across Africa especially when Liberia was plunged into civil conflicts in the 1990s. In those troubled days with many Liberians living in the Clara Town community and in various displaced camps needed food and hope, he was the model of giving without a limit. Whether his humanitarian gesture was done with an ulterior motive or not, his goodwill spirit may have sprung from the values instilled in him from this great family matriarch and it may have also been reinforced by his prolonged exposure to poverty and the venoms of society's elites' ill will and enmity toward people from the ghettos and slums in the tiny West African nation that he loves so dearly. Given those backdrops, he has come to believe that giving back to humanity and to the communities of the forgotten as the central theme of his life. He did it so diligently during the Liberian civil crisis that the United Nations called upon him to become one of their Goodwill Ambassadors of Peace.

Whenever he reflects on his days of excruciating hunger, lack of material and financial support from his parents, coupled with a life of punishing poverty that he lived in the ghetto of Gibraltar with his beloved grand aunty, he usually comes to tears. There is something that George Weah remembers about Ma Emma so well, it is her deep faith in the provisioning power of the Jehovah God she always prayed to. No matter how tough things were on Ma Emma, she would always try her best to put food on the table irrespective of how little the food was—her household ate two or three times a day. Being a retired marketer, selling fish and other commodities in the local market was not something that guaranteed continuous income to raise a household of over ten people.

While Clara Town may not fit into the perception of many of the people who know this worldwide figure, George Weah, it was an arbor that gave birth to everything he has become—prestigious leader to his followers, a wealthy man among his peers, and a powerful political leader and a motivator to many poor people at home and across black Africa. Ma Emma just happened to be the custodian of things yet to come—the man whose life would reinvigorate millions of youths within his country, in different African countries, and in faraway places around the world to strive to be better in pulling themselves out of the abyss of poverty by their own bootstrap.

To further dive into the life of George Weah when he lived at Ma Emma's house in Clara Town, Gibraltar, it is no doubt he had a very rough time as a teen growing up. George was a confused young man who didn't find himself earlier in life—this may be typical of most of the young teen boys in Liberia today. According to a family source, he was a lost soul who was always at loggerheads with his brother, Junior Boy and any adult who didn't understand his state of mind. There were times he felt lost especially when there weren't that many positive male role models at home (other than his older brother Junior whom he frustratingly looked up to for direction and fraternal leadership) whose good examples he could epitomize. He bounced around from place to place a lot—sometimes to play football, and other times to fit in with friends. He would often travel with Ma Emma to her hometown in Grand Cess to spend his school vacation with his grandfather who he dearly loved. One can only guess that his constant nomadic lifestyles came about because he was trying to escape the harsh reality of the Gibraltar ghetto—forthcoming chapters will give more details and the names of the more than two dozen places in and around Monrovia as well as out of Liberia where George Weah ever lived. George's fond memories of Grand Cess makes him bubble with mirth whenever he talks about his grandfather and his father's hometown. He always talks about swimming in the nearby river and would sometimes take a trip next door to Grand Cess to visit other relatives and the mysterious rock at the mouth of River Nugba. George Weah is a very good swimmer—he learned to swim in the Stockton Creek and the Mesurado River. Growing up as a teenager in the 1970s and 80s, things were so difficult that Ma Emma sometimes found it impossible to pay George and

49

some of the other children living with her tuition—young George was sometimes sent home from class for school related fees. The money she occasionally received from George's parents, or from the rent money (Ma Emma rented the shop that was attached to her house to a Fulani businessman whom all her children and members of the community affectionately called Jalloh) she got for the shop, and offerings from her prayer chapel as well as good will from relatives and friends was never enough to support the throng. Things were so difficult for George that he barely made it past elementary school, and junior high school—he did a lot of school hopping using football as a means toward a greater end. Without the little help he received from Ma Emma and his parents, completing his primary education would have been impossible.

Though George's early success can be attributed to Ma Emma, but his parents were also somehow involved during his early and teens years while he was still in Gibraltar. Throughout his stay at Ma Emma's house, they were regular faces there. As the story goes, Anna, George's mother made regular stops at the house whenever she had free time from her regular hustle and bustle. Though she had moved on with her life after splitting with her children's father, she made it her duty to continue her maternal role by checking in on her child regularly. As for William T. Weah Sr., he remained in close contact with his aunty, Ma Emma, and his children. While his children were still in Clara Town, Mr. Weah often gave Ma Emma the necessary financial assistance that he could afford for the support of his children. At the time, Mr. Weah was already married to Mary Gargar with his own family—his salary was not sufficient to have supported two households. There was no abandonment as had been speculated for years in the media and in so many side conversations about Ann and William's involvements with their two children living with Emma B. in Clara Town. In Africa, grandparents, abled brothers and sisters or other well-off relatives often play the role of the natural born parents in the life of their relatives' children, grandchildren, nephews, and nieces.

In Gibraltar, Ma Emma lived modestly, even after her grandnephew, George Oppong Weah became a professional football player in Europe. Being a woman of humble upbringing, Ma Emma was never boastful nor were she haughty about her grandnephew's newfound fame. While there had been many speculations about George helping his grandaunt, Ma Emma to sell in the local general market to sell dry goods and vegetables, those speculations are not true—that never happened. When George and William were taken to Gibraltar to live, Ma Emma was no longer selling in the local market as had been reported. She was only conducting a home-based business to support her household. After becoming a professional footballer, she lived in the same house until she was displaced from her family home by the civil war in Liberia during the 1990s. She never accepted Georges' offer to build a new home for her as he had promised years earlier. She maintained a low profile until her death. Ma Emma's modest lifestyle was passed onto her grandnephew, George Manneh Weah—his current homes in Liberia and everywhere he ever lived are evidence of his humbled upbringing. People that do not know his story, often criticize him for not living up to his legendary lifestyle like other world class football players. To his critics, he often asks them a simple human question, "What good does it do for a man of my stature to live in opulence while the rest of my people live in poverty?" As big as he became, he lived simple—he lived a life of simplicity by maintaining the common touch with those that know him and support him.

Ma Emma indeed made the greatest of impact on the young as well as the adult life of George Weah. Though he had lived through the eyes of abject poverty where he would sometimes go to bed hungry or hangout with the local neighborhood gangs at night in the hope of eating whatever the gangs cooked at midnight. George has never forgotten where he comes from and many of the people he walked with (though he has broken a pact with some of them as well as renewed friendship with others). Whether in wealth or in poverty, Weah has remained true to himself because he knows that in prosperity his friends know him, and in adversity, he surely knows who his true friends are. This aspect of human behavior was passed onto him by Ma Emma, the wise old lady who was George's rock and the true wind beneath his wings.

Chapter 5

Early Education: A Rocky Start

Primary and secondary education were not easy journeys for George Weah, just as they were not for many children like him with weak educational foundations growing up in the ghettos of Monrovia as well as in some of the country's remote counties and forgotten places. From childhood to around the age of six, he was mostly homeschooled. As a toddler, young George picked up things that he was being taught, though there were struggles along the way. By age five, he could barely recite the letters of the alphabet and could not count from 1 to 50 without struggles. He also struggled to develop the Ministry of Education's famous "SO SO" phonics and other basic reading skills. Due to a constant interruption from both his father, and mostly his mother who often took him away from Gibraltar to spend time wherever she stayed, impacted his early education. At the age of seven, besides football, books excited young George, especially picture books—he would flip through the pages of books to see pictures of any kind. Once he developed some reading skills in elementary school, his favorite book was "Fun with Our Friends" which had characters such as Sally, Dick, Jane, Spot the dog, and Puff the cat. By age 10, his interest in books diminished a little due to the constant interruption from his parents—when he was away from Gibraltar he read less.

As a student, George had a very rough early education

when he was growing up in Gibraltar. He did not have a solid education foundation like other children that grew in a household with educated parents present. His early tumultuous education experiences were due to his parents' constant fight over the school he should attend or who he should live with. For example, if Hannah, also known as Anna, moved to a new area, she would insist that Oppong and Junior Boy attend that school within that area. Unlike his children that had the option of attending any of the elite schools of their choice, his option was limited to the choices his parents or Ma Emma made for him and his siblings. Ma Emma not being educated—lettered enough to read the Bible, she took the place of Weah's educated father and mother in educating him, his brother Junior Boy, and the other children that lived with her. George Weah first began his early childhood education by being homeschooled by family members. Once Ma Emma realized that young George was fluently having logically good conversations with her and other members of her household around the age of four, she quickly had one of her relatives to begin teaching George his alphabet and numbers. By the summer of 1972, George Weah was enrolled in a public elementary school, Daniel E. Howard on UN Drive in Central Monrovia. He began playing football as soon as he'd learned to walk. Once he began to get the feel of learning, Weah soon took interest in the letter of the alphabet and the popular kindergarten song of that era that he was being taught; "A...B...C...D, E...F...G...H..." Though his cognitive and conversational skills developed very slowly for a child of his age, he later made up for many of his early shortcomings.

Gibraltar in the days of George Weah was like many poor slum communities around the world where many of the poorest of the poor inhabit, is a one-way and one-ticket journey for many of those who dare to enter. Often, it doesn't give many of its people an alternate picture to life, liberty, and success; especially the ones that truly want to defy the normal stereotype about people from the slums and ghettos. For George Weah, there were not that many positive educational forces that inspired him outside of football. His only inspiration came from Ma Emma who only knew how to read the Holy Bible, and sometimes his older brother who was mostly a bluffed boy. Emma B. always encouraged him to focus on education and God as he played football. Like many of the children in Gibraltar that struggle daily for survival, George Weah would have chosen football over education at any time had it not been for Ma Emma's stern stand on him going to school. But in the latter years of his life, Ma Emma's principle of education over football and every other thing would change when the opportunity came for George to make the ultimate choice between the two competing factors in his life, playing professional football or completing high school. As a child going to school, he hardly ate breakfast in the morning before leaving the house for school—sometimes Mom Emma's leftover rice from the previous day wasn't available. Food left over which is often referred to in Liberia as "Cold Bowl" is a lifesaver for many people who cannot afford breakfast which is considered by many people around the world as the most import-ant food of the day. He would sometimes go to school hungry and would return home hungry; that is if the school didn't provide food for the students. As part of the Liberian government's education initiative back in the 1960s and 1970s, every public school provid-ed breakfast and lunch for students. This program, known by many Liberians during those days as the 'Care Food Program', was a partnership between the United States Government and the Minis-try of Education of the Republic of Liberia.

With Ma Emma in George Weah's life, it was education and study first, church second (mainly on Sunday), and football third or the last on his daily to-do list. On the other hand, George Weah managed to blend all three competition priorities very carefully as he perfected his football skills which was his lifelong passion and his only ticket out of the Gibraltar Community in Clara Town. George Weah education took off when his grand aunty along with his parents took him out of his previous elementary schools and enrolled him at C. William Brumskine on Front Street which was formerly known as King Sao Boso Street in Central Monrovia. It was a double coincidence of 'wants' for George Weah to attend a school in pursuit of knowledge on a street named after Liberia's most powerful king when he himself would one day be named King George by his supporters for his great talents on the football

54

field. Unlike the previous schools he attended as a child where he sometimes ate breakfast and lunch, George had to sometimes walk almost five miles to school on an empty stomach—he ate no breakfast at home most mornings. If the school's cafeteria staff didn't prepare breakfast or lunch, he would spend the next five to six hours sitting in class while hungry and learning; and he would then walk the next five miles back home hungry. With such an extreme living and learning condition, no child would learn well or be successful in the classroom, but young George Weah tried his utmost best to learn and excel in school. In fact, school became his best escape from the harsh life in Gibraltar. He made a few friends whom he would follow to go and practice football or do other things that would keep him out of Gibraltar as well as get him into trouble. At school, young George felt liberated for the fact that he saw something positive outside of Gibraltar. Weah saw people that were not poor like many of the people from his neighborhood. He saw that his life would one day change if he got an education as Ma Emma always said or if he became a famous football player. Many of the residents of Monrovia loved the game of football, though some of the society's elites call football players unproductive deviants and street thugs.

As an elementary school student, young George would sometimes go to school and follow his friends to play football after school instead of going home directly after school as instructed by his grand aunty. He would sometimes carry only one notebook to school which he would roll up and tuck in his back pocket. For failing to follow Ma Emma's straight instructions of coming home directly after school or taking care of his books and notebooks, he would get physically punished by Ma Emma or an able relative (one of George's uncles) living in the house who happened to be an amateur boxer. Back in those days and even now, parents, school principals and teachers, caretakers, religious leaders, all believed in corporal punishment as a way of training and disciplining children—children got physical discipline by being spanked. Due to his love of football, Weah preferred being butt whipped for the sake of the game. He would use every opportunity he got to go out with friends and practice football and come home to face whatever consequence that awaited him. What Ma Emma, his uncle, and his young aunt, Rebecca Tehpahboe who was brought down from Sasstown to Monrovia in 1978 and was like a caretaker in the house didn't know back then is that George was trying to harness his skills of football in order to get out of Gibraltar. Therefore, nothing could deter him from pursuing his passion of football. According to family sources, whenever Oppong would come home from school after practicing football all afternoon, his uniform would be dirty with mud and dirty from the muddy fields he played on. After being punished several times for playing in his school's uniform, Weah found a way of evading punishment by practicing without dirtying himself—he would take off his shirt and school's pants before practicing football, often barefooted. He was a little slick teenage boy at that time, but he would always be caught in his shenanigans. If George wanted to do something and found that there was an obstacle in his way, he always found a way around that obstacle. This is a typical strategy used on the football field by highly skilled football players—if a player cannot go through or over an obstacle (often another player or defender) on the patch, that attacking player would find a way to go around that player or defender. In his professional football life, he displayed that skill by flipping the football around any defender that stood in his path and tried to stop him. Once George flipped the ball around that person, he would then run in the opposite direction to meet the football. Even as a popular politician he has used this technique time and again; he just might keep perfecting it throughout his life.

George's grandaunt might not have gone far in school, but she was no fool. Ma Emma had her own standard for all the children that lived under her roof. She never accepted any grade in the seventy percent mark to be considered a passing grade. When she realized young George's grades had dropped when he was still in elementary school due to him not being focused on studying his lessons, she stopped him from playing football. To continue playing the game he so loved, George Weah had to bring his grades up to a comfortable level that Ma Emma saw as a passing mark. For Ma Emma, education was the only way out of the ghetto and not football that was stereotyped by elites as being a sport for street kids and society's failed youth. On the other hand, his brother, William Weah Jr. was considered the smartest and the most likely one to be successful in the Weah's clan. Young George was always warned by his grandaunt with a glaring fact that it was impossible for him to practice football everyday when he had to walk to and from school; from Clara Town to Central Monrovia, study and do homework mostly on an empty stomach. In his little mind, young George thought he was superman to be able to mix school and football on weekdays. In her own simple and finite wisdom, Ma Emma would caution her grandnephew that two things could not occupy the same space unless one is able to pass through the other. Now as an adult and using hindsight, George Weah has seen the wisdom in Ma Emma's words. It can be assumed that he can be a good teacher and an excellent advisor to those young people who want to walk in his footsteps.

George Weah's rocky start in education is not an isolated case. If one looks at today's slum dwellers, especially school going children, life is now tougher than what it used to be some forty-five years ago. Some parents now cannot afford the very basics that would enable them to send their children to a public school due to the lack of employment in Liberia. Even with the proliferation of schools in some of these slum communities in Liberia, some children still do not have access to primary education, let alone access to good food or good sanitation. Abled family members are now unwilling to help less fortunate family members raise their children. Today's children are not willing to go through the tough disciplines their parents went through in the name of acquiring an education. Currently in Liberia, available schools are often overly crowded with many unqualified teachers along with the unavailability of instructional materials for both students and teachers to learn or teach from. It is against this backdrop that George Weah's grandaunt took him out of homeschool and enrolled him at Daniel E. Howard and then, C. William Brumskine Elementary School.

Education for George Weah was not guaranteed when he was growing up. He barely made it through elementary school due to financial constraints coupled with constant migratory living conditions at home. According to the Ministry of Education's policy on public education written more than fifty years ago, education should be free for all. Free and compulsory public education as enshrined in the United Nations Charter on Education is a policy that is preached by the Government of Liberia through the Ministry of Education. Contrary to enforcing free education in all public schools, the Ministry of Education charges parents several fees before enrolling students in schools across the country. Often, many poverty-stricken parents cannot afford these fees. As a result, children whose parents cannot afford the fees are forced to stay out of school during the school year. At times, many of these boys and girls are turned into breadwinners for the family. Many of them living in the rural areas are forced to work on their family's rice farm, get married at an early age, become street sellers or peddlers, become drug dealers, become prostitutes, and many other trades as deemed necessary. For George Weah, he did not have to do those things poor kids all over Liberia and in other third-world countries are doing to get an education or survive—Ma Emma's involvement in his life changed the narrative. Tuition may have come late, but Ma Emma made sure her grandchildren attended school even if she had to appeal to school administrators to give her an extension.

After more than five years of struggling in elementary schools, George Weah graduated from C. William Brumskine in the early 1980s before enrolling and bouncing between several government's run junior high schools in Monrovia—G.W. Gibson and Ellen Mills Scarborough. George bounced between these schools not due to him chasing better academics or a better dream in those institutions. It was merely for the football program; these schools were active participants in the National Public Schools League that was sponsored by the Ministry of Youth and Sports in Monrovia. Barely graduating from junior high school due to being distracted by his passion in football, Weah briefly enrolled at Muslim Congress Junior and Senior High School with a football scholarship in 1983 where his footballing skills became noticeable by a larger audience. He became one of those up-and-coming players that spectators were watching from the sidelines. By the mid-1980s, he had found his purpose in life—football and education. With these two powerful forces pushing him, nothing would stop George Oppong Manneh Weah from achieving his dream, but fate has its own way of altering a person's destiny, especially where there exists no third option that would propel the dreamer to the height that they want to climb. As the saying goes, "you cannot have the best of both worlds." Sometimes, the more a person chases their dream persistently, the more it really becomes a reality for them.

As a player on the Muslim Congress High School team, his talent never went unnoticed. Fellow teammates and coaches took notice of his amazing football dribbling skills. During a school league, he would score goals at will. He would almost dribble the entire playing field's length of the opposing team. What played to his advantage was his height and agility—he was slippery like a catfish in the water. He was about 5'11" in senior high school. He had the leg-span to outrun any average heighted Liberian defender. In Liberia, the average height of most men is 5' feet 5" inches. His playing style and amazing ball control had many high schools scouting him—this made him jump from school to school. After completing several semesters at Muslim Congress, he obtained a full scholarship to attend Wells Hairston High School on Mechlin Street in Central Monrovia. Back then, Wells was known as a school that promoted sports, especially Football, and of course, basketball. At Wells Hairston, Weah exploded on the national scene in the high school foot league that is organized by the Ministry of Youth and Sports and the Ministry of Education. He razzle-dazzled both opponents and spectators at the Antoinette Tubman Stadium with his dribbling and scoring skills that sometimes-made hundreds of fans walk behind him on his way home from playing. In the high schools' league, he was the top scorer for his school's team. As Weah's reputation for scoring and dribbling in the league spread far and wide, so did his urge to be better at what he was being noticed for—he put in extra time perfecting his football skills in local leagues on Clara Town Field, Walker Cinema Field, LPRC Field, Sand Field, New Kru Town and Point Four Fields, Barnesville Filed, and so many other places wherever there existed the opportunity to perfect his skills. Soon, scores of first and second division football clubs began to reach out to him in a bid to have him join their ranks.

It was at Wells Hairston High School that George Oppong Weah began playing for some of the country's elite football clubs. He made his debut at Bong Range United Football Club, which was a team located in Bong Mines, Bong County. The team was sponsored by the Bong Mining Company, a German-owned iron ore mining company. Following a brief stint at Bong Range, he was recruited by Mighty Barrolle Sports Association which was one of the oldest football clubs in the country. All this time, Weah Was still attending Wells Hairston High School in Monrovia. Sometimes football got in the way of his academics—though he was elected secretary of his class, his grades began to fall because of not studying, taking quizzes, tests, and doing his homework. At this point, Weah was not keeping Ma Emma up to date with his grades at school, though at times, he was seen studying with other kids in the community. Sometimes he would not attend classes or take tests especially when he had to travel out of town to play for his club.

Following a brief stint with Mighty Barrolle Sports Association, he crossed over to their archrival, Invincible Eleven (IE) Sport Association in Monrovia. It was with IE that he excelled in football with titles for his school and his club in 1986 and 1987 with back-to-back championships in the Liberia Football Association, LFA first division league. When Weah finally got promoted to the senior class (12th grade) in 1987, he had to drop out of school to pursue his football dream. This move would later come to haunt him as a leading football figure and a political leader for his party and a new generation of Liberian social agitators. It should be noted here that Weah has come a long way—a high school dropout who conquered the football world, later returned to the classroom to obtain his high school diploma, earned a BSc and a Masters', and became a successful disruptive politician in retirement.

Chapter 6

Introduction to Football

Like many poor children living in the Gibraltar slums, George Oppong Weah embraced the game of football from an early age—he heavily involved himself with the game of football as a simple means to his now successful end. Family members that saw him grow often say that George started playing football the moment he learned to walk as a child. What a phenomenon! Growing up in his little enclave of Gibraltar, George had heard names of famous local and international football players like Augustus Mitchell and Benedict Wisseh of Invincible Eleven, Wani Boto, Josiah N. Johnson (JNJ), and Borbor Gaye of Mighty Barrolle, Pele of Brazil, Johan Cruyff of Holland, Papa Kamara from neighboring Guinea and names of countless other great players from around the world and the African Continent. He ultimately made the game his favorite pastime, which ultimately led him to play barefooted, sometimes naked on unpaved dusty and rocky neighborhood pitches in the area whenever he was not at home helping Ma Emma with his share of the household chores or selling Kool Aid, donut, and other provisions for some of the community's merchants from whom he had taken jobs to sell their food products. As a child, young George would kick anything his little feet were able to kick. He would kick things such as empty tin cans, cups, orange husk, and countless other objects he found lying around.

As a young boy, he could not afford to buy a real football with whatever little money Ma Emma would give him for recess. But he and other boys made their own football out of balled up plastics, pieces of rubbers, and clothes to practice the game. For a very long time in Liberia, football was considered a game for abandoned and less fortunate street children who came from the poorest of the poor backgrounds in the capital and around the country. About fifty years ago, most educated parents in Liberia prevented their children from playing the game, let alone befriending a boy or a girl who played football. While this game might seem lucrative in our world today, it was not so in Liberia those days when a small group of elitists controlled more than 95% of the citizens of the country. This was a hard truth for George Weah and many boys of his time—he had no hope of becoming the man who everyone knows him to be today had it not been for the game of football. Not only was it his sheer determination that made him become who he became, it was his attitude that made him become the greatest African football player in the world.

In life, a person's mindset and attitude can make a big difference in their life. The question most people ask is, "Was George Oppong Manneh Weah born a football player or was he made into one of the great football players in the world due to environmental factors?" The answer may vary depending on who you ask, but in Liberia and in many places around the world, the name George Weah is to football as the eye is to seeing objects. This football maestro began playing football as early as he learned to walk as a toddler. As a child, he learned to first play the game shoeless in front of his grand aunty's house. By the age of four, young George was kicking just about anything his feet could come in contact with, empty cans, tennis balls, rubber bottles, bottle caps, just about anything that was kickable for his young feet. Those early formative years of objects kicking, and muscle flexing had a dramatic anatomical effect on the body of young George Weah. Unknown to him and to everyone, these early rock and other objects kicking exercises were shaping his body including his legs, arms, and every fiber of his muscle as well as his anatomy or his entire frame. When he was ten years old, he had already developed tensile strengths and skills in his legs and arms that enabled him to run, jump and leap in the air to headbutt an airborne football. When one comes to think about his formative football years, nobody can really be credited for introducing George Oppong Manneh Weah to the game of football. George Weah's inborn love for the game he saw other children playing attracted him to the game of football. Even as a politician and president (having now been elected), he still plays the game of football on the Alpha Old Timer Football Field in the Rehab Zubah Town Community in Paynesville City outside of Monrovia.

As a young football enthusiast in his Gibraltar neighborhood, he soon formed part of the little boys' football league that was being organized by J. Wortoh Anderson who was also heavily involved with the Liberia Football Association's National League. Back in those days, Mr. Anderson, and others like him used the little league as a platform to spot and sometimes recruit players for other football teams. Young George Weah joined his first football team, Young Brazil at the age of 12. On the team, he played goalie, but he would later choose to play upfront as a striker. After several tryouts in the local football little leagues, he settled for the goalposts—becoming a goalkeeper. As a young goalie, George Oppong Weah was terrific as he became the most sought-after young goalie in the community. It was from between the goalposts that he developed another perspective about the game of football—he saw players' mistakes, goalkeepers' errors, scoring angles, and how to score impossible, but amazing goals. From manning the goalposts, he saw all the errors made by both players and goalies. He saw how easy it was for a player to shoot for a goal and score when he was under pressure from advancing defenders and an attacking goalkeeper. After leaving the goalposts, George Weah developed the keen ability to map out opponents' locations on the field and would create various playing scenarios inside his head on how he would dribble past the opponents to score a goal. By his early teens, young George Weah became the prime goalkeeper for his community teams, Massa Invincible Eleven, aka Massa IE, and later Feh Feh Football Club. With Weah between the goalposts, the team was always sure of victory, though there weren't that many skillful strikers that would score goals like Weah would later come to be known for. He was seen by his many teammates as a natural born versatile football player. Whether he was between the goalposts or leading the attacking force, George Weah had the ability to make fans fall in love with him. When he was in his mid-teen, he was tall, handsome, and shiningly dark as if he had been waxed up like a polished Carbonado that is only found in the Central African Republic and Brazil.

Before transitioning from being a goalkeeper to a goal scoring striker, Weah watched most, if not every football game on television during his days in Liberia. He never missed any world cup match or any European football leagues and the English FA Cup which was then called 'The Road to Wembley' that was shown in their community video club or on ELTV, the country's national television station. While still a goalie, he admired the playing styles of great players like Edson Arantes do Nascimento, also known as King Pele, Frank Beckenbauer, Johan Cruyff, and years later as a striker, Diego Maradona. After perfecting his footballing skills on local football fields, he then combined all four of these professional players' playing and scoring techniques into his own footballing skills. With such a concocted combination, one can only imagine how potent and skillful a player would become if a single player had all the playing qualities and attributes of those great football giants combined into one person. It is of no dispute the reason George Oppong Weah is the greatest living African foot legend ever. Mr. George, as he was referred to in France, embodied the techniques of four of the world's greats. He possessed the strength of Diego Maradona, the agility of King Pele, the attacking and sweeping ability of Frank Beckenbauer, and the artistic feat of Johan Cruyff who wore the famous number 14 jersey for the Dutch national team. Like Cruyff, George Oppong Weah also donned the number 14 jersey for his national team, the Lone Star, and many other clubs he played for. His achievements on the football field in Europe were superbly unsurpassed. No other African player will ever come anywhere close to achieving what George Oppong Weah has achieved—not even in a thousand years will there be any African player like him.

Before transitioning from between the goalposts for one of his first football teams Feh Feh to becoming a striker, George Weah kept having these occurring dreams in which he would see himself playing football in front of large crowd, sometimes in front of thousands of screaming fans and scoring goals; lots of goals— lot of goals that would mesmerize and razzmatazz people in his dream. Perhaps though, it was his destiny being revealed to him by the God whom Ma Emma told him to have faith in. Though an uncle of his who was an amateur boxer in Monrovia wanted him to become a boxer due to his height and wingspan, young George had to follow his destiny and his soul's calling. Weah's dreams of footballing greatness did not come easy—he had to work hard to make it come true. As it is often said, to be great, one must use four things in becoming great: dream, sacrifice, discipline, and commitment. Undoubtedly, George Weah possessed these four secrets to success. Anyone wanting to be successful, need to copy him.

His early days as a football player, perfecting his skills on the muddy Clara Town's field and places he practiced, caused him to sometimes skip Saturday's lunch due to practice or dued to playing in areas' football league. By his early teens, food was not an object for young George because he was eating off the streets or at his friends' homes against Ma Emma's warning. Ma Emma had warned him years early against eating at neighbors' houses. Her warning was not only an effort to protect him from the physical harm of being poisoned by some wicked community member that saw him as an annoyance, but it was for not letting anyone know if she had no food in her house as well as any poor living conditions that may be existing at their home. She didn't want people within the community unfairly gossiping about how she was not feeding her home, though she made sure food was on the table, at least most of the time—even if it was just a Liberian style "Dry Rice". As the proud Kru woman she was, she would never go out on the streets of Monrovia to beg around for arms like some of the unemployed single mothers with dozens of dependents did back in her time. George, knowing these facts about his grandaunt, learned to deal with the harsh situation in his own way—using football as a means to a financial end.

Playing football as a goalkeeper gave young George a better view of the field. According to people who played with him during his early days, he had the canny ability to zoom out of the football field to visualize the layout of his opponents. With a bird's eye view of players and their various positions on the field, he knew exactly where the weakest link on the opposing team was. He knew where the best route to scoring a goal lies after mapping players' relative as well as their absolute locations on the field. George Weah sometimes used an inner boost of testosterone to drive himself to the opposing teams' goalposts as he would weave in and out of players' obstacles as he made his way to putting the ball at the back of the net. During his early days as a goalie for Feh Feh and other local football teams, he had the reputation of sometimes taking the ball from his own eighteen yards box and dribbling past players of opposing teams for a goal. By his early to mid-teens, George Oppong Weah who was now approaching six feet, had developed a passion for playing in the frontline instead of the back as a goalkeeper. Soon, he was recruited as a striker for the area's second division team, Young Survivals Football Club.

In retrospect, Vai Town's football field, West Point's football field, Walker Cinema's football field, Clara Town's football field and the countless other football fields where George Oppong Weah practiced and played in many football tournaments, were all breeding grounds for many of Liberia's football heroes and a home for many football clubs. These football fields were testing grounds for great football players like George Oppong Weah, Joe Nagbe, Philip Kamoh Sayon, Nyennehtu 'Santos Maria' Brown, Anthony Gray, Mealie Freeman, Joka Wlaka, Johnny Grant, Sarkpah Myers Nyensuo (aka "The Rock of Gibraltar or Zig Myers"), Westmore Nagbe, Thomas Freeman ("T Free"), John "Monkey" Brown, David Momo, Garrison Sackor, George Sackor, Wanibo Toe, Borbor Gaye, James Salinsa Debbah, Thomas Kojo, Jonathan Boy-Charles Sogbwe, and several other dozens of top-notch players who made the Liberian national team as well as played for other international clubs around the world. While great players arose from these muddy pitches, only one person rose up and became the greated legend in Liberian football—George Oppong Weah is that player. Some of the most prominent football teams in the Gibraltar area were: Red Eagle, Feh Feh, Young Brazil, Bahjaenekay, and Young Survivors. These teams produced some of the finest and talented football players the country ever saw.

Chapter 7

The Dream of a Ghetto Kid

When George Weah kicked his first object, whether it was an empty can of milk or a tennis ball, this simple act was a sign telling those around him and the world that a legend was in the making. Growing up in the ghetto of Gibraltar, there were not that many choices for George Weah and so many of the children with big dreams to make. As the saying goes, "You cannot become what you do not see". As a young person living in the ghetto, especially a male child, there is not that much one can do to change their circumstances. Often, a person is born in the ghetto, lives their life in the ghetto, grows up in the ghetto, and they may sometimes die in the ghetto. For most people in those environments, the cycle of poverty is a way of life because it is the ghettos that choose many of the children that are born in them. Most ghettos and slums have a stronghold on many of its dwellers. In some instances, only a few of the ghettos' inhabitants are able to escape the iron grips of these uncompromising ghettos found all around the world. On the other hand, if you are a child that is born in the slum or the ghetto and you really, really want to change your destiny, then you need to have one of three things—education, talent, or money. Though the third item is the product of the former two items, you need to possess one of the 'THREES'. No amount of church going or prayers going up to God or Allah can help a person to escape the strong grips of the slums and the ghettos. Escaping the venoms of the ghettos requires hard work and persistence.

Every child has a dream no matter their social, genetic, or economic predisposition. For George Weah, by the age of thirteen, he had created a mental image or dream about who he wanted to be. Aside from dreaming of being a musical artist and a great football player, George Weah wanted to join the United States Military and become a U.S. Marine. Going to the U.S. and becoming a Marine was Oppong's dream growing up as a young boy in Liberia. He did not only love the flashy U.S. Marines' official uniform; he loved the tough disciplines that are instilled in a United States Marine. Young George loves seeing these elite-fighting men in action, mostly in Hollywood movies. As a teenager, he also wanted to be a great football player and a good dancer like John Travolta who he so admired after seeing the 1977 movie "Saturday Night Fever". He was even nicknamed John Travolta by his football friends due to his dribbling and his dance moves whenever he was in possession of the football. In reality, George Weah is a great dancer.

Every night, young George would sit on the broken blocks of his neighbor's unfinished foundation opposite Ma Emma's house and stare at the stars above and thousands of thoughts would race through his mind. Knowing the situation in his Gibraltar neighborhood, he didn't want to remain in that community forever. But how could he escape the painful life when his birth parents couldn't afford to provide for him and the almost one dozen children they had in total. Sometimes whenever he was playing football on the neighborhood's field and saw a plane flying overhead, he would stop in his tracks and stare intently at the floating object above. "I will one day sit in a plane", he would tell himself or some of his friends. Whenever he felt the need to tell these friends his dream of flying in a plane, many of them would only laugh at him and tell him how impossible it is for him to fly on a plane. Some of his young friends would ask him questions such as, "Who will put your poor ass on an airplane? Do you even have money to buy a plane ticket or to fix a passport for your poor ass to use?" He would confidently tell them that he would one day fly on a plane or own one.

Most slums and ghettos communities in Africa are not the most desirable places for a child with high aspiration to be. Often, only children that are truly ambitious have always found their way out of the ghettos, either using arts, education, innovations, and sometimes through sports—just like George Oppong Weah, the skinny black kid from Gibraltar did using his tremendous football talent more than thirty years ago. On the pragmatic side of the "Born in the ghetto and die in the ghetto," assertion that most people make today in connection with George's "From rags to riches" story, what if a person born in the ghetto or slum did not possess any talent like George Weah? Can one say then that they are doomed forever? Let people not be too quick to judge others by using the "George Weah's standard" for success and escape from poverty. Though George Weah had developed his footballing skills at an early age, he wasn't automatically destined to be this larger-than-life personality Liberia and the world now know him to be due to that footballing choice and many other choices he made along the way. For him, there were many humps and bumps on the road to his success. He had to battle several forces to get where he is today. In fact, he was not considered by many people within his community or in his own household to become successful in society—William Weah Jr. was seen as the most likely to become the most successful person from Emma B's house. The fact that is worth knowing is that the ghetto had chosen George Weah way before his birth because of family predisposition. But George dreamt big, and he chose football and success as means of getting out of Gibraltar. In order to attract the success dreamt of, he had chosen and dreamt of, he had to break away from several negative influences and habits so he could harness his skills into a craft that would ultimately make him marketable in order to live the life he now lives. As an athlete, he had to quit smoking marijuana, drinking liquor, gambling, and following the wrong friends that were going nowhere and wanted him to remain right where they were. As a teen, George Weah recognized earlier enough that if he didn't make an adjustment to his attitude early enough, he was going to end up like the rest of the unprogressive boys and adults that lived in his Gibraltar community, many of whom were still living with their parents, and other relatives.

With George Weah, dwelling among shipwrecked dreams and losing himself in wishful thinking was not the solution to the tribulations brought upon them by those that rule over his country. Identifying cracks and apprehending the defaults in his life was essential for him to find a way to get out of the ghetto and to start a search for a new haven that only he could see beyond the borders of Liberia. He didn't like the way people cherish the ghetto, as if it's some royal palace or kingdom. He also didn't like the way people treated each other within the Clara Town slums and his Gibraltar Community—conflict over land, thievery and infidelity between husbands and wives. He wanted to be different and do those good things his God-fearing grand aunty wanted him to do. When he was still young, he noticed that it was very hard to find love, trust, and respect in the Gibraltar Ghetto. For some reason, he didn't find too many people that wanted to do better for themselves in the community because so many of them seemed to be satisfied with where they were at that point in their lives.

As a young man living in Gibraltar, George Weah wanted the best things life had to offer. He didn't want to have to keep borrowing pants, shirts, shoes, underwear, socks, or deodorant from his brothers or from friends in the community. He desired to wear some of the finest clothes, shoes, sunglasses, gold chains and wristwatches, date beautiful women in the area, and whatever it was that brought joy and prestige to a person. Weah wanted to dress up well and go to nightclubs like Black Sugar, Roxy Pool Room, IK, Sha Na Na Disco, Lips, Bannister, La Joy, Carlton Disco, Bacardi Disco and many other hanging out places for boys of his age. He often hung out in Roxy Cinema poolroom to play pool with friends. He wanted to dress like John Travolta or some of the actors he saw in Hollywood movies, but he could not afford his expensive tastes in material things. As a poor ghetto boy, George normally dreamt bigger than himself while he was still sleeping on the hard concrete floor in mosquitoes infested room at his grand aunty's home. In fact, at times, George Weah slept anywhere he could find a space to sleep due to overcrowding in the house. Some of his friends and relatives he shared his dreams with reminded him of the stark realities in their Gibraltar ghetto. "Get your head from in the cloud and bring it back down to Earth and to reality, Oppong. You cannot afford any of those expensive things you're dreaming about," some of his destitute friends as well as some family members who couldn't see a way out of Gibraltar would tell him. Though he was sometimes frustrated from sharing his dreams with the wrong people due to the lack of encouragement, but he never stopped dreaming and worked hard toward attracting his dreams into his life. He soon realized that there was something wrong with his family and many of the friends he was sharing his dreams with. He noticed that most of his family and friends were always hungry for immediate things, especially wants. Many of them were also emptied of dreams and high aspirations. He also noticed that the hungrier they were, the weaker they were in pulling themselves up by their bootstraps out of poverty. In fact, many of them never had the least instance of a booth with straps. He too was hungry in another way—he was hungry for success and a way out of Gibraltar and Liberia. Due to hunger of different types, it became obviously difficult for many of his poor ghetto friends and some of his unstructured family members to think clearly because they needed to have a sober thought to work out a way on how to survive from day to day. Some of them were primarily concerned on how to get food into their empty stomachs. Many young men and women in Clara Town and Vai Town were sure they could still work if they could find work, and they could look for it if only they could find food to eat to strengthen their bodies. But how were these people going to get food for themselves, for their children, for their wives or husbands, for their parents when there were no jobs available? Had There been some form of social service provided by the government, a small dent would have been made in the lives of the poorest of the poor in Clara Town and in many of the slums and ghettos around Liberia. But there were simply too many people within those shanty homes for any government without the financial capacity to cater to.

Manageably, food was always on the table in Ma Emma's house no matter how little it was for the large group that lived there. On the other hand, one could only wonder how other peo-ple fed their families when there weren't that many jobs available in Monrovia with its growing population? God being God in His infinite wisdom, He always provides for His children. In most poor countries where unemployment is high, people often starve to death, but this was not the case in Gibraltar. Even the poorest resident of the community often found a way to eat. Often, if a person goes to bed hungry for a day or two, they become mental-ly dead which leads to wrong decision making. Contrary to the hardship in the community, George Weah being the lucky person he is, never stopped dreaming while growing up in Gibraltar and elsewhere around Monrovia and Liberia. He knew if he worked harder, his dreams would come to reality. Young George realized at an early age that a person's dream only becomes illusive when they stop chasing it. Therefore, to realize his dream, he kept pressing on by putting one foot in front of the other while maintaining a laser sharp focus on his destination.

It was at a very young age that George Weah discovered the power of dream. For the men and women in the ghettos, the dream is their greatest asset because with dream comes hope. Hope is what fuels upward mobility and success. Everything that humanity has ever achieved began with a simple dream. For most people, as do the residents of the slum communities across the world, the dream is all humanity has. Though one might not have the financial franchise or the political network, but the dream is all that a person has as a living entity. As George Weah did, everyone must protect their dream. A dream must be nurtured, and it should be attracted into the life of the dreamer once it is strengthened by the power of hard work. Dream is a powerful thing, and sometimes it can be worth dying for.

As humans, people need to be careful who they share our dreams and aspirations with on their journey in life. There are so many dream killers among families and friends. No matter where a person is in life, they must beware of Psychic Vampires also known as "PV". These are people who whenever they are around you, they will suck all the energy out of you by sometimes dragging you into meaningless arguments with baseless reasons why they think that your dream will never be possible. Whenever these people leave your presence, you feel very worn out, tired and hopeless, especially about pursuing the dream that you're so passionate about. As for George Oppong Weah, his dream did not matter to many of the PVs who he shared it with, though he later became very selective in sharing his dream due to past lessons learned. Other than surviving from day to day, many of his family and friends in Gibraltar were stuck in life or had no dreams of making it big like he was dreaming of doing. Many of his family and friends wanted him right where they were in life. Until they saw him living his dreams, they were all in shock when he became a highly sought-after footballer in the country or when he signed his first semiprofessional football contract with one of one of Liberia's biggest football clubs, Invincible Eleven, IE. He baffled the naysayers and the many frenemies in Liberia when he climbed at the apex of world football when he won the Federation of International Football Association, FIFA's World Best Player title.

Growing up as a teen and as an adult, George Weah never allowed his dream to be sucked out of him by the community's Psychic Vampires, many of whom called him a troublemaker and nuisance. Weah never shared his intimate passion and dream with everyone; he only shared it with those who he could trust, and those who he saw as being worthy of knowing those things he holds dear to his heart. Besides Ma Emma, he sometimes shared his dreams with Junior Boy, Philip Karmo, and a few of the people in the house. On his journey to the top, understood that negative thinking and negative acting people along with Psychic Vampires only came into his life to suck out the positive energy and leave him with fatigue, both physically and mentally. Dreaming about success is one thing and attracting that dream into one's own life is another thing. For George Weah, it took sweat, pains, sacrifice, and blood—his own blood on the football field, sometimes on practice grounds and during football matches. As a man born of lowly birth who was doomed to fail by virtue of his social status, he never stopped dreaming and working on attracting his dream in his life. He remained humbled with a renewed mindset and a very good and receptive attitude in acknowledging his shortcomings and taking corrective measures to remedy them. Where others saw impossibility, George Weah saw opportunity—just like he did on the football pitches and scored many otherwise impossible goals.

Chapter 8

The 1979 Rice Riot and the 1980 Coup

At the age of twelve, George Weah's world came crumbling down when the city of Monrovia was embroiled in a torrent
of violent demonstrations on Saturday April 14, 1979, by political
agitators in the likes of Baccus Matthews and his People Alliance
of Liberia, PAL along with other progressive movements. This was
the first time George Weah saw dead bodies lying on some of the
principal streets of Monrovia. The April 14 riot which is commonly
called the Rice Riot would later lead to Liberia's discordance into
cycles of violence in later years. The Rice Riot impacted Weah
in so many ways. It made him see adults as unreasonable and
self-centered. The riot helped him to know the vulnerability in Liberian society—how quickly sentiments can flare up and turn into
a national disaster if it is not addressed.

Prior to the 1979 Rice Riot, the Liberian elite that are
often referred to as Americo-Liberians, have acted with a mixture
of obedience and resistance to US influence in Liberia since the
founding of the country. The most significant era of obedience and
alliance with the government of the United States of America was
that of William V.S. Tubman administration which lasted for some
twenty-seven years from 1944 to 1971. As a result of Tubman's
"Open Door Policy" that we mentioned earlier which was a period
that many scholars referred to as an era of economic growth and

prosperity for the Liberian economy and the people of Liberia, dissidents kept a low profile. But the policy created a wide income disparity between rich and poor in the long run. This gap was a catalyst that sprouted the upheaval in Liberia in the 1980s up to the early 2000s.

By 1970, Liberia found itself at a tipping point. When President Tubman, who was a stooge for the United States but ruled the country like a monarch, died after undergoing a Prostate Cancer operation in the UK in 1971, his successor and Vice President, William R. Tolbert Jr., resumed resistance to US influence in Liberia. Under his leadership, the Liberian Government began to reorient the economic system from liberal capitalism towards state-led, planned economic systems, focusing on food self-sufficiency and industrialization. In the early days of his administration, to gain support for this policy, Tolbert established relations with socialist-oriented countries such as the USSR, the People's Republic of China, and Libya. During Tolbert's short stints in the Executive Mansion, more than 30 state-owned enterprises were established, and the government began to set restrictions on the US, for the use of military facilities in Liberia. Concession agreements with foreign companies were renegotiated, creating serious tensions— particularly with the Firestone Rubber Company that was then headquartered in Akron, Ohio. Tolbert saw the bigger picture for Liberia in the long term.

Additionally, the Tolbert administration advocated for pan-African unity against neocolonialism and promoted the Declaration on the Establishment of a New International Economic Order, adopted by the United Nations General Assembly in 1974. Tolbert was directly involved in the formulation of the Monrovia Declaration, adopted by the Organization of African Unity, OAU, the forerunner of the African Union during a meeting held in Liberia in 1979, few months after the rice riot. This declaration led to the influential Lagos Plan of Action for the Economic Development of Africa. This declaration frowned on the exploitation of Africa that was being carried out through neo-colonialist external forces which seek to influence the economic policies and directions of the African States. This declaration stands in sharp contrast to the World Bank's Berg Report whose major focus was on the balance of payment deficit among many African countries. As of date, the economy of over 90% of African countries is still controlled by African countries' former colonial masters. Many of these countries like France, the United Kingdom, Belgium, and the United States of America, call all the shots when it comes to the foreign exchange rate in the various African countries. In truth, Africa is truly not freed from western powers' economic and political dominations. There is no clear path insight as to how the Lagos Plan for the Economic Development of Africa will ever be achieved when African countries' Central Banks are currently located in Europe and the United States.

In the mid-1970s the CIA reacted to Tolbert's policies by supporting Liberian civil society groups in opposition to the Government of Liberia, in particular the Progressive Alliance of Liberia (PAL), headed by Baccus Matthews, who was in close contact with the CIA (many political thinkers believe that Baccus was a paid CIA informant). The fact is that during the Cold War, the CIA recruited spies to work within governments they suspected of having ties with the USSR. Liberia being the biggest CIA's spy base in Africa, had more spies and CIA operatives working in and out of the government than in any other African country. The PAL movement often used Marxist rhetoric to denounce Tolbert's administration. The most significant event took place after the government accelerated the national plan for food self-sufficiency by stimulating local rice production through an increased import tax on foreign-produced rice. The PAL claimed that this was a way to boost the profit of rice importers and promote Tolbert's own private rice production. This was a preposterous assertion on the part of PAL and Dr. Gabriel Baccus Matthews. Tolbert was looking ahead into the country's future. It was insanely stupid for many of the supporters of PAL to have believed the assertion that was being made against the administration the led to the violent protest and death of several dozens of poor citizens from the ghettoes and urban areas around Monrovia.

In a confidential White House memorandum issued about six months later, it noted that the riot in Monrovia had severely damaged the Government of Liberia and that it was unlikely Tolbert would "survive until the end of his term in 1983." Six months later, the country saw what the CIA had in its treasure trove for the small West African nation that was run by America's puppeteers for over 130 years.

According to Emmanuel Bowier and other eyewitnesses, this is how it all began when George Weah's innocence was removed. In early 1979, President William Tolbert, without warning, increased the price of a 100-pound bag of rice from $22 to $26. This impromptu and unheard-of price increase, especially considering that most Liberians at the time and even now lived on less than US $1 Dollar per day could not afford their staple food. Hearing about the overnight price increase of the nation's staple, opportunistic PAL seized the moment to unleash the country's first ever staged demonstration. Using political rhetoric and divisive sugar-coated statements on the uninformed common majority, the PAL leaders were able to convince many of their supporters and sympathizers that they could import metric tons of 100 pounds bags of rice to Liberia and sell it for US $9.00 per bag. They secretly organized a protest the price increase. Considering that rice is Liberians' staple, the protest or demonstration drew a massive crowd, unparalleled in the history of Liberia. Many of the PAL movement's supporters were mainly university students and people from the ghetto who only wanted their living conditions to improve. Many of the ghettoes and slums dwellers were never interested in politics or a change in government—they have been suppressed by William V.S. Tubman administration and others before him. George at that time was never interested in politics besides playing football and having food on his table. From the ordinary Liberian perspective, the increased price would have mainly hurt the poorest people living in slums and in urban areas, as it currently happens in Monrovia and around the country.

On the other hand, the justification for the price increase as was later explained by Florence Chenoweth, President Tolbert's

Minister of Agriculture was for the empowerment of local farmers. In a nutshell, the government of Liberia wanted local rice farmers to increase their production capacity of rice instead of the country relying heavily on the importation of rice from foreign countries like the United States of America, India, and other far-eastern nations. Looking back from where the country is now, this was a brilliant and a darn good strategy had it not been used by power-hungry opposition politicians to make it a trap for many of the uninformed and uneducated demonstrators who took to the streets that April morning to demonstrate and wind up dying for an unworthy cause. The increase in the price of rice called into action the main political agitator of that era, Dr. Gabriel Baccus Matthews who was a bitter political opponent of the government.

Early that Saturday morning in April, many ordinary citizens including market women, school students, civil servants, readied themselves as usual and went about their business. Some people got ready for church, some people were going to the market to sell or buy Sunday's meals, others with youth in their favor like George Weah were looking forward to playing their favorite sport that day. Unknowing to many of them, it was a day betrayed by the PAL movement. Days early, rumors abound about the impending demonstration which was nothing to be concerned about—at least this was how many people saw things from an ordinary person's perspective. At Ma Emma's home that morning, Rebecca, having been in Monrovia less than a year, had just completed serving breakfast with the dry rice and some leftover food from the previous day. Rebecca being the oldest girl in the house, did most of the cooking for the family as asserted earlier. Several days earlier, Dr. Matthews and his PAL colleagues including, D. Kahn Carlor, Oscar Quah, Michael George, just to name a few, had organized, mobilized, and called for the peaceful demonstration in Monrovia. As planned, the group would have marched from the intersection of UN Drive and Camp Johnson Road in the Buzzy Quarter section of Monrovia, up toward the Executive Mansion to protest the proposed price hike. Conversely, soon the news of the demonstration spread like wildfire and nearly 20,000 people joined the demonstration against the government and the Ministry of Agriculture.

At that time with imported parboiled rice being the nation's staple food, people would go to the extreme to protect its availability on the Liberian market and they would prevent any government from changing the price they were used to buying. Few minutes into the march, it soon turned into one of the largest riots the small West African nation ever experienced. Within 8 hours, violence erupted in the city's streets as ill-trained police officers went out on a killing spree and subsequently killed nearly fifty protesters in the first few hours, while more than 500 people were injured. Many of those killed were ordinary civilian looters that took advantage of the situation to join some members of the Armed Forces of Liberia to break into Lebanese and Indian merchants' stores to loot.

Soon, the demonstration spread into the various suburbs of Monrovia. Many residents of Clara Town, West Point, Slipway, New Kru Town, and many other slum communities joined the demonstration in their own little way—breaking locks off storefronts and doors to loot away goods. Soon, Florence Chenoweth was replaced as minister of agriculture after publicly admitting that she had erred in proposing the rice's price hike. The damage had already been done to the Liberian economy—most of the stores and businesses were not insured in Liberia during that period. But the people of the slums and ghettoes had a huge payday because many of them got even with the government and with dishonest traders one way or the other. During the demonstration, Ma Emma warned her children and grandchildren not to participate in the looting of stores within the Clara Town or Via Town areas. In fact, she didn't want any of them leaving the home that day for fear that something bad would have happened to them. President William R. Tolbert's political mistake came when he back peddled on the price hike strategy during a radio address by reassuring the country of the government's continuous commitment to subsidizing rice, and that the price would be kept at or below $22 for a 100 pounds bag of rice. Today in Liberia, the price of a 100 pounds bag of rice is twice that amount while the price for the same quantity and a higher quality of rice in places like the United States, India, China, and other rice producing countries remain the same or even lower.

CLARKE & TUKPAH

The Tolbert and many critics of the West believed that PAL and other progressives like Dr. Gabriel Baccus Matthews, Dew Tuan-Wreh Mayson, D. Khan Carlos, Dr. Amos Sawyer, and many were being played and manipulated by the United States of America and other Western powers to overthrow the Tolbert's Administrator because it has moved further and further away from the West and was now having closed and cozy ties with the Russians and Eastern Bloc countries. Earlier in March of that year, the government arrested George Boley who was an assistant minister of Education along with twenty other suspicious figures for associating with PAL. They were charged with treason and seduction and were scheduled to be executed on April 14, 1980, which would have been the one-year anniversary of the Rice Riot.

When the dust of the demonstration had settled, Baccus and members of his PAL movement were arrested and put behind bars. Once that was done, things returned to normal—but this was just the beginning of a long-drawn-out conflict that would haunt Liberia, a small nation for more than two decades.

The fact remains that rice is eaten as breakfast, lunch, and dinner in most Liberian households. The current national annual demand for rice in Liberia is approximately 625,000 metric tons while production is estimated at 300,000 metric tons. In 2016, Liberia imported rice at a cost of over $260 million USD. If the 1979 proposal for the increase in the production of local rice was accepted, Liberia would have been a major producer of rice in Africa, if not in the world—Liberia is blessed with good soil and an agriculture friendly climate. What Tolbert and his administration wanted for the country was for Liberia and its people to eat what they produce, and to only produce what they can consume and to market the excess on the global market. Instead, PAL put a negative spin on Tolbert's policy and made it a trap for many of the fools that got in the street to protest their own interest. While Ma Emma protected her family from the self-sabotaging demonstration orchestrated by some self-serving politicians, the event kept the ordinary citizens on edge.

When a semblance of hope seemed to be returning and people were beginning to put the April 14, 1979, Rice Riot behind them, then April, 12 happened. In the early morning of Saturday April 12, 1980, a group of 17 armed men, mainly noncommissioned officers in the Armed Forces of Liberia, AFL, entered the Executive Mansion shortly before midnight and shot President William Richard Tolbert while he was in bed. The President had just returned to the Executive Mansion having spent almost nine hours at a religious conference, World Baptist Alliance Conference at the E.J. Roye Building on Ashmun Street in Central Monrovia. People familiar with the incident claimed that the CIA's fingerprints were all over the coup. One of the soldiers who participated in the coup, Albert Toe, openly admitted that after having killed Tolbert, the coup plotters contacted the US Embassy near Monrovia. The Americans endorsed the coup and promised to provide all the necessary support for the military junta. Though the 1980 coup was believed to have been orchestrated by the 17 noncommissioned officers of the AFL, inside sources like J. Henneh Johnson, a former aide to the President, the First Lady, Victoria Tolbert, and dozens of others confirmed that it was not the 17 AFL soldiers that overthrew the President. Rather, it was a unit of Israelite and American Commandoes that stormed the Executive Mansion through a drainage system and murder the president in cold-blood. Fearing a backlash from the international community and their Cold War nemesis, USSR, the CIA hurriedly handpicked few of their informants, Samuel Kanyon Doe who was a CIA informant, and scapegoated them as those how tactically overpowered Tolbert's elite security guards and assassinated him. The morning after the coup, the leader of the coup, Samuel Doe surrounded by dozens of soldiers and imprisoned politicians from the April 14, 1979, Rice Riot that were now freed, announced on the government's owned ELBC national radio station that a military coup had taken place and that a military junta under the name of the People's Redemption Council, PRC had taken power under his leadership. Following the radio announcement, Monrovia exploded in jubilation by the news of the coup. Tens of thousands of citizens, mainly from the slums and ghettoes got out on the streets of Monrovia jubilating with songs such as "Native woman born soldier, soldier killed rogues". That day, Doe and members of his military junta suspended the constitution and ruled the country by military decrees.

The PRC era ushered in a heavy dark cloud of uncertainty over the country—military men were the lords and gospels in the land. In fact, the U.S. Embassy was very much instrumental in forming the PRC as a military junta immediately after the coup. As it was during those dark days, all civilian communications were shut down in Liberia, and American advisers were assigned to key Liberian ministries. As a show of U.S. support, American Soldiers were deployed in the streets of Monrovia to help get looters and shooters off the streets. Samuel Doe had not really expected to be where he was at that time—he was lucky to have been handpicked by his CIA handlers to lead the country. During the early days of the PRC, Doe feared that forces were coming from all corners to attack him, and he wanted America to send him strong military and economic support.

Few days after the coup, the PRC established a special military tribunal that charged 13 key government officials from the Tolbert administration with high treason, corruption, and misuse of public office and sentenced them to death. On April 22, ten days following the brutal coup, the 13 accused government officials were tied to light poles and were executed by firing squad on the Barclay Training Center Barracks' beach in Monrovia. The execution was broadcast by national and international media. Among those executed were Frank Tolbert, Richard A. Henries, James A.A. Pierre, E. Reginald Townsend, C. Cecil Dennis, Cryil Bright, Frank A. Stewart, P. Clarence Parker, John Sherman, James T. Philips, and Joseph Cheeson. Following the execution, the PRC destroyed the records of the Tribunal. This incident was George Oppong Weah's second exposure to public killing—he witnessed the hanging of people convicted of ritualistic killing in the country years earlier during the Tolbert administration.

From the 1980 coup going forward, Liberia found itself on a downward spiral. It began with infighting among members of the

PRC. As the popular saying goes in Liberia, "the revolution soon began to eat up its own babies." The internal turmoil finally led to the murder and execution of several PRC members. By the end of the 1980s, the PRC Government that had changed from being a military junta into a civilian government after rigging the country's first democratic election since 1943, found itself in a full-scale civil war with the National Patriotic Front of Liberia, NPFL lead by one of Doe's presidential appointees, Charles McArthur Taylor.

All the while these events were happening in the country, George Oppong Manneh Weah was still hounding his football skills. He stayed away from controversial issues—though he some-how practiced politics in high school as a student.

Part II

The Legend

"Heroes are remembered, but legends never die."

Max Holloway

Chapter 9

Growing Up in PRC Liberia

Getting adjusted to a bad situation and not making it a mind-sore while focusing on one's passion is what George Weah did as a teenager during the People's Redemption Council, PRC's reign in Liberia during the 1980s. Like many slum dwellers living under the draconian rules of the People's Redemption Council's Government, George Weah was neither a big supporter nor an ardent opponent of the junta that ousted the Tolbert's True Whig Party in April of 1980. In years to come, he would become a bene-factor of the regime. Upon coming to power, Samuel Doe and his sixteen friends had the support of more than 90% of the Liberian people. For George Weah and many others, they lived with what was given them as common citizens. Many of their supporters were people of indigenous background—Liberians from 15 of the 16 ethnic groups. For the ordinary Liberian, the new government that murdered Tolbert and others with the help of America exerted their heavy-handed authority in a more repressive and brutal way—the PRC ruled Liberia with iron-fists. No one dares to stand up to the men in military uniforms.

Growing up under the PRC's regime, life was filled with mixed experiences for young George Weah who was now in his teens with an uncanny footballing ability. He witnessed the government's brutality against its own citizens, and at one point, he saw neighbors turning against neighbors during an attempted coup in 1985. By the early 1980s, he was still fine-tuning his football skills having transitioned from being a goalkeeper to now playing forward for his community football team, Young Survivals. The periods between 1980 to 1985 were dark times in Liberia for politicians and anyone who dared to openly criticize Samuel Doe or the government of the PRC. Those with the nerves of steel were dragged out of their homes at night and thrown into prison or sometimes, they were summarily executed in secret by the state's death squad or secret security. The cloud of uncertainty ended when President Samuel Doe made a public pronouncement that he was putting an end to summary execution; by then, many innocent people had already lost their lives.

Following the 1980 coup, the military promised to raise the living standard of the Liberia People; especially the military who according to the coup leaders had long been neglected by the Tolbert's government. Specifically, the regime made a pronouncement to raise the salaries and provide other incentives for the soldiers and civil servants in the country. However, the prevailing economic conditions in the country combined with corruption within the ranks and files of the military, the government was unable to fulfill the many promises made to the nation. Concerning PRC's promise to the military, there were two main barriers that prevented the government from implementing these promises. Firstly, this pronouncement to raise salaries prompted the business community to double or triple the prices of all commodities within the country. Secondly, and perhaps most importantly, prior to the military takeover and years that followed or by the decade of the 80s, the price of iron ore and rubber which were then the two main exports and primary sources of income for the government had dropped on the world's commodity market. Furthermore, the international financiers especially the World Bank and the International Monetary Funds (IMF) including other donors became resistant to trusting the military government with money to finance its agenda or subsidize civil servants' salary.

As a result of these barriers, combined with the fears of

losing the support of the armed forces which was crucial to the survival of the government, the People Redemption Council focused its attention primarily on the soldiers for the fear of them starting a mutiny to overthrow the government. Having reneged on its promise to the ordinary civilians, it was therefore the responsibility of civilian officials within the administration to be the bearer of bad news by telling citizens that the government could no longer offer free primary and secondary education throughout the country. There was also a shortage of teachers and little infrastructure available around the country. In the mid-1980, the government could not freeze the price of Coca-Cola, or the local franchise-holder, USTC which again was a subsidiary of the Firestone Rubber Company. If they did, the USTC would stop producing it. With these revelations, the soldiers' hope sank, and they demanded from their leaders a fulfilment of a promise made to them—they were not accepting excuses from the PRC. To avoid an internal coup, the PRC government had to find the cash to pay AFL Soldiers, even if it meant not paying schools teachers and other civil servants of the government for six months or more.

Clara Town and the Gibraltar communities were not in the best of shape during the 1980s. The PRC's coup added to the sufferings of the already struggling people in Gibraltar and various communities around the country. George Weah and some of his siblings were still struggling for survival—if Ma Emma didn't provide meals for him, he would not have a decent meal that day. As a survivalist, if there was no food at home, he found food by whatever means necessary to fill his hungry belly—be it joining the older boys in the neighborhood to cook midnight food or something they referred to as, *"Join before you chew/clear (JBC)"*. As it is a well-known secret, the ingredients for many of the midnight food came from many different sources. Often, boys in the neighborhood would work cooperatively to make their midnight cooking happen every night. For George Weah, it was a source of food for him, even if he didn't contribute to the cooking. As the slogan of the PRC went, *"In the cause of the people, the struggles continue"*, his struggles indeed continued until he transitioned from elementary schools (Daniel E. Howard, C. William Brumskine) to junior high schools like G.W. Gibson, Ellen Mills Scarborough, Muslim Congress, and Sr. high school in Monrovia.

Throughout the PRC's era, George began participating in school politics. For those who knew this quiet young man from elementary school to junior high school and even high school, he would always run to become secretary of the class. Now in his mid-teen, he became more open socially due to his growing football talent. Balancing football and education were a very tough call for the young man. When his grades were taking a downward turn Ma Emma urged him to quit football if he didn't bring his grades up to a comfortable level. As always, he cut back on practice time to focus more on doing schoolwork. To obtain better grades, he would go to friends' homes to study and do homework if there was no electricity at his house. Sometimes, the light would go off for a while when Ma Emma didn't pay the electricity bills.

On the other hand, the PRC's promise to the masses of total redemption from poverty, inequality, the lack of opportunities, and corruption was a promise betrayed. They did exactly the opposite of what they promised—they became tribalistic, nepotistic, and sectionalistic (coined). The young men that removed the corrupt government soon replaced it with another corrupt system that was not based on meritocracy. They weren't only corrupt, rather, they were brutal to everyone or anyone who tried to expose them. Their murdering sprees of ordinary civilians and many of their own friends send fear and shockwaves in every civilian quarter. Those with the guts to confront the PRC often disappeared, killed, or if lucky, found themselves behind bars in filthy prison conditions. Growing up under Samuel Doe's PRC, there remains a stark reminder of the constant danger lurking for critics who would dare to stand up to the strongman. People of the slums and ghettos including West Point, Gibraltar, Terminal Island were controlled by Jimmy Ringo, a notorious criminal. This well-known criminal provided a sense of security for many of the residents in his territory.

When the military junta of the PRC decided to change from wearing military uniforms into wearing civilian attire, the lives of over 90% of the people did not change for the better. By then, George Oppong Manneh Weah had found his true calling. The game he loved to play so much was paying off for him. He was now attending school on a football scholarship and earning money from playing in the local league. Though the money he earned was inadequate to buy him all that he needed, he no longer felt the pinches of poverty which were marked by extreme hunger, and sickness from malaria and other tropical diseases that he usually suffered from due to playing on dirty football pitches, eating uncleaned street food, and sleeping on the concrete floor on a mat next to other family members like Atlas, Teah, Bobby Moore, or his young aunt Rebecca. In later years, Weah would come to benefit from the former PRC government as he became one of the pride players of the Liberian national team the *"Lone Star"* and one of the prides of the leader of the new government, which was now the National Democratic Party of Liberia, NDPL that reigned from January 1986 until he departed the country in 1987. He formed part of the Liberian national football team that traveled to Brazil to undergo both fundamental and some advanced training at a football academy in that country. Upon his return to Liberia, his football skills just became better as he literally exploded on the national football stage in Monrovia. By the mid-1980s, he formed a cozy relationship with President Doe who was seen by many as a killer and a bloodthirsty leader. At that time, George became a constant guest of President Samuel Doe's Executive Mansion on Capitol Hill. In the 1980s, President Doe was the chief patron of sport in the country. Weah was given full access to the Executive Mansion by the President—who would do anything to be in the company of any of Liberia's football greats. Whenever George came to the Executive Mansion, he would be escorted into the President's office or his private residence by then Minister of State for Presidential Affairs, Mr. G. Alvin Jones. As a payoff for his talent, George Weah would never come to the Executive Mansion and leave empty pocketed—Doe would give him a load of cash to take care of his needs. Weah was one of Samuel Doe's best friends. Though Samuel Doe was a brutal dictator who killed those who sought his downfall, he was a great fan of football and a very kind generous man to those he admired.

In the height of his reign, Doe would often give money to the poor and to schools and organizations that he thought needed it. For football players in Liberia, he was indeed their chief patron who cultivated the game and wanted to take Liberia to the African Cup of Nations and the World Cup, if possible. Samuel Doe and George Weah's relationship grew way beyond the football field. He became like a little brother to Doe. When George Weah moved to France, Doe would often send him thousands of United States Dollars to buy him some of the finest French tailor-made suits and clothes to bring for him upon his return to Liberia.

Growing up in PRC Liberia, George Weah was compelled to witness brutalities that were being committed by the regime, but these events never affected his passion for football. People of the ghetto were not immune to the harsh reality that was playing out on the national stage. The effect of the PRC brutalities was felt everywhere, including in his Gibraltar neighborhood. Doe was a very heavy-handed leader. He often accused his fellow soldiers of plotting to overthrow him. Those suspected of orchestrating a coup against the PRC often went underground. Many of them were sought after in poor communities and ghettos around the country. Next door to Gibraltar, was another dangerous ghetto community called, Terminal Island and Struggle Community. These places, West Point included, were the hideout for many disenfranchised political critics of Samuel Doe and his PRC gangs. These communities were often raided by heavily armed government troops. In 1985, George Weah's neighborhood along with the Clara Town and Vai Town communities were raided by Krahn-speaking AFL soldiers that were on the hunt for Gio and Mano-speaking men and women that were suspected of being co-conspirators to the November 12th coup that failed to oust President Samuel Doe.

Upon his departure from Liberia to play semiprofessional football in Cameroon, the country was at a tipping point from ethnic tension between the Krahns of Grand Gedeh County on the one hand, and the Gio and Mano people of Nimba County on the other hand. The decades old tribal conflict between the Gio, Mano of Nimba County and the Krahn of Grand Gedeh County would come to affect every citizen within the country. The buildup of tensions would culminate to the decimation of the entire country, its infrastructure, its economy and the deaths of hundreds of thousands of innocent men, women, children, and animals.

Chapter 10

Early Football Journey

The name "George Oppong Weah" is to football in Africa and Liberia as water is to wet. Without the game of football, George Weah would have amounted to nothing. He would have been born in Nimba County, grown up in Gibraltar, and would have probably died in Gibraltar without anyone knowing his name like many others. From the moment he put on his first football jerseys for his neighborhood team, Young Brazil, Feh Feh Football Club in Clara Town, to the time he signed his first semiprofessional football contract, George Weah's life had never been the same. Having had a brief stint in Clara Town with Young Brazil and Feh Feh, and many of his neighborhood teams where he named himself "Oppong" after a Ghanaian football star Charles Oppong who once played for Ashanti Kotoko and the Ghana Black Star, George Weah moved on to play for another area teams Bahjaenekay and the Young Survivals Football Club which were two clubs at the lower-end of the Monrovia football scene. It was with Young Survivals, a fourth division football club within the Liberian Football League at the time that George's football career took off. Though he was a rising star, there were several things lacking in the young man who would one day become one of the world's most explosive football sensations—he was lazy and lacked the physical strength. At the time, George held onto the football for too long, and locked his sight on the ball while dribbling opponents without lifting his head up to find the goalpost or a teammate for a final pass or goal. Notwithstanding, people could see his raw talents far beyond his many flaws—he was a complete mesmerizer and a sight to behold on the football field during those early days on his road to stardom. During his early days as an amateur player, whenever George Oppong Weah came on the field to play, he would score a goal or two for his side. In local football leagues, there were no games that George played, and he did not score a goal or two. What helped him at that time was that he developed a strategy of looking beyond every defender and imagined himself standing one-on-one with the goalkeeper. He developed a quick and robust thinking skill at an early age because in the game of football, players must be fast thinking. For a person to become a great scorer like those great players George admired, he had to become shrewd and quick like a fox. The game of football is fluidly dynamic such that it requires a fast thinking and fast acting person.

To amp up his football game, George Oppong Weah had to teach himself how to control his breathing and his anxiety level whenever he was in possession of the ball or whenever the ball was taken away from him. He had to learn how to hold his breath and breathe more slowly while in possession or in pursuit of the ball. Football, which is a very physical game, requires a person to have stamina and Weah had to learn to build endurance and stamina over time. Most professional football coaches that encountered him, saw him as skillful, but a lazy player who needed a lot of development. For he was tall and skinny with not much meat on his body. His fellow teammates openly told him that he was lazy and didn't know how to share the ball wherever he held onto it. To overcome these shortcomings, he had to work on it by putting in extra time doing long distance jogging and ball control and release. He had to develop the eyes of an eagle and the strength of a cheetah—he had to develop speed, strength, and eyes for goal. Once he had overcome his lapses, he was ready for primetime.

George Oppong Weah's sudden outburst of speed and agility made him a formidable force on any team he found himself on. Whenever George was in possession of the football, he would formulate several playing scenarios in his head on how to dribble past several defenders on his way to the opposing team's goalkeeper and football net. In the Liberian Football League, amateurs often targeted the most skillful player to wound or destroy them. Given that background, Georg learned to avoid brutal fouls from players that were targeting him during games. He had to learn to jump over an approaching defender after swiveling the ball around him. To avoid being hurt during a game he had to keep moving back and forth and around the field. People who didn't understand his strategy during his early days often labeled him as lazy or a 'Bunker' which is a Liberian word for a slacker. In his early days as a striker in Liberia, he suffered several minor injuries on the field, but those injuries did not stop him from playing his favorite game, football.

From the onset, coaches with the eyes for talent and greatness knew that George Weah would one day become a great football player if he continued perfecting his craft on the field. With every goal he scored, and every celebratory dance he did for every goal, only increased his fame both in his Clara Town community and around the city of Monrovia. From the muddy red field of Clara Town up to the sandy field of West Point, along the way to the human defecation football field of New Kru Town, and from Walker Cinema to rocky Slipway Field and everywhere in between; his skills and talent gained popularity and his fame went far and wide in Monrovia and its suburbs. Admirers and fans would sometimes run into him and would give him money in admiration of his amazing talent. The game of football changed George Weah's life forever when he entered the first division league of the Liberia Football Association, LFA. Local fans showered him with gifts of all kinds. Liberian women threw themselves at him for free sex and marriage which he never gave them. Even men tried to sexually exploit him of his innocence and his youthfulness. Though he was talented and handsome, he remained humble most of the time. He was no angel because he often got into confrontations with others.

As a teenager trying to perfect his game, young George experienced a lot of emotional issues—puberty without being properly mentored by a great male role model, lacking nice clothes to wear much more. He was put down a lot because of his unruly behavior by some family members and community members who only saw his flaws and not who he could become. In 1974, when George sustained a terrible third-degree burn by hot water and was taken out of Gibraltar to seek medical treatment. While sadness overtook some of his friends during the time he was away, some of the adults felt relieved for the few months he was away from Gibraltar. Prior to the incident, he and his older brother, William Weah would sometimes fight all day. As a preteen and as a teen-ager, George was very temperamental. Back then, he got in a fight with anyone who picked on him—he never backdown from a fight even if he got a beatdown. He would not listen to anyone's advice other than, Ma Emma. But in 1980, things changed around for him for the better. There was a Ghanaian Teacher that lived in the community who everyone called Brother. Brother was related to Abraham Kay of St Joseph's Warriors Football Club. Brother took on the responsibility to mentor young George after seeing his great talent. Brother's intervention helped change his negative behaviors or the negative way he came across to most adult within the community. He helped George from being this hot-tempered and rude boy to someone different. He was like a big brother to all the young men in the community. Brother took young George as a little brother. To earn extra cash, George would do Brother's laun-dry, clean up his one-bedroom apartment. It was through Brother's tutelage and mentoring that George became transformed. His confi-dence level went up and his grades improved for the most part.

By the mid-1980s, George could now afford to buy shoes and pants that fitted him instead of burrowing pants or shirts from childhood friends that were not his length to wear. Though his fame back then was not as mammoth as it is today, George Weah endured so many things—the good, the bad, and the ugly while growing up as a poor boy from the ghetto of Gibraltar. What needs noting is that football has brought Weah many good things. Be-sides the expectable consumables of wealth, he garnered during his early days which also included fame and prestige, insightful people using hindsight would say the most valuable prize he ever won was the chance to have left his home in the ghetto of Gibraltar in Liberia, and to have left Africa in particular. Historically in Liberia, football players had no future in the nation's political future—they belonged to the underclass and were relegated to the lowest fringes of Liberian society. No Liberian elite wanted their daughter to marry a football player, but George Oppong Weah changed that negative stereotype into something sexy and beguiling, not in a deceptive way. Undoubtedly, his trip to Europe was a one-way ticket out of poverty which brought him gleaming sports cars, penthouses, beautiful women both white and black, after having had a front row seat to poverty.

To be a successful football star, George Weah recognized at an early age that he had to be different. He worked on his leadership skills when he was with friend. He knew he had to practice more, run frequently, play more games with older players far beyond his age, and pray more just like his grandaunt, Ma Emma had instructed him to do. With Ma Emma as his backbone, he knew that someone was cheering him on, telling him, "You can make it. Just take one more step, run one extra mile, do one more practice, play one extra match, study your lesson for one more hour, and you will be a man, my child." He recognized that every young boy, in Liberia who didn't come from the wealthy elites, saw football as a game of unity, liberation, and equilibrium. At a young age, he had come to realize that football would one day bring him shoulder to shoulder with the high and mighty of the Liberian society and those who often called him such names like, "Street kid, Grown up boy aka Gronna boy, or Good for nothing ghetto boy, as well as Slum dweller". Some of his labelers or 'name callers' lived within his community and in other places around the city of Monrovia. He realized that to be the best, it would require hard work, sacrifice, commitment, and discipline that are mixed with a little bit of humility. With those thoughts in his mind and burned on his brain, George Weah went to work in transforming his body, his mindset and mode of thinking, to become one of the greats in the game of football.

Whenever George Weah was not out selling popcorn and

frozen Cool-Aid for the Aido family that lived within their Gibraltar neighborhood, he would either be on the dusty or sometimes muddy Clara Town or Via Town field practicing football with other young boys from nearby communities. During those early days of his football life, the game of football was all he had, and it meant everything to him. Being a poor boy who felt abandoned by his father without the necessary sponsorship to further his skills, he and some of the teenagers would grab their half-torn leather covered football and run up to the Walker Cinema's muddy or dusty field, depending on the season in Liberia, to practice their beloved game. It was on those dusty and muddy fields that young George developed his goal scoring ability. He learned to visually-mind map opponents on the field by creating possible scenarios inside his head of the next opponent's location or position once he had dribbled past an opponent—he developed a quick analytical and decision-making ability. In modern day technology, it is referred to as Artificial Intelligence based on predictive analysis. These skills he would carry over into his professional and political lives years later. This early developed skill has made George Weah enigmatic to many of his friends and people outside his immediate domain.

Unlike most street or ghetto boys who played football and got involved in fist fights on football patches, George rarely got into a fight with other football players. Unlike the occasional clashes he often had in the community with adults, other boys as well as his brother, William Weah Jr. aka Junior Boy due to his bad temperament, he never transferred any aggression to anyone on the football field. Perhaps though, he might have had more respect for the game of football than the adults and his brother who he felt misunderstood him and called him names like "stupid pekin" (a Liberian slang for stupid kid) etc. At the age of fifteen, he was more of a pacifist than a fighter or grumble maker. Though he would sometimes get in fist fights alongside his teammates whenever one of them were attacked by the opposing team, George was never always the first to throw the first punch. If he was picked on, he fought back with everything he had. Growing up in Gibraltar, one had to be tough and learn to fight and stand up for oneself. In the slum of Clara Town, Weah had to develop the animal instinct of survival while adhering to his grand aunty's moral codes as a guiding compass both in society and on the football pitches. Once he emerged on the national scene, he came to be known as a fine and professional gentleman who played the game of football organically and with a passion that has never seen since the day of David Momo who was one of Liberia's best players who was rumored to have turned down a contract because of his love for his country.

In sickness and in health, George Oppong Weah prevailed as a young boy living in Clara Town. As a kid living in the ghetto of Gibraltar, Liberia's many tropical illnesses like Malaria, Typhoid, jigger, lice were his constant visitors. Unlike William who was the sickliest child at the time, George constantly got sick during the Raining Season. While many of the illnesses killed dozens of residents within his community and hundreds of people around Liberia, young George was one of the lucky victims that overcame illnesses Chickenpox, Measles, Malaria, Diarrhea, and many other tropical diseases. According to the World Health Organization, WHO, Malaria kills more than four hundred thousand people in sub-Saharan Africa every year. Living in a heavily congested and unsanitary environment, George Weah got sick of Malaria almost every month as a youth. Often, his young body would sometimes succumb to the Malaria causing parasites that invaded his immune system. Whenever he would contract the sickness from the bite of the Anopheles Mosquitoes or Malaria Vectors that carry the five parasites of which two are the deadliest, P. Falciparum and P. Vivax, George Weah would get a complete system breakdown. He would vomit until he would taste the bile from his stomach in his mouth. As it is with most Malaria patients, he would run a high temperature, sometimes in the 105 or more. The sickness would cause him to stay indoors under his worn-out blanket in bed or on his little mat on the hard concrete floor as the parasites wreaked havoc in his body. Lucky for George, he did not succumb to the illness like many people do across the African continent and in many developing countries around the world. As a way of self-medicating, he found a way to fight back. He would go on the nearby football field to practice whenever he found himself on the other side of the illness. As it is a common belief in Liberia and across Africa, the best way for an athlete to overcome an illness is to fight that illness by using physical exercise to sweat it out of the body. George Weah sweated many of his illnesses out of his body. Whenever he got too weak to practice and sweat out the Malaria, he would take Chloroquine or Quinine along with Paracetamol to help reduce the headaches and fever. At times, many of these drugs reacted adversely by making his body itch and his ears to ring bells of different amplitudes inside his ears—a sound only he alone could hear.

As an aspiring football player whose passion was above his own physical health, George Weah never allowed mental or physical illness to stop him from succeeding and playing the game he loves—a game that would bring him to prominence, great wealth, and political power. Apart from all the hardships life threw at him which he often referred to as insignificant minor obstacles, he remained true to his passion and never stopped loving his family and friends. George Weah is a trusted friend to so many of his friends, but he has never gotten the same loyalty back from many of his family and friends. Many of the friends he met during his embryonic football journey, he'd never stopped being that good friend they know him to be.

Chapter 11

The Taste of Fame

Like a hungry prizefighter, George Weah knows the taste of victory and the agony of defeat. In defeat, he's a man who never gives up—he always bounces back to continue fighting for what he believes in. Beside his paternal grand aunty, Emma Forkay Klonjlaleh Brown, commonly known as Ma Emma or Emma B who watched over his furthering steps, he owes everything that he now is or owns to the game of football. Without hard work and fame that followed him on the football pitch from Liberia, there wouldn't be any George Oppong Manneh Weah, the youngster that the veteran Cameroonian striker, Roger Milla once called "Black Diamond of Africa". Having gone through the ranks and file of various football clubs in and out of Liberia, George Weah realized that the game of football is a symbol of status, wealth, and prestige for many of the impoverished Liberian youth as well as thousands of young men and women across Africa and around the world. The game of football truly changed George's life from being a poor hungry conflicted street kid who had no direction in life with a bleak future, to being a man that is now bigger than life itself. George has now become a benchmark for many aspiring African players across the continent. The question many critics often ask is, "Does George Weah deserve the fame and all the accolades he now enjoys?" For many of his fans and political supporters in and out of Liberia, the unanimous answer is "Absolutely Yes!" Mr. Weah worked very hard to be where he is in life today. He has so many physical scars on his body to show for his success as well as mental and emotional ones. Himself have left so many scars on others. He had weathered all the storms of life by taking in all the ill wills and enmities that life and the Liberian society threw at him. While other Liberian football stars rose and fell along the road to success, George Oppong Weah's fame has never diminished—it has only gotten bigger and bigger, but it has done so at a huge cost.

As always, fame has more enemies than anyone can imagine. Many friends and family would rather want a person to remain right where they are in life than rise above their circumstances. George Oppong Weah has often been bastardized and marginalized by trusted friends, critics and some family members who misunderstood his true intentions for doing whatever he believes is in the interest of himself and majority of his countrymen. When he stood the tests of time and remained true to himself and the struggles, fame came running toward him. From the very first day his taste buds and palate experienced the taste of fame, he held onto it, and has made it his own forever. Some critics will say that ever since George Weah became rich and famous, he developed a "hunter-gatherer" mindset as a way of preserving his wealth and status. Many of these critics have come to believe that he is a greedy man who does not love to share his fame with others or allow the spotlight to shine on his close friends around him. This is true to an extent due to the competitive world of football he grew up in and the constant competition he was always in with his older brother, Junior Boy. On the other hand, if George Weah was really a greedy man who did not share his wealth with family and friends, he wouldn't have gone broke at the end of his footballing career.

George Oppong Weah's fame began at the Antoinette Tubman Stadium in Monrovia when he scored his first goal in front of thousands of cheering and jubilating spectators. It was with youthful exuberance he celebrated along with thousands of screaming fans after scoring an incredibly impossible goal for his team, Mighty Barrolle Sports Association in Liberia Football Association, LFA Championship League in 1986 at the Antoinette Tubman

Stadium in Monrovia. That same year, George Weah helped his team, Mighty Barrolle, to win the LFA National League Championship. Soon after, some of the perks that came with the championship and dozens of other goals were money and gifts from team's officials and fans alike. Both young and older women offer their own gifts of free sex, and unknown admirers also offer various monetary gifts to George Weah because of his talent of the field. As Weah's fan-base grew bigger and larger, so did his huge appetite for good food and luxury things—with money, he could now transport himself to school from Gibraltar and visit friends outside of his community. Instead of walking or taking the public bus to school or practice, he was now taking Monrovia's famous yellow taxicab wherever he wanted to go. With fame and still in his teens, George Weah was now beginning to develop some bad habits like missing prayers service at the family home chapel, missing church service at Georgia Paton United Methodist Church where his grand aunty, Ma Emma usually dragged him to. He also began sleeping out of Ma Emma's crowded house and coming home late in the night or in the early morning, smoking marijuana with friends, drinking alcohol and having many girlfriends in the neighborhood and in different parts of the city as well as out of town. But as a famous and naïve teen who was influenced by his community, these things were bound to happen, especially with the absence of a strong male figure in his life. The upside to all of these was that George Weah never allowed these bad habits to define him or stand in the path of his success. He had the mindset to succeed and the attitude to change these bad habits that he'd copied from friends. To attract into his life the very things he had dreamt of, Weah had to stick to his success game plans—practice hard and play harder.

Following his transfer to the Invincible Eleven, IE Football Club which was an archrival to Mighty Barrolle, George Oppong Weah became the favorite player for the fans of Liberia's darling football club, IE, and the Lone Star of Liberia. By 1987 with his newfound fame and favored by football craze spectators, Weah's life slowly changed—he could now afford to help Ma Emma with money to support the large family at home as well as buy his necessities as a young boy. While other boys of his age were still struggling for survival, Weah's life story had changed due to his sheer will power and help from people like, Samuel N. Burnette, Archibald F. Bernard (his current legal adviser), Carlton A. Karpeh, Adama Sirleaf, and dozens of unsung heroes and heroines of Invincible Eleven. Many people in his Gibraltar community had written him off as another failure because of his earlier unruly behavior toward adults in the community and his lowly birth's story. While most people will attribute Weah's success to his talent, it should be noted that Weah is a very pleasant and humble soul who values hard work over everything else. As an athlete and up to now, he still wakes up at 4:00 AM. He is an early bird who wakes up before dawn everyday, even if he goes to bed late. Being a man of limited words, which can somehow be attributed to his early speech development and his struggles in elementary school, Weah never boasts of his football exploits or the many titles he won during his football career. Unlike few self-absorbed and pompous Liberian players of his time, many of whom were very talented but failed to reach the apex of their football careers in Europe due to pride and lack of discipline, George Weah's humility and hard work brought him the fame he deserved. As flawed and vindictive as he is seen by many, his work ethics as a footballer was unsurpassed. When fame came, he never took himself like a prima donna—he never allowed honors and glory to change him. Sometimes in life, a person's attitude and their mindset can make all the difference for them and thousands of others around them.

By the age of 18, Weah's fame went beyond Liberia's borders. In Cameroon, his playing styles and dribbling skills brought him a huge following. As the only Liberian playing in that part of Africa, Weah's skills didn't go unnoticed by football enthusiasts in Yaounde. He was lauded by Paul Biya, President of Cameroon, and Cameroon's football legend Roger Milla. For his mesmerizing performance for Tonnerre Kalara Club at the Ahmadou Ahidjo Stadium in Yaounde, Roger Milla nicknamed him the 'Black Diamond of Africa'. This was the reason why Tonnerre didn't want to give him a transfer to play for AS Monaco when the opportunity came for George—he was an asset to the team. Compounded with that, his contract had not yet expired, but President Samuel K. Doe intervened on his behalf.

In Europe, his fame only grew bigger and bigger, beyond his wildest imagination. By the early 1990s, George Weah could now afford just about anything the poor kid from the ghetto of Gibraltar could ever dream of—luxury cars, flying first class in any plan of his choice to some of the most exotic places so many Clara Town residents could ever dream of. At the height of his career, George Weah was chartering the Concorde, the French's iconic supersonic jet to fly him from New York to Paris, France, sometimes for game or for pleasure. The Concorde only took three hours on the seven and a half hours journey. Fame and the money that came with it made George to live large and to give his children the life he was denied because of his predisposition to poverty.

Not only was he famous as an international football super star—he represented the Liberian people when war was ravaging his tiny country. During the 14 years long civil wars, George Weah had everything in the slowly decaying nation. He had family members including Ma Emma, his mother, brothers and sisters, friends, loved ones and his heart. He never forgot where he came from and the people he met along his journey to stardom. For love of country, he risked his life and came back to Liberia many times during the height of the bloody civil wars. He traveled to displaced camps around the city and refugee camps around the West African sub-regions in the spirit of Liberian solidarity. On many of his visits to see yearning citizens of Liberia, he often gave financial support to refugees and stranded war weary Liberians. As the only famous son of the land, he became the face of Liberia to the international community. At the time, the name George Weah was the only good thing that came out of Liberia. He never forgot what his paternal grand aunt, Ma Emma told him, "Never forget where you come from, and remain true to yourself". Whenever he came home from Europe for vacation, he would bring gifts for his friends and his many girlfriends. At the time of being George Oppong Weah, the most famous football player in Liberia or in Africa, he was alluring to many young girls. He lured many underage girls to having sex with him. Some of these girls were in their teens—below the age of legal sexual consent. He and his boys would go women or girls hunting at the Sports Commission on Broad Street, Cathedral Catholic School, Wells Hairston High School, St. Theresa Convent, the College of West Africa, and many other places and schools in and around Monrovia. Many of these high school teens were the 10th, 11th, and 11th grades, and were between the ages of sixteen, seventeen and eighteen years of age. Many of these teens were taken to his 9th Street residence in the 1990s and at his Rehab Road home. Fame also gave Gave George an exotic taste both in drinks and in food. Before departing Liberia, George Weah drank Guinness Stout, whisky, and sometimes gin of all kinds. But with fame and being in Europe, that continent gave him a taste of exotica, especially drinks like Bacardi and Coke, Hennessy Paradis, Remy Martin Louis XIII, and food like Chateaubriand, many others.

In Europe, Weah represented something new out of the African continent. While he may have left Liberia and Africa as the 'Wizard Dribbler', Europe changed him to a goal scoring machine. He became the new gold standard for measuring African players' output on European soil. Some European team coaches openly asked new African recruits if they could play football like George Weah or Mr. George, as he was called in France. His fame was not only meant for him alone—it rubbed off on those that had encountered him years earlier. Many Liberian football players used his name to land football contracts across Europe and in other places. They would sometimes tell coaches that they had played football alongside George Weah as a kid or on the professional level. At the height of the Liberian Civil Wars, George Weah's name was also used by many Liberians and Africans that took refuge in Europe and in other places around the world to open locked doors onto themselves. Often, Liberian migrants and war affected refugees would tell immigration officials that they were related to George Weah in one form or the other, and they would get a pass. Many Liberians acquired immigration status in different European countries by using George Weah as a conduit to obtain a legal status. While he was placing himself at the pinnacle of football, he was also unknowingly creating opportunities for his fellow Liberians and Africans in general.

The taste of fame was not George Weah's alone; it belonged to those who dared to go out of their comfort zones to be different. At the time, George Weah was different from the self-centered establishment. He created an avenue so others could thrive while walking in his footsteps or under the shadows of his wings. As evidence to this day, look at the avalanche of African football stars that are now playing in Europe, it would not have happened hadn't George Weah shattered the artificial barrier erected by Europeans ill will and enmity toward black players over the centuries. While there may have been great African players before him, none enjoyed the level of glory and honor as he did. George Weah did not only make his employers happy, but he made millions of fans fall in love with him and made hundreds of football players cry his name after every victory and defeat that won his team a title. Though there is not yet any past or current African player that can match the fame and achievements of George Weah, one cannot rule out the possibility that it will not happen after a thousand years. Maybe there might just be someone from the African continent that might be as good as he is, within a hundred or perhaps a thousand years.

Growing up poor and wanting what every successful football, basketball, and Hollywood star had, has always been on George Weah's radar. As a kid growing up in the ghetto of Gibraltar, he wanted fancy clothes, jewelries, good food, beautiful women, and luxurious cars. He even dreamt of owning his own plane like the rich and famous actors in Hollywood did at the time. Wanting something is one thing and working hard to achieve what one wants is another thing. With the help of good coaches and God being on his side, his talent brought everything he longed for. While struggling to achieve his dreams against all odds, Georg Weah never allowed his dream to fizzle or go dry like a raisin left alone in the sun. He worked, and worked, and kept dreaming and tweaking his dream on the game he loved so much. As he began to earn his own money, his appetite for gathering the finest of things grew bigger and bigger as the years went by. To live his dream, he used a portion of his earnings to buy expensive European cars, clothes, jewelry, and expensive sunglasses along with wrist watch-es. As a wealthy man, he went to places where only the rich, powerful, and famous frequented. George Weah's fame afforded him the ability to charter jets and many other planes to take him to his intended destination around the world. While he's often criticized by others for living a wastefully luxurious life, he lived his life as he had planned. He lived life to the fullest. He kept a family, and never lost the common touch with those that mattered to him the most—the poor, the dejected and the social rejects of Liberia.

A few of George Weah's closest friends have broken paths with him for what many term him as being, "repugnantly vindictive, domineering, and the one man in the room behavior". Being raised by a God-fearing grand aunty, outsiders might think these characterizations are not something to be attributed to George. As humans, people grow and evolve behaviorally. But again, one needs to be careful when it comes to passing judgement on others including George or believing some of the allegations that have been brought against him by former friends. While many of his supporters do not see him the same way critics and former friends see him, Weah being human may have had a personal difference with many of these critics. In life, people can form their own impression of a person after an encounter or tense incident with that person. If Weah had had such an overreaching behavior during his early football and political days, his supporters believe that he has outgrown such officious and the one man in the room syndrome or behavior. As a mature man and a politician, he may have created rooms for dissent, and a diversity of view. As a person grows, so will their associates. A leader often makes new friends and maintains old and trusted allies as he or she advances in their career or stature. While shining, they might sometimes allow others to shine as well. On the other hand, Mr. Weah's critics and many of his friends think the opposite. According to a close friend he once played football and partied with, he still thinks George Weah hasn't gotten over his childish petiteness. He is seen as intentionally callous due to his treatment of people he disagrees with. Many of them feel that fame has given George an entitlement mentality. For he thinks he's entitled to having his friends' women because he's George Weah. Many of these friends fear bringing their women around George who has eyes for pretty women. He is said to boldly stares at other men's wives or girlfriends and sometime seemed to undress them with his eyes. While he may projects a friendly persona of a welcoming friend, he hates being overshadowed by those around him or anyone within his immediate proximity. Many of his close friends assert that George also hates being alone— that's why he often travels with a large entourage to provide for him an extra layer of self-confidence and security. Perhaps though, he still suffers from the low self-esteem problem he struggled with as a teen. To keep being in his good grace, one has to keep whispering gossips in his ears about others. Often, people around him constantly whisper wicked things in his ears about each other within his entourage. In his football prime days, whenever he and his friends went into a nightclub to hangout and met Liberians and Nigerians' scammers who tried to outspend him with their stolen money, George would out spend them with thrice the amount they would spend. For example, if the scammer group spent $50,000 on drinks and entertainment, he would spend between $150,000 to $200,000 that night. Back then, he would have one of his trusted friends hold his spending cash, bank debit card, or sometimes his credit card whenever they traveled or went out to party.

Chapter 12

The Liberian Civil Wars, 1989—2003

No ordinary Liberian citizen expected it to have happened; not George Weah, not even Ma Emma, his God's fearing grand aunty who raised him from childhood until the day he became a professional football player. It caught everyone by surprise. In fact, people thought if the civil war reached their safe haven of Monrovia, it would only last for a few days or maybe a week, but everyone was wrong. The Liberian Civil War was a war created from mere tension between two men, Samuel Doe, and Thomas Quiwonkpa due to their failure in settling their personal differences. The sheer stupidities of Doe and Quiwonkpa that were strengthened by ethnic tension between the people of Nimba County and Grand Gedeh County, and exploited by western countries, mainly the United States of America, Britain, and France led to the death of hundreds of thousands of innocent citizens of all ethnic groupings. The civil war should not have been fought in the first place, especially when there emerged no clear winner at the end of it all. Liberia and Liberians were the losers in these civil wars that were fought for more than 14 years. Liberians should never again allow anyone to agitate, fan the flame of conflict or mislead them into destroying themselves under the guise of a revolution.

The Liberian Civil War was designed and orchestrated by the Central Intelligence Agency, CIA or the "Cocaine Importing

Agency" as most black people in the United States refer to the U.S. spy agency. Charles Taylor was a CIA inside man working within Samuel Doe's People's Redemption Council Government. While working within the Doe's administration, he passed secret government's information to his CIA handler stationed at the U.S. Embassy near Monrovia, just as Doe, Ellen Johnson Sirleaf and others had done to the Tolbert administration years leading to the 1980 coup. When Charles Taylor stole money from the PRC Government, he made a successful run for the United States. After being accused by Doe of embezzlement and imprisoned in Massachusetts, Taylor was taken out of jail by the United States government and transported to New York for debriefing about a secret training the CIA was sponsoring in various places around the world including Africa for a full-scale assault on the Samuel Doe administration that had fallen out of favor with the United States Government.

It all began after Doe had gotten enlightened as a true Liberian patriot and threatened to deny the United States Government full access to its strategic facilities in Liberia, one of which was the Roberts International Airport, RIA in Margibi County. Up until the time of Samuel Doe's threat, the U.S. Government through the CIA used the RIA, to conduct clandestine operation activities throughout Africa. Liberia was used as a hub for transporting weapons across Africa by the CIA for the destabilization of countries the U.S. saw as having Soviet ties and for the support of African dictators. Denying the Americans something they have unquestioned access to was a slap in the face of George H.W. Bush's administration. Before Bush, Samuel Doe was one of President Ronald Reagan's puppets in Africa. Like previous Liberian leaders, Reagan used Doe like pinball to do whatever he wanted him to do. In return, Doe got military and other financial aid from the United States, but most of the money went into Doe and his cronies' pockets. With Doe's threat, it was only expedient for the U.S. to do whatever she had to do in protecting her interests in Liberia. By the mid-1980s, the end of the Cold War was nowhere in sight. For the United States Government, the RIA was not only a strategic asset, it meant everything to her, though she had other installations like the VOA relay station and the OMEGA Navigation Tower that was being used to spy on the Soviet Union's activities across Africa and the Middle East. But for the CIA, the RIA was irreplaceable, and they could not afford to lose access to it.

Against that backdrop, the George H.W. Bush's administration welcomed the arrival of Charles Taylor and his ban of Libyan, Cuban, and Burkina Faso trained rebel fighters with open arms. They aided Taylor and his men by giving them strategic insight on the status of the Armed Forces of Liberia, AFL as well as providing him with financial support and military hardware. The Liberian Civil War proved that the United States does not have a permanent friendship with Liberia. Rather, the Government of the United States of America only has a permanent interest with Liberia or any other country for that matter. As long as those interests exist, the bond of friendship will remain. But when the interest no longer exists, the United States Government will turn her back on her friends and embrace the country's foe. The U.S. Government could have ended the Liberian Civil War had it wanted to. As the greatest military force in the world at the time, the U.S. Government could have put an end to the carnage in Liberia with a single battalion of United States trained Marines or even a handful of Green Berets from the U.S. Army. Instead, they told the rest of the world that the war was an internal matter, as they worked behind the scenes to prolong it by fanning various kinds of flames that prolonged the violence and suffering of the Liberian people. For a fact, the United States had always dealt Liberia a double hand—throwing stones and hiding her hands behind her back in most instances. Young and forward-thinking Liberians will one day come to the realization that the United States of The American government is not a true friend of the Liberian people—the ordinary none racist people are the true friends. The Liberian Civil War hurt not only the country's infrastructure, but it also killed dreams and so many promise keepers that never had the time to help a country that was slowly dying under its own weight. Who knows, maybe some of the victims of that insane war could have been great scientists, doctors, inventors, writers and so many things that could have changed Liberia and the lives of millions of its citizens.

The civil war displaced almost two million people from Liberia. During the war, it was the Krahn minority vs. everyone because the NPFL was a popular movement that comprised almost 13 of the 15 tribal groups in Liberia. With such mass support from more than 98% of the citizenry, the NPFL exerted its sphere of influence throughout the 14 counties, now fifteen counties of Liberia. The Liberian Civil War was based on mere male ego. As stated earlier, it was a war created by the failure of two men in settling their personal differences and fueled by the United States Government's hatred for one man, Samuel Kanyon Doe—a man they helped to make but got smart at their own games. The history of the Liberian Civil War cannot be written in one context because it has many little moving pieces. The war afflicted and affected everybody, rich, poor, Christians, Muslims, straight, gay, everyone in between, and George Weah who was now playing professional football in faraway France. From France, George monitored the war and tried to remain in contact with family members and friends daily. While he was thousands of miles away from the conflict zone, his heart bled everyday due to the images he saw of the war on French televisions and other international news flash. Arsene Wenger, who was his coach at AS Monaco in the 1990s, said that George Weah would stay in his room all day crying for his people in Liberia. According to Wenger, he often wondered how many twenty something year-old men could do such a thing today, but Weah's love for his people and country was organic at that time and it is believed to still be that way today.

Throughout the Liberian Civil Wars of the 1990s, fighting occurred not only across the major divisions within the country, but also within each side of the warring factions and as individual groups splintered. For the most part, civilians became the main target for violence in three main patterns. First, the conduct of the war as various armed groups tried to claim, consolidate, or expand areas of control, second, competition between armed groups for control over economic resources and extracted resources from the civilian population, and finally, it was a deliberate targeting of ethnic groups associated with different armed groups. Gios and Mano killed Krahns and Mandingoes, and all other tribes sought to

establish dominance in one form or the other—lesser-known tribes
rose to prominence at that time in the 1990s. However, as sadly
and as cold as it became, separating violence against civilians from
combatants proved very difficult. ECOMOG fighter jets from the
Nigerians and Ghanaians contingents occasionally bombed civilians' targets in areas occupied and controlled by the NPFL. For this
act, the NPFL killed thousands of civilians in Monrovia by raining
howitzer long-range mortar rounds on residents in Monrovia. As
Charles Taylor put it at the time, "If Gbarnga cries, Monrovia will
cry also", the rocket killed dozens of people in the only safe hav-
en that frightened civilians knew. As the ECOMOG peacekeepers
fought back and killed NPFL's soldiers, the NPFL continually recruited and trained fighters as a means of perpetuating the war. To
swell their ranks, NPFL and other warring factions also went on a
widespread recruitment of children as fighters. Many of these often
hastily assembled and ill-disciplined armed forces that were used
for their reign of terror had no idea why they were fighting. Many
of them only knew that they were 'fighting for freedom' and called
themselves "Freedom Fighters".

As a result of the war, an entire generation of children
in Liberia has known nothing but war for much of their lives.
During those dark days in Liberia, most of the child soldiers only
knew one Liberian, George Oppong Weah as a model of perfection during their involvement with the Liberia Civil War. He was
the light in the darkness for many of them. Now as grown men
and women, many of these former child soldiers have come to
hold loyalty to only George Weah, just like they had done to their
commanders in their earlier life as child soldiers. For many who
may not know the stories of these war-affected children, it is easy
to give up on them and write them off as part of the unfixable
damage caused by poverty, unrest, and deep-seated ethnic and
governmental hate. For the analyst, child soldiers are a relatively
recent phenomenon, there is not much information on the long-
term consequences of child soldiers that fought in the uncivil wars
in Liberia. However, lessons learned during the brief ceasefire in
Liberia in 1997 and from rehabilitation efforts in other countries
suggest that there are rays of hope in a community-based approach

to rehabilitation of young boys and girls affected by the protracted 14 years conflict.

While the series of skirmishes were taking place, George Weah continuously engaged Liberians both home and abroad; he would send relief items to refugees in Ghana, the Cote D'Ivoire and internally displaced people in Monrovia. George Weah himself had been accused of providing financial support to MODEL Rebels, which was a Krahn rebel faction operating in southeastern Liberia. The accusation arises from a statement George Weah made years earlier when he was at odd with Charles Taylor and Edwin Snow who was the son-in-law of Mr. Taylor. But most people believe that the accusation was based on Weah's close ties with Samuel Doe and his humanitarian support for some of the Krahn refugees living in Cote D'Ivoire. George Weah's close tie with the Krahns stems from his friendship with former President Samuel Doe who supported Weah both financially and morally.

Looking at the period from 1989-1997, there were numerous failed efforts to bring the country into experiencing peace. The civil wars which were a pure creation of the United States CIA, had spiraled out of control—the genie could not be put back in the bottle. Those eight years of fluctuating fighting were marked by the blood of brutal ethnic killings and massive abuses against the civilian population, especially women and children. In the first two phases of the civil war, thousands of Liberian men, women, and children were killed and subjected to torture, beatings, rapes, and many other forms of sexual assault. The acts of inhumane treatment of civilians resulted in the massive displacement of Liberians both inside and outside the country. Though it is believed that the civil conflict goes as far back to the founding of the country, it was just fueled by the involvement of Western Powers, mainly the United States, the United Kingdom, and France. While the U.S. was a major player because of its fallout with the Samuel Doe government, it played a subversive role behind the scenes, sometimes arming various warring factions in and out of Liberia.

When one looks back at the civil war, one will find the

United States fingerprints all over the Liberian Civil Wars whether the younger generation of Liberians know it or not. Though the fall of the former Soviet Union and other former Soviet blocs helped to power the Liberian Civil War with the supplies of leftover weapons from the Soviet era, NATO and the United Nations could have easily stopped the inflow of weapons in the conflict zones during the early stage of the war. Instead, everyone was cashing in on the bloodlettings that were taking place in Liberia and neighboring Sierra Leone. Many European and Western powers turned their eyes the other way and allowed major gun traffickers from the United States, especially the CIA and many others across Europe and the Middle East to constantly supply guns and other military hardware to warring factions across Liberian and the African Continent.

When one looks deep into the genesis of the Liberian Civil Conflicts that took away the lives of thousands of men, women, children, and animals, one would see a lot of invisible hands operating in the shadow—western agitators like the U.S.A, UK, France, and regional enablers like Cote D'Ivoire, Sierra Leone, Ghana, and Nigeria. Prior to the start of the civil wars in 1989, Liberia was mostly an unknown country to many people across the world beside its most famous son, George Oppong Weah. It seemed like many Liberians forgot their violent past of the 1980 coup and the November 12, 1985, abortive invasion which led to the mass exodus of hundreds of Gios and Manos men and women from the country. Those Gios and Manos that made it safely out of the country later organized themselves with the support of regional and western governments to launch a decade and a half long war on the poor and mostly innocent people of Liberia.

The Liberian Civil War started in the early morning of December 24, 1989, when a handful of Libyan trained Liberians rebels mixed with Burkinabe dissidents attacked a border post in the border town of Butuo in Nimba County. The group was under the name, National Patriotic Front of Liberia, NPFL which was led by Charles McArthur Taylor. These armed men have been transported to the border by the Ivorian government under the leadership of Felix Houphouët-Boigny who had been a stooge for his French colonial masters in Paris. He hated Samuel Doe who he blamed for reneging on his promise and murdering his son-in-law Adolphus Benedict (A.B.) Tolbert after the PRC violated international law by breaking into the French Embassy where A.B. was given political asylum by the French. After the arrest in June of 1980, he was imprisoned and later murdered by Doe's PRC junta following his mysterious disappearance from the prison. The site of his burial hasn't been found up to this day.

On the same note, Taylor was assisted by Burkina Faso for the fact that the Burkinabe's President, Blaise Compaoré's was then married to Daisy Delafosse-Tolber, the former wife of A.B. Tolbert. Daisy Delafosse was the goddaughter of Ivorian President and dictator Félix Houphouët-Boigny. Delafosse and her godfather had a strong influence on Blaise. This created a double dose of enemies for Samuel Doe, with the combined forces of Houphouët-Boigny and Blaise Compaoré acting against him. It is believed that it was Taylor's men that helped Compaoré to overthrow then President Thomas Sankara in 1987. The geopolitical nature of the Liberian Civil War helped prolong it. The dissidents under the leadership of Charles Taylor who happened to be a CIA informant remained in close contact with the United State Department of States throughout the war. The CIA and the State Department helped Taylor and his ragtag NPFL fighters draw out the battle plan for the war against Doe and his Krahn dominated AFL soldiers. In the grand scheme of things, Taylor was being used to get rid of Doe who was posing an imminent threat to US's interests in Liberia.

According to a leaked U.S. State Department's document that made rounds on the Internet a few years ago, the game plan for the civil war in Liberia was to get Samuel Doe out of power by all means. Then U.S. Assistant Secretary of State for African Affairs Herman Jay Cohen proposed to Taylor that they were going to force Samuel Doe to resign and have his Vice-President Harry Moniba take his place as president. Moniba would then appoint Charles Taylor as the new Vice-President of Liberia and then himself resign as head of state a few months later. During his presidency, Taylor would be forced to organize an election in October of 1991 according to the Constitution of the Republic of Liberia. The U.S. Department of State and the CIA arranged with the President of Togo, Gnassingbé Eyadéma to have President Samuel Doe be granted asylum in that country. For Americans, their favorite candidate for the highly coveted seat was Ellen Sirleaf, and not Dr. Amos Sawyer. Amos Sawyer was too much of a liability for the Americans—for he had long been viewed as a dissident politician by so many in the international community. To facilitate the transition of power, the United States government through the U.S. Department of State had an aircraft available in Freetown ready to pick Doe and his immediate family from Monrovia. Prior to all these happenings, Doe had evacuated his wife, many of his girl-friends and children from Monrovia. According to the CIA's plan, Herman Cohen was to fly or sail into Monrovia under the cover of darkness and say to Doe, "Okay, now is the time. Get your family and everyone and get on the plane and let's go to Togo." On the other hand, Doe wanted every stranded Krahn citizen of Liberia that lived in Monrovia to be evacuated as well. This was a huge problem for the Americans that didn't want to be seen as meddling in the internal affairs of Liberia. This was the reason whenever any U.S. State Department officials when being interviewed by the international media about the Liberian Civil War, especially Liberia being seen as a country founded by the United States, they would always say, "The conflict is the internal affairs of Liberia. Therefore, Liberians need to find an amicable solution to their own problem". The evacuation plan soon changed; the U.S. Department of Defense had overruled the U.S. Department of State's plan for Liberia. According to Cohen, Robert Gates, the deputy national security adviser to George H.W. Bush, shot down elements of Cohen's plans and ordered deployment of the US Marine Amphibious Readiness Group in Liberia. The group soon arrived offshore of Monrovia between the 3rd and 4th of June 1990. The combat ready group were prepared for deployment in a war zone. The Department of Defense, DOD didn't follow-through because they didn't want to take moral responsibility if anything went wrong during the deployment of the U.S. ground force in the conflict zone in

Liberia. What the Marines did when they realized Doe and several of his loyalists were held up in the Executive Mansion on Capitol Hill in Monrovia, they shelled the building from the sea; pretending as if it was the Independent National Patriotic Front of Liberia, INPFL forces of Prince Johnson that had taken control of the western side of the city. Several months into the fight with Samuel Doe, Prince Y. Johnson captured and killed Doe in September of that year. Early that year during the civil war, Prince Johnson who was then a battlefront commander of Taylor's NPFL, broke away and formed his own elite fighting group that he named "Independent National Patriotic Front of Liberia. As the fight for the removal of Samuel Doe continued, the DOD and CIA backed off. Like the U.S. State Department, they too deemed the civil war as an internal affair of Liberia. Many Liberians believe that if the United State of America wanted to truly put an end to the Liberian Civil Wars it could have done it with ease to stop the carnage that took the lives of an estimated two hundred thousand people.

The United States was working behind the scenes, and later sensing the unpredictability in their front man, Charles Taylor, they walked back on many of the things they had strategized. They came to the realization that if Taylor was allowed to taste state power as was seen in his rebel territory, he never would have held presidential and general elections that would ultimately bring their preferred candidate to power. They became very afraid of him becoming president because he had become heavily indebted to unfriendly governments like Libya, Burkina Faso, and Cuba.

To stop Charles Taylor in his tracks, the U.S. Department of State and the Department of Defense along with other intelligence services quickly rally West African countries, mainly Ghana, Nigeria, Sierra Leone, Guinea and later Senegal to muster reactionary forces that would bear the brunt of the war, if anything of that nature ever happened. The U.S. would provide funding, logistics, intelligence and other strategies for the Economic Community of West African States Monitoring Group, alias ECOMOG the military group leaders of the subregion agreed to form. During the formation of ECOMOG, the U.S. Government informed the West

African Leaders that the military group needed to be seen as an African initiative—Africans working together to solve an African nation's problem. Prior to the formation of the West African Monitoring Group or ECOMOG, the U.S. Department of State, in secret, directed West African leaders to form an interim government that would replace President Samuel Doe since the U.S. Government initial plan had failed. Consequently, during the summer of 1990, then Gambian President, Dawda K. Jawara, Sierra Leone's President and several other West African leaders congregated in the Sierra Leoneans' capital of Freetown and set up the Interim Government of National Unity, IGNU. This government would later come to find itself fighting on several fronts upon arriving in Liberia. All the while these things were playing out behind the scenes, the civil war still raged on, and hundreds of civilians were being slaughtered by both the NPFL of Charles Taylor and Samuel Doe's Krahn dominated AFL.

Amid the NPFL war of the 1990s, Charles Taylor armed anyone he saw fit to fight, this included, young boys and girls, the mentally ill, the disabled, and mercenaries from Burkina Faso Sierra Leone, and the Gambia. For the NPFL, the use of children as soldiers date back to the start of Liberia's uncivil war in 1989. In the 90s, Charles Taylor and his NPFL gangs became infamous for the abduction and use of young boys and sometimes girls to increase the size and strength of the fighting forces. Other Liberian fighting factions like ULIMO J and K, LURD, LPC and many others soon followed suit, and this tactic was eventually adopted by other groups in neighboring Sierra Leone during that country's civil war. Reason behind the recruitment of children was simple, little boys were favored because their immaturity made them more likely to take risks and less likely to question authority. Also, young boys, particularly the ones with little to no education from the rural areas didn't always understand the war, so they could be indoctrinated with beliefs more easily than an adult. Those days, if someone asked any of the child soldiers why they were fighting, they would simply tell that person that, "They were fighting for freedom." Many of the Gios and Manos called themselves "Freedom Fighters". Many of the child soldiers were made to believe that looting, stealing, and other activities were just the games of war. They were told by older commanders that they were impervious to bullets—that they could not be harmed or killed by bullets because they were protected by voodoo charms. Many of these child soldiers were eager to taste battle and to prove themselves to their commanders. They were all enticed with incentives such as promotion in rank, food, material things, and sometimes women to have sex with. Many of these boys were killed by ECOMOG forces.

While the mayhem was taking place in the 1990s, George Weah was playing host for many of the Liberians fleeing the killing field in Liberia to Europe and Ghana. He used his personal funds to rent homes for families in need and rendered other services to his compatriots. This kind act of humanity infuriated George's newly wedded wife, Clar Marie Duncan. She temporarily separated from him in France and moved her and her young son Timothy back to the U.S. Many who encountered George Weah felt the magic of his kindness. As a twenty something year old man, he was very entertaining outside of the football field. Unbeknown to him, he was making his way into the hearts of many of his countrymen.

Chapter 13

Professional Football Career in Europe

Playing professional football in Europe and winning the fans' love was not difficult for George Oppong Weah who had been preparing himself for the task his entire life. From his amateur football days in Liberia to his semiprofessional days in Cameroon, he marveled at the star-power of professional players in Europe. He envied the lifestyles of some of the professional players he grew up watching on Liberian television. When George finally arrived in Monaco the fall of 1988, it was not something of a pageantry—Weah had to justify his inclusion on the team and then on the squad. His being on the squad started on a rocky footing because he lacked certain technical skills the game required. George Oppong Weah did not grow up like many young European football-loving boys that had the privilege of attending youth training at football academies across the Continent. Weah's only exposure to being trained by professional coaches was when the government of Liberia sent the Liberian national football team, the Lone Star to Brazil at one of that country's many football academies. Besides his self-taught skills that he developed on muddy football fields in Clara Town and on rocky grounds around Monrovia, along with trainings given him by coaches of the various local teams he had played for in Liberia, and in Cameroon, George Weah would have failed had it not been for his sheer perseverance and a positive mindset.

Upon his arrival in Monaco, he was seen by well-established players as raw, lanky, and lazy. Seeing his raw talent and explosive power from video footage during his time in Cameroon, AS Monaco's coach at the time, Arsene Wenger decided to nurture the 23-year-old George Weah. Wenger kept Weah on the sideline for six months in order to allow Weah to get himself familiar with everything around him, fan, lighting, weather, players, and training. Realizing the level of interest his coach had in him, the determined and focused George Weah accepted the offer from the man who would take him as a son and would later teach him something more than football—Wenger taught George Weah about life and the career of a black football player in France and on the European Continent. With Weah accepting the help and Wenger willing to help the success hungry George Oppong Weah, the combination turned out to be something phenomenal. The result would bring fame and glory to George Weah and the people of his native Liberia while it turned Wenger into one of the most sought-after coaches in Europe.

After spending hundreds of hours in professional skills building training and thousands more in strength and skills training, the full force of the Liberian legend in waiting was unleashed on the field of Monaco and on the European Continent. George Weah gained strengths in his legs and upper extremity and was powerfully built by the age of 24. He became the wonder boy of AS Monaco. Having left behind the hardship of Africa, Weah morphed into a commandingly handsome young man with sharp cheekbones, intensely sparkling eyes, and the height that gave him a view into the future. His beautiful dark-brown skin became so luminous that some French people thought he was sometimes lighting up from within. Both black and white women threw themselves at George Weah for varying reasons—sex, love, identification with the star, and for cash. Being a twenty something years old young man with money, fame, and glory along with the look that goes with them, George Weah had his field day with every female that crossed his paths during his professional football days and even as a politician. In Liberia and in other places around the United States, he had several of his home boys scouting women for him to have sex with. When George wanted a beautiful woman, be it young or old, all he did was to point out that woman he wants to have sex with to one of his scouts who would track them down and would make the necessary arrangement for they and George to have a private moment together wherever George desired. In Monrovia and around Africa, he would drive in his fancy car packed with his entourage around school campuses, sporting activities, displaced and refugee camps, and at places where young women congregated. Some of Weah's former friends believe that this predatory behavior continues up to this day. According to many of his friends within his cliques as well as many of the females he has had sexual encounter with, George Weah is very indiscriminate when it comes to women. He objectifies women and believes having sex with them will raise their social status—they would boast about having sex with him for fame. If he met a group of beautiful women that are all friends, he would try to have sex with every woman in the group. This behavior often causes friction between friends. There were also frictions between George and many of his Posses or friends over women that led to him breaking friendship with them. Many of his friends see him as a sex predator.

Upon catapulting into stardom and being able to afford just about anything he wanted, George believed that he was being taken advantage of by some of this family members and his circle of friends. Breaking friendship or path with many of his friends was a matter of principle for him. For George, he believed that many of the guys within his circle were only leeching on him. Since he had the money at that time, therefore he calls the shots. If he felt disrespected or betrayed by anyone within his immediate domain, he did away with that person and would instruct others not to talk to that person. If George heard a rumor about any of his friend going after one of his girlfriends, he broke friendship with that posse. Furthermore, George Weah's relationship with most of the women he encounters is not a permanent one—he is a transactional person. According to one of his close friends, he often considers his sexual encounters with women as a fling, or a one-night stand. If George was done having a sexual relationship with a female, he would often pass that female down to one of his posses for their sexual pleasure. He treats many of the women he encounters like a use and recycled pass-along objects. For those women who he didn't pass down onto one of his friends, he had them on the rebound or reserve list to be rewind (a Liberian slang for substitute) by him a any given time. Many of these women willingly gave themselves over to Oppong as prize for his personal pleasure. Often, they did this to remain on his good or gracious list because as easily as he made friends, he easily broke away from those he felt he didn't have use for. Many of this friends see him as a purely transactional guy—needing a friend who brings a benefit to him.

While this pattern of behavior from a man that was raised by a God's fearing woman and in a Christian home might seem abhorrent to many westerners, it is a common thing among African celebrities and politicians. Some analysts blame many of these women (victims and survivals), both young and old for giving themselves over to George Weah and his henchmen to be feasted on. One can only say that these women are infatuated with his status, or maybe, they are self-prostituting for cash and for identification with George Weah.

With fame and wealth all around him, one would think that George would have forgotten where he came from, or he would have buried all the bitter memories of his hardships behind him when he was on top of the world as the greatest African player in the world. But he never forgot from where he came or all the roads he'd traveled to get to where he was. Whenever he was in the company of friends, he would retrospect and narrate his story of personal struggles and hardships in Liberia, especially how as kids, he and his older brother, Junior Boy, scrap metal at dumpsites or sold Fufu (a popular Liberian food that is made from fermented Cassavas' dough, which is cooked and served with varying kinds of sauces) in the local market in Camp Schieffelin for their uncle's wife when they lived with him for a short time. They would sometimes get in trouble if they came up short with the money at the end of their selling day. He would also tell friends of how he would follow Junior Boy to the Freeport of Monrovia to work as day boys by unloading container trucks in warehouses for $2.50 or $5.00

at the end of the day. Or how he went onto garbage dump sites to gather emptied glass bottles and aluminum cans and wires for sale to local tradesmen. His struggles came to a slow end when he signed up and donned the number 14 jersey of Invincible Eleven, IE in the mid-1980. George got his first real job with the Liberia Telecommunications Corporation, LTC as a Switchboard Operator. He also got a contract as the face of the Liberia Electricity Corporation, LEC—advertising the company's services on national television in Liberia. This contract which he included his brother, William on, didn't work well for the twenty-something year-old. As a professional football player, he established several businesses that failed. Many of these businesses were being managed by women he was having romantic relationship with or with people that he was too closed to. He also owned several businesses in the United States, Cote d'ivoire, Ghana, Liberia, and in Europe, etc. All those ventures failed due to poor management.

In the 1990s, George Weah thrilled millions of European football fans with his amazing skills on various football fields in Francs, Italy, Russia, Germany, and in many cities across Europe. On the football field, he had the uncanny ability to predict an opponent's future location before reaching said opponent with the football. According to George, if he wanted to score a goal, he would imagine the football at the back of the net before reaching the goalkeeper. By having the destination of the football in mind, getting through the many defenders was just a matter of location mapping of each player that he would create in his head as he dribbled his way to the goalpost. For George, getting to the goalkeeper and putting the ball in the back of the net with opponents coming toward him or pursuing him for the ball was a thing he trained his brain to do while using his feet to implement the scenarios that his brain had formulated. In the 1990s, George Weah was an amazing football genius—he would freeze an attacking defender in their tracks using his famous 'Double Shovel' technique. He would often blaze past hapless defenders to score goals and win championships for the game's elite clubs like AS Monaco, PSG, AC Milan, and Chelsea FC. At this stage in his football career, Weah had matured to the point that he had control over his dribbling skills, his breathing, and his goal scoring ability. He was fast, strong, and shrewd like a fox for most defenders in the world at that time. For George Weah had come to master the art of the game and the act of scoring impossible goals that made football fans cry both in defeat and in victory. He had long discovered and developed the mental nature of the game, its players, and his opponents' styles on the other teams. He often told his teammate that, *"Football is a mind game."* To be able to outperform one's opponent, Weah believes that the tactic must first be played inside the player's head using many kinds of scenarios before passing what the mind has developed onto the feet for final implementation. He would mind map his opponents and create scenarios on how to get the ball at the back of the net. He once told players of Junior Professionals, a team he formed and coached in Liberia, the reason he scored amazing goals is his ability to buoy and mentally zoom out on the pitch in order to see the positions of his opponents. With his skills and strength, once in possession of the ball, scoring a goal would be inevitable. This is an ability that is found in many successful football players-—it cannot be taught by any coach in the world. A player either has it or does not have it.

To many of the millennial generation (children born after the 1980s) in Liberia, Georg Oppong Manneh Weah symbolizes everything their country lacked at the time of their birth because he possessed wealth, honest achievement, love for country, international prestige, and a closed connection to people of lowly birth and humble origin. While many of these millennials did not watch him play football on European fields, many of them are of the belief that he is the future of their country that has been plagued with so many unfortunate things and leaders that do not love Liberia and millennials.

George Manneh Weah never forgot his humble origin with all the glamour and fanfare he enjoyed in Europe. Weah always answered his nation's calls to action—football action to be specific. After arriving in Europe, he kept his ears back home and encouraged fellow players to take a leap of faith from the harsh reality in Liberia to the lush green turfs in Europe. He often told his fellow

Liberian players that the game in Europe was far different from the one played in Africa because it was more intense, fast, technical, and rough at the same time. He arrived in Monaco after being lured to France by Claude Le Roy who was then the head coach of Cameroun's Indomitable Lions. After seeing Weah perform, Le Roy was certainly very impressed with the exploits of the young Liberian brilliance in Cameroon. It was then he sold the young talent to Monaco's head coach Arsène Wenger. Upon his arrival and after a brief training session, George Weah made his first Ligue 1 debut on August 17, 1988. That game ended with a 2–1 defeat for Monaco by A.J. Auxerre. For George Oppong Weah, it was a colossal loss for a first timer on French soil. For his coach, it was a good loss—it made Georg train harder and to adjust himself to his new environment to justify his inclusion on the starting squad. Before leaving Monaco after a blissful four-year stint, George scored 47 goals that made him a legend at AS Monaco. Soon he got comfortable, Weah did not disappoint the man whom he called 'Father". He played his life away during every game whether Monaco won or lost. At times when the game was tough or their side was down by several goals, his teammates would turn to him and ask him to perform the magic from Africa. *"Give us some of those African voodoo, Mr. George,"* they would joke. In return, he would deliver a goal or two, to the delight of his fellow teammates and adoring fans. For many of the European players who watched George Weah play football during his career in the 1990s, they believed that he was indeed the best player of his generation that played the game. He brought joy to millions of fans and sent millions more crying for their defeated teams. He made many African proud and fell in love with the game of football when their hope in the game was at the verge of dying. For Africa and Africans, George Oppong Weah was the trickle of light in the darkness for them. His prowess in Europe re-ignited many young players' hope for the game a decade later. The result can be seen in the exploits of players like Nwankwo Kanu, Samuel Eto'o, Didier Drogba, Yaya Touré, Mohamed Salah, just to name a few.

Having been seen by coaches of top European teams as he played and scored amazing goals AS Monaco, George Weah moved to the French football giants Paris Saint Germain, PSG in 1992 long before Arab money made the club the powerhouse it has now changed into. With PSG, Weah won the French League title two years later in 1994 and he became the top scorer of the 1994–95 UEFA Champions League. His fame spread far and wide such that in 1995, he signed for Italian football goliaths AC Milan. This happened after Milan had lost the Champions League final of that year to Ajax, their bitter archrivals. At Milan George Weah became the king of the pitch as his name became a household name on the lips of many Milanese as well as millions of residents of big cities, villages, and towns across Italy. Weah's skills helped to fuel AC Milan's two Serie A titles. His more memorable performance was when AC Milan played Verona. That day, George Oppong Manneh Weah burned his name on the hearts and brains of millions of fans and spectators across the world when he scored a solo one-of-a-kind goal. This happened at the dying minutes of the game when King George Weah, as he was named by fans, picked the ball up on the edge of his own penalty box and began to run. With an outburst of testosterone running from his adrenal cortex, he ran and ran as thousands of fans cheered him on and on as the former Italian President Silvio Berlusconi in a child-like gesture urged him to keep moving along. Like a good driver, George Weah meandered his way in and out of the obstacles and human traffic that were headed toward him. His speed was incredible as he jockeyed and jinxed and ran toward Verona's goalpost some more. Without thinking about the magnitude of his action, he ran on and on, while dummying and dribbling past virtually every single player from Verona. Before everyone's eyes, George Oppong Weah had run the full length of the field in just under 40 seconds and scored the most brilliant individual goal any professional football fan has ever seen in their life. European television broadcast the goals for months. For weeks, newspapers across the world wrote numerous articles about the stupefying goal of George Weah. That goal transformed George into a living legend—elevating him to the level of a football god and one of the greats of AC Milan.

After conquering Italy and leaving his footprints in France, for a reason still unknown, he fell out of favor with the coach and management of AC Milan. With a stellar record behind him, George Oppong Manneh Weah moved to England on loan to Chelsea where he helped win victory for the "Blues", as they are called in the English League. From all indications, George Weah wanted to finish his career with Milan as other great players have done. As his career started to wind down, he moved to Manchester City, Olympique Marsielle, and Al-Jazira in the UAE in 2003 where he finally retired. It should be known that throughout Weah's career, he proved he was not an ordinary footballer. He is still the one and only player ever to hold the African, European and World diadem for the best footballer at the same time.

Without a doubt, Liberian football wouldn't have produced great legends and made great news hadn't George Weah harnessed his skills in France during the early days of his spectacular career in Europe. That year, 1988, George Weah French training rubbed off on his country's struggling national football team, the Lone Star of Liberia during the country's 1990 World Cup qualifier against their Ghanaian football nemesis. Earlier that year, Liberia held Ghana which was led by its superstar Abidi Ayew Pele who was also an attacking midfielder on loan for the French side Lille to a goalless draw in Accra. The return match in Monrovia sealed George Oppong Weah's legacy as a football hero forever. This is a game that older Liberians will forever remember because then President Samuel K. Doe declared the following Monday August 22, 1988, a national holiday, urging the nation to celebrate the Lone Star's 2-0 victory against Ghana. Historically, Ghana Black Star had always walked over the Lone Star of Liberia on the football field. A well-known fact was that Ghana has always been a heavyweight football opponent to Liberia as the rivalry dates to the 1970s.

With the Black Star of Ghana paired against Liberia for the 1990 World Cup qualifying rounds, Samuel Kanyon Doe vowed to change this trend of recurring defeat of the Lone Star. He personally got involved by encouraging the players of the national team to play the game like they have never. The ruthless dictator and sport-loving president gave the players cash allowance and took the extra step by giving each Lone Star player a piece of land to build their own home. For many sports lovers, Samuel Kanyon Doe groomed and nurtured the game of football that George Weah became an ambassador of by making football his own when he took the name of his country into the Continent of Europe. The defeat of the Black Star of Ghana was a clear manifestation of how impactful the involvement of an absolute president can be on any sport within a country.

At the Samuel Kanyon Doe Sports Complex in Paynesville that blissful day, George Oppong Weah did not only engrave his name on the hearts and brains of the Liberian people forever; he made them love and sing his name in unison and danced rhythmically with an everlasting resonant that even the Du River shook at its very bottom. With Oppong fresh out of France and armed with advanced skills and onto the SKD Sports Complex pitch surrounded by over forty thousand cheering, adoring, and shouting fans, the Black Diamond of Africa could not afford to disappoint them—he had to play like his life depended on it. That sweltering Sunday afternoon, history was in the making when President Samuel K. Doe arrived with the national team riding in some of his personal Cadillac convertibles at the football stadium named in his honor. In fact, it was President Samuel Kanyon Doe that made George Weah the captain of the national team that day. That Sunday afternoon in Monrovia, George Weah and a few other players rode with President Doe in his open-top Cadillac. Following an intensive first half play, the Wizard Dribbler (a name given to George Oppong Weah) and the Black Diamond of Africa found the back of the net of the Ghanaian team with a free kick that was too quick for Black Star's goalkeeper Mohammed Odoom. The goal sent a huge wave of celebration across the nation. The name, "George Oppong Weah" was plastered across the lips of every Liberian across the land and abroad. What seemed to be a local victory became an international topic of discussion as news media across Africa and the world talked about the great talent of George Weah who became a Monaco's sensation that year and the years that followed.

"Oppong opened it, Debbah closed it," which meant that

George Weah opened the scoring spree and James Salinsa Debbah closed the scoring spree with a final goal; was the song football lovers sang after the referee blew the final whistle to end the historic match between Liberia's Lone Star and the Black Star of Ghana ninety-six minutes later. Earlier that month, President Doe and the Liberia Football Association through the Ministry of Youth and Sports launched a football campaign called, "Operation Eliminate Ghana". To seal the game, Liberia's Most Celebrated Football Player (a name given to James Salinsa Debbah) who later became coach of the Liberian National Football Team, scored a solo goal at the dying minutes of the game to securely send Liberia to the group stage of the 1990 World Cup qualifier.

Though he was unable to take the Lone Star of Liberia to the World Cup during his blissful football career, George Weah's talent put Liberia on the map of world football. Another way to put it simply, while George Weah's talent put Liberia on the map of world football, his achievements and fame put the map of human's endeavor and a personal story of rise from rags to riches on Liberia. His exploits on the European football fields have raised the bar so high that it will be impossible for any other Liberian or African to reach—for he literarily conquered the football world and won every imaginable football title a typical child born in Liberia and raised in an urban ghetto in the sleepy city of Monrovia can even dream of.

For Liberia failing to qualify for the 2002 World Cup, George Weah was blamed for throwing (selling) the game to the Nigerians. That defeat was so hurtful to Lone Star's fans, that it made many of the supporters turn against George Weah. Some even hauled verbal insults at him and his mother. Feeling hurt by the fans' ungrateful attitudes, Weah vowed never to play for the Lone Star again. In later years, he would play a backseat role for the national team. Conversely, other professional players on the team blamed Weah for his domineering and overreaching behavior. Many of his teammates accused him of being a football dictator— wanting to play coach, financier (George Weah personally funded the Liberian national football team during the war's years of the

1990s. He gave players stipends and other financial benefits just as the government did during the Doe's era of the 1980s. In return, George Weah got refunded by Liberian football authorities), team manager and president of the team. This feat of being everything on the team was very impossible for anyone to achieve. Often, he and Jonathan Boy-Charles Sogbie would sometimes get into a heated argument about who to play and who not to. Sogbie was one person who vehemently opposed George Weah's everything attitude on the national team. The constant in fighting among players brought down the morale of the team. Evidence of the conflicts were often witnessed on the field during games. For example, if Boy-Charles was in possession of the ball and Weah was open for a pass, he never gave the ball to him. Rather, he would look for someone else. Liberians being a people that easily forgive and are sometimes patronizing, looked beyond Weah's immature and vindictive behaviors. They treated their national hero, George Manneh Weah with uttermost respect reserved only for a king. Hundreds of admirers would line the streets to cheer him along as he rolled by in his Porsche, Mercedes or his BMW.

George Weah's critics cited that he was not playing his best because he feared being injured in Africa would have impacted his lucrative contract in Europe. Many of these critics believed that if George Weah had played as hard as he did for his European clubs, no African team would have defeated Liberia in any match during his primetime in the game. Whether these assertions are true, only George Manneh Weah can validate these claims. In Liberia, spreading rumors is a culture—people eat rumors for breakfast, lunch, and dinner. Whether these allegations were truths or lies, Weah fame only grew bigger than the country he was being accused of under-representing.

At the height of his professional football years in Europe in the 1990s, to bring some stability into his life, and to forever seal his legacy, George Weah took off some time in the summer of 1993 to marry his long-time girlfriend, Clar Marie Duncan who he had met at a Chase Bank branch in New York. This wedding was witnessed by thousands of people both in Liberia and in the U.S.

Weah's Mother and his siblings along with several family members and friends were at the occasion to support the 27 years old. This wedding was a subject of discussion in many Liberian quarters for many months. Resolute Weah had made a choice for a wife that nobody could dissuade him from—Clar was the one the King's eyes beheld.

Clar Marie Duncan-Weah who was born in Jamaica and moved to the United States of America with her parents, won the heart of George. After spotting the beautiful young woman at the bank's branch for months, he sensed something different in her— he asked her out on a date. The day Clar agreed to go out on a date with him, he could not wait for the day to come by. He realized that she possessed all the qualities that a man looked for in a wife— beauty, discipline, love for family, outgoing and fun loving, smart, and committed. After George Weah met beautiful Clar, it was love at first sight for the young and handsome Liberian professional footballer. Many of his friends thought their relationship wouldn't last because George Weah was a big womanizer at the time. He had shared his time and his beds with so many Liberian women—had children with them and told them his innermost dream. In France, he had several serious relationships with Liberian women that led people thinking he would have married, but he didn't see many of them fit for a wife or for other reasons. One of such serious relationships was his blissful romance with Miranda Seyon, the daughter of former University of Liberia President, Patrick L.M. Seyon who was believed not to be in favor of his daughter and George's relationship because of George's lack of education. As hurtful as it was for George Oppong Weah, he moved on with his life until he met Clar in New York.

Meeting Clar Duncan was a birth of fresh air for George who was at the time going through different types of women at the time. He believed that Clar was special in a very heartwarming way—she was at the time independent and didn't come across as a gold-digger like the many Liberian women that have crossed his path. Deep within his spirit, she was the type of woman he knew would have his back besides bringing stability into his busy life.

He was fascinated with her charm, her simplicity, and good manners. Unlike the many Liberian women that threw themselves at him because of his status and for other reasons best known to many of them, she did not. She played a kind of hard-to-get modesty with him as he pursued her. This attitude made George Weah want Clar the most. In confidence, he told close friends that other than her amazing characters, one of the main reasons he chose to marry Clar over a Liberian woman or any other woman for that matter was because she was tight vaginally, versatile in the bedroom, and actively aggressive in bed during sex. He further explained that she does not remain laying on her back throughout their love making session like most of the women he had been with do. Rather, she takes charge of him during sex like a real Jamaican woman. Often, his love for her brought tension between him and his sometimes cantankerous mother. For example, during family time when they would play George's favorite board game, Ludo, George would rather take his mother prisoner than his wife. This behavior often angered Anna to a point that she would leave the game without completing it. A close friend of the family said that during one of those family time Ludo games in New York, Anna asked George, if they, George, Clar, and herself were in a boat that was taking on water and it was about to capsize, who would he first save? To Anna and everyone's surprise, George said Clar. He further said, "Old ma you naaaaa enjoy your life ooo, so I need to save my wife first and come back for you later". This answer and explanation made his mother upset as she got up and scattered the game before walking away. She didn't speak to George and Clar for several days.

While there may have been so many reports in the media about their relationship, their love for each other somehow endured. Clar is a very simple woman who takes things one day at a time. She is not perfect in any shape or form, but she epitomizes class and self-worth of a virtuous woman. Their circle of friends knows her to be mostly a lay back person who allows George Weah to be George Weah. This was the one rare quality George found in her that made him love her more than any other woman he had been with. She too loved him without a doubt. But on the other hand, she does not support George's womanizing and promiscuity. She separated herself from him on so many occasions—twice in Europe and multiple times when the family relocated to the United States. Prior to him meeting Clar, George Weah did not find the supportive and unflappable quality in any Liberia female he had dated in the past. According to his close friends and family members, most Liberian women only came to him because of his money and because he was George Oppong Weah, the professional European football super star. Following their initial meeting at a local New York Chase Bank where George had an account, George called a few of his close friends to tell them about the beautiful Jamaican girl he had met at the bank and was going out on a date with. One can only imagine how exciting that moment was for the man who would conquer the football world in Europe. Days later, they had their first date. He was very much impressed by the intelligence of the young woman and decided to take their relationship seriously, though he was still based in France and having fun with other women. As the saying goes, a thousand miles poses no barrier to true love—he had money that gave him access to one of the world's fastest commercial planes, the Concorde supersonic jet that took only 3 hours from Paris Charles de Gaulle Airport to John F. Kennedy Airport in New York instead of the seven hours journey.

His decision to marry a non-Liberian was solely based on some of the previously mentioned qualities that he hadn't found in many of the Liberian women he had dated or fathered children with. George Weah needed a woman who could tolerate his lifestyle or a woman who could somehow restructure his family life as well as manage his future. As it became obvious as he rose in stature, the George Weah of Gibraltar and of the past was not a superman to have managed every aspect of his life—he needed the right helpmate who would influence his life in a positive way. Without Clar, George would have never made the investment decisions he made. He could never have succeeded into the man the world now sees him to be. Therefore, following more than ten years of being in several unstable relationships with women and perambulating socially on different continents, young George Weah found his perfect match in Clar Marie Duncan. Being one of the most eligible bachelors in Africa and the world at the time, Weah decided to go for someone less known; someone from a humble background like himself. He wanted someone who did not like the spotlight as much as he was in it. Now that the dust of time had settled, he'd found that person in his beautiful wife, Clar Marie Duncan-Weah, the only woman who has given Weah true love, the voice of reason, peace of mind, stability, and magnitude to his career.

Together the couple have raised three beautiful children, Martha Teta Weah, George Weah Jr. (aka Champ), Timothy Weah. Of these three beautiful children who are now men and women, one of which is Clar's only biological child, Timothy. These three children all grew up in love and under the firm disciplinary eyes of Clar. If anyone saw these three children, there was no telling if they weren't Clar's biological children—she treated all the children like they were her own by birth. In Liberia and some other African countries, some females discriminate against children brought into marriages by their husbands. Before their wedding in 1993, George Weah and Clar had a frank family discussion about raising the children and the family values they would uphold. Having been raised by his God-fearing grand aunty, Ma Emma almost in the absence of both parents, George Weah wanted to be there with and for his children. Clar was more than a mother in the home for the children, she played dual roles in the home because George Weah was often on the road playing football and earning a living for the family. When she relocated the children from France to Milan and then the U.S., she had to give up her career and took on the role as a full-time mother, raising their children and managing other aspects of George Weah's career.

Being the typical African man and a celebrated sport's figure who has several weaknesses, it has been allegedly reported that George Weah has also fathered several other children with half a dozen women, but his beloved Clar has always stood by his side. The abiding love that Clar and Weah share is unquestionable. Clar is a very strong woman who has always stood by her man no matter what others say or think about him. While rumors swirled about George Weah's infidelity, and her involvement with other people, they never stopped loving each other. Both lovebirds while they might had been hurt due to the discovery of one another's secrets, they reprimanded each other in private. While some Liberian women may have reacted differently for similar things, Clar reacted magnanimously and stayed above the fray. This hard-found character is rare in our modern world today. Clar's family value should be mimicked by Liberians and women across the generation. While she might have parted pathways with him on many occasions, she never stopped loving him and carrying for their children.

Chapter 14

A Broken Hope and a Broken Society

While Stephen Crane, the first ever battlefront or war corre-spondent who covered the Spanish and American War in the 1800s may have written this great poem, 'War is Kind' as a means of depicting the horror of war during his time, the Liberian Civil Wars of the 1990s and 2000s were most assuredly not kind. The absurd civil war that brought voids and terrors into many Liberians' hearts and lives was very devastating. It caught everyone by surprise—even those who initially welcomed the coming of the rebels to take out Samuel Doe and his majority Krahns dominated government. As Charles Taylor and Prince Johnson's rebel fighters advanced onto the city of Monrovia, they murdered anything and everyone they perceived as their enemy, this included men, women, children, and even animals. Whether the enemy was physical or imaginary, rebel fighters took them out per the instructions of their command-ing officers or COs. The unsophisticated and stupendous display of insanity was heartbreaking during the civil war of the 1990s. Frightened civilians stood by and watched their loved ones being herded on roadsides and summarily executed by boys as young as twelve years of age. As a result of the unprecedented carnage that was brought on the Liberian people, hopeless civilians lived at the will, pleasure, and mercy of the rebels. Many were being used by the rebel as human shields and various types of slaves—sex slaves, diamond digging slaves, food producing slaves, guns totting slaves, economic slaves and the list goes on.

As the Liberian Civil War raged and dragged on throughout the country and the decade of the 90s, George Weah or Mr. Georg as he was called to by fans in France, became a man without hope. The mental image shown on European televisions of the Liberian war affected him, but it was not something he would have shared with the coaches on the teams he played for at the time. He could not take his mind off the savage fighting that was ravaging his native Liberia. George Weah closely monitored the events of the war on Radio France International, RFI, the BBC, CNN and on major European television stations while he was still playing in Monaco and later at Paris Saint-Germain FC in France. According to family sources and close friends, George Weah had occasional nightmares about the slaughters that were going on in Liberia. The nightmares of the carnage in his homeland were so powerful that he would wake up from sleep in the middle of the night and he would work the phone in the early morning hours and sometimes all day in a hope of reaching some family member or a friend that might still be held up in Liberia or in a refugee camp within the West Africa sub region. Sometimes the heartbreaking stories coming out of Liberia impacted his performance on the football field during games while he still played football at Monaco and PSG. George lost several family members and several friends to the wars in Liberia. The horror of the civil war was unbearable for those who lived through it—people are still traumatized to this day. George Weah, while still a twenty something year old player, was forced to balance the impact of the war on his psychic as a human being and on his performance as a professional football player. Knowing that he wanted to be the best player in Europe, he had to bury some of the horrific news deep in the further recess of his awareness and zoom in on his football career. As tough as it was, he endured. He was able to bring victory to his team.

Most civil wars, especially the one in Liberia, was not fought to totally annihilate the enemy soldiers. Like many of the civil wars that have been fought in Africa and around the world, the fighting in Liberia killed more civilians than the combatants that were involved in the fight. At the end of the war, most Liberians later came to realize that war never chooses its victims. Everyone, especially the unarmed civilians are the true victims during the period of the fighting no matter how far away they are from the war that is being fought. No matter how far away he was from the way, George Weah became a direct victim of the senseless carnage that was waging in Liberia. For the lives that were being wasted by bullets, he wanted it to come to an end so badly. As kind as he was to many of his friends during their time of need, the warlords and fighters were not being kind to him. War is not kind at all. As George Weah usually said at that time, *"What is kind, is for everyone to be kinder to one another and stop the fighting."* The civil wars of the 1980s and 90s gave Liberians insight of what war really is. Many of them openly make comments such as, *"Whenever two people argue, they need to find a solution to their problem instead of plunging others into their madness."* The Liberian Civil War had no clear winner. Many of George's supporters believe that those who committed gruesome violence against people and think they have gotten away with murder, will one day face justice in one form or the other.

Egregious crimes perpetrators during the Liberian Civil Wars, many of whom are now living with the firm and false belief that their crimes will dissipate in the dust of time, have it wrong. While many of these perpetrators might now be enjoying impunity from a crony political system that rewards murders and criminals, but history is never wrong because their sins will definitely find them out. While he may not have made a public pronouncement about his support of bringing the perpetrator of war crime to justice, George Weah strongly supports bringing to justice individual perpetrators of crime against humanity. Many of these criminals that have broken the hopes of millions of Liberians and caused the death of so many people's loved ones and left Liberia as a broken society will be sought, and they will be brought to justice in the not-too-distant future. The Liberian Civil Wars and the crimes committed against innocent people have changed Liberians into something they were not—wicked, liars and thieves, fickle and flatterers, deceitful and ungrateful, and blind followers that dance to the drumbeats that are played by those misleading them in the wrong paths. Since the end of the ugly and ungodly civil wars that destroyed Liberia, many Liberians have unlearned some of the religious and ethical mores that were instilled in them by the church, by Islam, and by their parents. Many of them hold no loyalty to anyone if it is not in their interests—they do not keep their words or promise to anyone. They will praise and stuff you up with flattery words that they do not truly mean. The hopeless nature of the civil war revealed the worst in Liberians. One can only surmise that these behaviors are truly who Liberians are, but it only took the war to bring it out.

The Liberian Civil War indeed turned Liberia into a completely broken society with no modicum of hope for a return to its prewar moral status. The war robbed many Liberians of their self-worth, dignity, and humanity. Now, the people are lovers of themselves rather than lovers of God and their neighbors, or the country they claim to love and pledge allegiance to. From the look of things within the country, one can squarely say that the deepest wounds of the wars are difficult to see and slower to heal. Some of these wounds are the psychological scars of war; and even after a decade of peace, they are crippling people of all ages and creeds. According to a report from the World Health Organization of the United Nations, more than 40 percent of Liberians suffer symptoms of post-traumatic stress disorder (PTSD) related to the wars of the 1990s and 2000s. Many of those affected by the wars do not have access to mental health services that would help them cure their problems. Successive governments have done nothing to help many of these traumatized people since the wars ended more than eighteen years ago. Most of the victims are still suffering in silence with no help on the horizon for them or their family.

Former combatants and child soldiers, many of whom now in their 30s suffer from so many forms of mental health issues and other forms of psychological disorders. To soothe their pains away, a high percentage of these former combatants have taken on the use of illegal drugs, alcohol, and other controlled substances. In many of the ghettos of Monrovia and in the rural areas, the rates of post-traumatic stress disorder, PTSD and other mental illnesses are higher. The mistake of the previous governments in failing to structurally counsel, de-traumatize, reintegrate ex-combatants and other war victims is now becoming a social problem in every community within the country with the presence of drug users and abusers. Sadly, the government through the Liberia National Police, LNP occasionally raids communities and arrests drug addicts with the hope of cleaning those communities and eradicating the problems of drug abuse and vagrancy that were created by Liberia's prolonged civil wars. For many of the people that are currently suffering from illness attributed to the prolonged 14-years war, there's almost nowhere to turn for help. Liberia does not have a lot of psychiatrists or many psychiatric hospitals for a population of 4 plus million people. Many people will continually suffer in silence because mental illness is normally stereotyped in the country.

The civil war made people living both in rebels' held territories and in peacekeepers'-controlled areas very hopeless. People earnestly prayed for an end to the madness no matter where they were. It was unimaginable living in rebel held territories like Gbarnga or in ECOMOG controlled areas of Monrovia and its suburbs without worrying about being killed by Charles Taylor's rebel fighters or ECOMOG peacekeepers' clustered bombs that occasionally fell on civilians' homes. In rebel held territories, civilians lived at the mercy of the rebels and their commanders because the rebels were the lords and gospels in those areas. The rebels had the power to take life at will, and the power to give life to those who they didn't want to kill. In rebel-controlled areas like Gbarnga, Kakata, Ganta, Robertsport, Tubmanburg, and Buchannan, it was common to see rebel soldiers freely pick up any young girl off the streets, take them home, rape them, and then keep them against their will. In these rebels'-controlled areas, there was no civil authority to seek redress for these acts of violence.

Like the rebels, the ECOMOG peacekeepers too were the lords and executioners in Monrovia—they had the freedom to take lives if they wanted to. They also arrested and detained anyone that they suspected as being a rebel fighter or Charles Taylor's supporter. The peacekeepers were at least more merciful than the rebels because many of them operated under the Geneva Convention on Warfare—at least some of the time. Some of the peacekeepers operated like Mercenaries—interested only in their handsome paychecks and what they could reap from their host country, Liberia. Many of them raped and sexually exploited young Liberian girls and sometimes boys. Like the rebels that raped women and forced underage girls into sexual slavery, some peacekeepers subjected many young Liberian girls into a subtle form of sexual slavery by inducing them with such things like food, money, clothes, and protection. Girls as young as 13 years of age were seen having sex with men that could be their fathers or grandfathers.

Liberia became a complete failed state during the periods between 1990 and 2003, for the war had negatively affected every Liberian living inside and outside of the country. At the end of the war, everyone hungered for hope and total redemption. Contrary to being impacted by the madness in Liberia, Mr. George continued to dominate the professional football landscape in Europe. In 1997, He was the biggest African football player in the world. Recognizing the magnitude of his star power he was chosen by the United Nations Children's Education Fund, UNICEF to become the UN agency's Peace Ambassador to Liberia to help end the civil war and help reintegrate child soldiers into civil society. This position enabled him to raise awareness and shed light on the plight of child soldiers fighting in the Liberian Civil Wars. He also used his title to raise funds to strengthen the capacity of the UN to cater to the welfare of war victims, especially the child soldiers. At the end of the civil wars, children that were successfully disarmed and reintegrated into society were not given the necessary framework and tools that would enable them to become meaningful contributors to Liberian society. Today, many of these children have returned to the streets in Monrovia and in other places around the country. Many of them are now engaging in different types and forms of vices—armed robbery, prostitutions, drug dealing and using, money doubling schemes (Black Money), soldiery and mercenary and many other crimes. The broken society that was left behind by the civil wars should never be ignored because it is going to impact

Liberian society for a very long time. It would take a leader with the right mindset, insight, and unsurpassed love for the country to nurse the wounds that the wars inflicted.

The civil war of the 90s took a lot of Liberians by surprise. By surprise, it is due to the scale of unimaginable deaths and destruction that were brought upon the small country. At the onset, most people living under the suffocating regime of Samuel Doe and his death squad in Monrovia thought if the war reached Monrovia, it would have lasted for a few days, and everything would return to normal. But this thinking was very far from reality. The 1990 fighting exposed Liberians to killing and the sight of death and destruction. As far as most Liberians can remember, death was not a commonplace in the somehow divided but close knit tiny West African nation that boasted of being the first independent country in Africa during an era of Europeans scramble for Africa in 1886 and the subsequent colonialism that followed. Prior to the civil war, Liberians were mostly shy, welcoming, and friendly. Majority of the people loved strangers and hated the sight of a dead person. But that innocence was taken away from them by the April 12, 1980, coup and its aftermath that was culminated by the public execution of the 13 officials of the former regime. As mentioned in previous chapters, the coup that was orchestrated by the U.S. Central Intelligence Agency, CIA put Liberia onto a path of a downward spiral. As a result, when Charles Taylor was being used by the U.S. Government to take out their number one nemesis, Samuel Kanyon Doe, death and killing were no longer a stranger to some Liberians because they had been practicing the act of killing for almost a decade. As cold as it may sound, the wars of the 1990s and 2000s only revealed who Liberians truly were—lovers of cruelty, satanic and lacking the fear of God, greedy for power and prestige with no love within their hearts to lookout for the less fortunate, opportunistic to the core with eyes to grab what is not theirs, and enemy to justice. This stupid American-made conflict decimated Liberia and made the country into a pariah state and a laughingstock among the comity of nations.

As the war raged on, with Monrovia being the final target for Armageddon, citizens that saw the city as a safe haven, were left vulnerable as they found themselves in the crosshair and became the target for slaughter. To avoid being killed or caught in the crossfire, those who could run, ran to the neighboring countries as well as places far away from the killing field of Monrovia. The warring factions trusted no one—members of the Armed Forces of Liberia killed all real and perceived enemies while the NPFL rebels of Charles Taylor and other rebel forces committed some of the same egregious atrocities against their fellow unarmed citizens. The rebels killed and rape women of all ages; they were involved in forced displacements, force labor and terrorized the countryside. On the other hand, members of the AFL, mainly the remnant of the Krahn tribe that found themselves fighting for survival after the death of their clansman, Samuel Doe, killed whoever they saw as an enemy. The insanity that seemed to have no end rendered many Liberians at home and abroad hopeless. While in displaced camps and other self-imposed exile, many Liberians hopelessly gave up on Liberia. Some people sold their properties and vowed never to return to the land of their mothers and fathers' birth.

These victims and survivals of the stupid and self-destructive conflict were simply tired of living under the cloud of uncertainty and constant harassments. Some Liberians living abroad were labeled as cannibals by their foreign friends, neighbors, and the society they found themselves living in. Not to think of their pain, many of them opted to forever turn their backs on the country that has given them a bad reputation. While George Weah and scores of other Liberians have returned home to rebuild a shattered country, there are currently thousands of Liberians and friends of Liberia living in the Diaspora that have never returned to Liberia since departing the country in the 1990s. Many are fearful that if they returned home, the bad memories of pains, suffering, mayhem, destruction of their hard earn properties, and the murder of loved ones that they witnessed will be relived. Some of these survivors were forced to take up citizenships of other countries that opened their doors to them. Many of these exoduses now have children and grandchildren that have never stepped feet on the soil of Liberia, a land of their ancestors. With the return of peace and a fully functioning government, all one can hope for is the return of Liberians from the Diaspora to restore hope, bury their hurtful past, and rebuild the country that they once loved and almost give their lives for.

Chapter 15

Honors and Glamor

For some people, especially Liberian and African males, a few of them would allow fame and honors to get to their heads, blind them from seeing things clearly, and make them lose the common touch with their past. On the contrary, George Manneh Weah was born humble and remained humble like a lamb, even at the height of his football glory. While he may have lost lots of friends that he considered to be dead weights and for other reasons best known to him, George Weah has somehow remained true to himself and his calling. For those strangers who have crossed paths with George often talk about his kindness and humane spirit, while some of his close friends consider him as arrogant, uneducated, petty, vindictive, reviled, thin-skinned, immature, dictatorial in nature, and greedy for power and profit. George Weah is also a man who never forgot the calming words of his beloved Ma Emma, *"humble yourself before the Lord and He will lift you up."*

Like many mega sports stars of today that place themselves out of the reach of their fans, ordinary people, and journalists, George Weah was never a hard-to-reach football star in Europe or in his native Liberia and everywhere he traveled. He managed fame and glory very well. He was down to Earth, fun loving, a people's person, and he understood human's sufferings and hardship. As the only flagbearer for Liberia during the troubled days of the country, he never forgot to look back. On the football pitches of Europe, George Oppong Weah was the crown jewel of football which the African Continent was sharing with Europe and with the rest of the world. He was everything that a wanting coach could ever look for within a football player. He was skillful and talented, keen to score impossible goals, entertaining to watch, handsome and outgoing, full of energy, and was loved by millions of fans and admirers. He was the pride of Liberia—when nothing good came out of Liberia, Europeans and the world saw George Weah as the only model of perfection or goodness that came out of the small self-destructive country located on the West Coast of Africa. Without being stopped by the burden of the Liberian carnage, George Weah would go on to win many prestigious titles such as the coveted Ballon d'Or ("Golden Ball" which he is the only African football player to have won), UEFA Champions League Top Scorer award, Coupe de France, Ligue 1, Coupe de la Ligue, Serie A title, English FA Cup title. Weah also won the Liberia Football Associations, LFA title with his side, Invincible Eleven, IE and many others awards and honors.

Hard work always pays off no matter how long it may take. George Weah put in the work and the rewards that followed were monumental. With troves of honors being bestowed upon him by dozens of international organizations, millions of football fans fell in love with the skinny black kid from Gibraltar. At the height of his career, most footballers in Europe, Africa, and around the world who saw the exploits of George Weah believe that he is not one of those talents that come along once in a lifetime. Rather, King George Oppong Manneh Weah comes along once! That is the reason he will always be the greatest African Footballer. While there may have been hundreds of great African players before him, and a hundred more will come after he's gone from the face of the Earth, there is going to be only one George Oppong Manneh Weah the world will forever remember.

For most of the fourteen years George Weah played professional football in Europe, he reaped almost every award that is known in the football world. These are awards that have been given to all the great players who have played the game of football. While he was being given glamorous awards, he gave back to the poor through the United Nations, other humanitarian NGOs. For his good deeds, he gained the respect of the world. History and historians will tell and retell the wonderful and unique tales of George Oppong Weah, the high cheekbone boy who grew up on the riverside in Monrovia, in an impoverished, unstable ghetto community with no stab at a second chance of success and became one of the best football players on the planet. At the peak of his football career in 1995, King George reigned as the world, African, and European best footballer of the year. These honors were a trio of crowns never worn simultaneously by a footballer before or since George Weah got all of them. He was also named the African Continent's Player of the Century. Listed in the table below are some of the awards and honors this great son of Liberia and Africa has in his collection of accolades and achievements he has in his honor vault:

Year	Award	Organizations
1987	MVP Championship	Invincible Eleven IE (Liberia)
1988	MVP Championship	Tonerre Klara Club (Cameroon)
1988-1999	Captain,Liberian National Team	Lone Star (Liberia)
1989	African Player of the year	International Journalists
1991	French Cup Winner	AS Monaco
1992	European Cup finalist	AS Monaco
1993	French Cup Winner	AS Monaco
1993	Married Clar Marie Duncan	New York, USA
1994	French Championship	Paris St. Germaine
1994	African Player of the Year	International Journalists

1995	African Player of the Year	International Journalists
1995	European Player of the Year	International Journalists
1995	World Best Player	FIFA
1995	Onze Mondial Award	Onze Mondial Magazine
1995	FIFA Fair Play Award	FIFA
1996	MVP Championship	A. C. Milan
1997	UNICEF Goodwill Ambassador	UNICEF
1997-2000	Vice President International Affairs	Liberia Football Association
1999	MVP Championship	A. C. Milan (Italy)
1999-2000	Technical Director, Lone Star	Liberia
1999	MVP Championship	A. C. Milan
1999-Present	Member, FIFA Players Committee	FIFA
2000	African Player of the Century	International Journalists
2000	English FA Cup	Chelsea
2004	Among FIFA's 100 Greatest Players	FIFA Magazine
2004	20th of 100 Greatest African	African Magazine
2004	ESPN Arthur Ashe Courage Award	EPSY
2004	Great Britain's Eagle Award	London, England
2005	UMN African Student Association	Twin City
2005	African Hero Award	

It can be said without a shred of doubt that George Weah's football career has impacted the world and those around him.

Many of the honors and awards were not based on political affiliations, neither influenced by any form of pay to play nor political back-slipping. Instead, it was all based on his achievements on the football fields, and his love for life and humanity. He has always projected a humanitarian image to the world—raising millions to support the United Nations causes around the world. Looking at his actions from afar during the Liberian Civil Wars, one can say that George is a man of peace! As the pacifist he was taught by Ma Emma to be, he is truly an enemy to cruelty and lover of peace and justice—though people within the Liberian body politics have accused him of being a financial supporter of the MODEL Rebel that killed scores of people during their war against former Liberian President, Charles Taylor. Wherever he traveled, honors have always followed him. Up to the writing of his biography, he has gotten more and more awards and honors than any single Liberian or African can boast of. In October of 2017, he will again position himself to run for the presidency of Liberia. If he wins, another title which he has been fighting to add to his plethora of titles since 2005 will finally be won. As it has been with his 1995 World Best Player title, there has been no former professional footballer that has been elected president of a country on the African Continent or anywhere in the world. With all his honors and the glamours that accompany them, his fans believe that he is not haughty or naughty, pompous or ignominious to others, but humble and loyal to family and friends. While fame may sometimes cloud and alter a person's worldview in a negative way, George Weah had always remained true to his core belief of being a people's person and doing the right things, at least most of the time.

When he began playing football, winning the Ballon d'Or (Golden Ball) and morphing to become the only African to become world best player was not something on young George Weah's mind. All he ever wanted to do was to play football—and he played the game with passion, commitment, discipline, and sacrifice. To achieve what he wanted, he worked hard at every twist and turn along the way to success. He sometimes asked the right people the right questions when he could not see his way clearly. Though he's a man who now loves to eat good and big food, he would sometimes forgo a meal or two as well as sleep just to complete a training session or a practice regimen. When he was young and still living in Gibraltar, he barely ate at home. His older brother, William Weah Jr. would sometimes eat his food—especially when he was tired from football practice. As a kid, if anyone asked young George Weah to make a choice between football and a hot plate of dry rice mixed okra, bitter ball, pepper, Smoked Herring, pork, luncheon meat, diced with Maggi Cube, and raw palm oil, he would choose football over the delicious plate that any boy of his age would run to. George disciplined himself for the sake of self-development and achieving his stated goals and dreams in life. If any young man or woman wants to be successful, George Oppong Manneh Weah is that model that needs to be used daily.

Though Georg Weah garnered all the honors the game of football ever had, these honors were not his alone—it belonged to Liberia and Africa. For the king of Liberian football, these honors were special for him, but he acknowledged that hadn't he gone through the toughest of times, he would not have finetuned his game, disciplined himself, changed his mindset and his attitude, and humble himself as he climbed the ladder of success. George Weah has left his footprints forever on the pitches of Liberia, Cameroon, Monaco, Milan, England, and the UAE. He is a happy man because his footprint has been immortalized in Monaco's "Promenade des Champions. While his fellow Liberians may never know the magnitude of his success, the one thing evident is that he has forever changed how African players are rated all over the world. Now as a leading politician of his country, many observers think that if he's not surrounded by the right teammates, he may not be able to score that badly needed winning goal that will give Liberia the victory it really needs to move forward. A victory that will bring a total liberation and transformation of the country and its youthful population.

Chapter 16

Looking Back to Where He Comes From

No matter how bad of a shape Liberia found itself in before or during the civil wars, George Manneh Weah "de deh" (a Jamaican word meaning, "to show up") every time. He never abandoned Liberia, not once! He gave everything he ever earned on the football field back to Liberia and Liberians. There are two diverging views of George depending on who one talks to about this global icon. Many of George's childhood friends from Gibraltar believe he is more of a giver than a taker or even a keeper. He never allowed his past impoverished life to stop him from helping those that needed him the most. But many friends who he has parted-way with say the contrary. They know him as a narcissist, attention loving, spotlight hugging, a showoff, and a man who loves to have sex with other men's women, but he hates other men chasing after his women. Some see him as a man who keeps speech (a Liberian slang for a grudge keeper) from others like a female, loves to throw hints at others, speaks in parables to those he suspects of wrongdoing, unforgiving, and harbors hatred for anyone who disagrees with him. Many of these former friends assert that George will quickly end his friendship with anyone over a girlfriend more than he would do over money. They believe that his relationship and friendship with others is purely transactional—he will drop you like a hotcake once he thinks you have nothing to offer him.

Irrespective of his many flaws, he came through for many Liberians in the 1990s during the country's dark days. Unlike many Liberians that were once poor and are now rich and living comfortably, and have forgotten where they came from, Mr. Weah has never forgotten his humble origin—he'd always looked back and has given back to society and to Liberia. If he were like some bad-hearted Liberian that experienced the venom of hardship and the pinch of poverty in Liberia, he would have turned his back on Liberia forever and enjoyed his wealth elsewhere. But how could he forget a place he holds so dearly to his heart? How could he turn his back on so many people that looked up to him as their future? Why would he turn his back on the only country that Ma Emma loved like many people before her had done? How could George Oppong Weah not look back at Liberia when it is the beginning of his everything—his dream, his legendary status, and the man he has now become. While he may have come from a lowly birth in society, he had always dreamt of greatness. He propelled himself to greatness by changing his thoughts and adopting a new mindset. Being a world-renowned football legend with a recognizable presence, George Weah dedicated much of his life, time, and resources to the passionate pursuit of humanitarian causes in Liberia. He had always believed in the oneness of our world and had worked tirelessly to use his fame and global presence to advance the causes of humanity, especially children, the disadvantaged or marginalized people. Weah's humanitarian gesture gave the world a bird's eye view of this remarkable personality who believes his responsibility to humanity and his fellow countrymen is only just beginning and may not end after his death.

George Weah used his celebratory status to travel the world and meet great people for many different reasons. On his first official visit to South Africa after retiring from professional football, former President Nelson Mandela described George Weah as *"Africa's Pride"*. During a meeting he held with the only moral African statesman who has ever lived, Weah was encouraged by the noble statesman to engage in politics and never to forget the cause of his people. These words cut to George Weah's heart and soul during the visit and after leaving South Africa. Ever since that meeting,

George Weah had worked tirelessly to earn such praise from his fellow citizens and members of the international community. With all that has happened and continues to happen for him, he has never forgotten his roots nor his family and friends from Gibraltar, and all other places he had lived and played the game of football. George's life experiences have made him a greater person both mentally and spiritually. Along his journey to the top, he developed some insights in human's behavior.

Too many people may never know how much George Weah has contributed to Liberian society—his humanitarianism has often been underrated by the media and those who revile him based on their interaction with him. George Weah is a flawed character just like everyone else. Like every human being, he has many short-comings which he openly acquiesces to. He understands that he would never be loved or liked by everyone. Often, a person's good intent will be twisted by naïve and frenemies to make it a trap for fools. When he gained financial leverage as a professional foot-ball star, he developed a habit of helping those he could identify with. Whenever George saw the need for students to be educated within his Gibraltar community, he would pay the tuition with his personal funds for those needing students. Weah knew that sitting at the apex of world football did not mean that he would be there forever. For him, he knew that one day he would come back down and meet some of the same people he'd left behind. To empower them, he engaged in several self-help projects as a means of im-pacting the lives of people on a larger scale. Unlike other Liberian professional players stationed in Europe and elsewhere, George Manneh Weah often came back home to identify with the poorest of the poor without having a political intent or an ulterior motive of gaining for the good he was doing his people. For those who benefited from his kindness and his humanitarian deeds, are among his diehard supporters to this day.

George knows a lot of places in Liberia. He has lived in more places in Liberia than any other Liberian. Growing up, he and his brother Junior Boy constantly bounced from place to place. But playing football enabled him to live in so many quarters within

Liberia and around the world. Before football took him overseas, he lived in places like, Gibraltar, New Kru Town, Sayon Town, Slipway, Lakpazee, Smythe Road, Perry Street, Bassa Community, Worwein (Capital Byepass) in Montserrado County; Sasstown in Grand Kru County; Bong Mines, in Bong County; Bahblozohn in River Cess County; Buchanan in Grand Bassa County; Marshall, Camp Schiefflin in Margibi County. Outside of Liberia, he lived in Yaounde, Cameroon; Monte Carlo, Monaco; St Germaine, France; Milan, Italy; Manchester, England, London, England; Abou Darbi, United Arab Emirates; Accra, Ghana, Staten Island, New York City, Queens, New York City, Pembroke, Hollywood, Florida.

As a way of giving back to his Gibraltar community, he built an elementary school that was named in his honor—though it may not be to international standard. With this contribution, children are getting educated and are preparing themselves for national and global leadership. He had always wanted to give back to his community and to humanity. In his prime, he became a voice for the disadvantaged, the homeless and the youth. It was not by mistake that on April 7, 1997, he became UNICEF's Goodwill Ambassador. In his work as UNICEF's ambassador, he supported HIV/AIDS and Educational programs in Liberia, Ghana, and many other countries around the world. In 1998, George Weah and other famous stars launched a CD called 'Lively Up Africa'. Proceeds from sales of the CD went to support children's programs in Liberia and in other countries. During the Liberian Civil Wars that lasted for over 14 years, Weah pleaded with the UN to help his country's young boys and girls that were being used as soldiers. Many of these child soldiers were sexually abused, mentally tortured, educationally denied, and humanly violated of their inalienable rights. With pure love for his country, he found himself at odds with Charles Taylor who felt disrespected by George Weah for meddling in the Liberian Civil War and for not taking off his sunglasses when Weah had gone to pay him a visit and was speaking with him. Weah's visit to Taylor was to retrieve his properties (vehicles) from Reginald Goodridge, one of Taylor's henchmen who seized Weah's cars and other properties in Monrovia, during a bloody fight for control of Monrovia in 1996. At the time of the war, Benjamin Yeatan the leader of Taylor's Death Squad led rebel soldiers to George's 9th Street home and raped some of Weah's female family members. Due to George Weah's popularity, Charles Taylor feared that he was trying to overshadow him and become president himself. In an outburst of frustration over Taylor's behavior, George Weah told some friends, *"Taylor thinks he's the only one who can carry war in Liberia. Some of us can carry war there if we want to."* This statement reached Charles Taylor. *"George Weah wants to be president,"* Charles Taylor once told the people of Liberia. True to Taylor's words, Mr. Weah threw his hands and feet into the race for the presidency of Liberia years later when Charles Taylor was booted out of the country by LURD and MODEL rebels with the help of the United States of America.

At the height of Liberia's Disarmament, Demobilization and Reintegration of child soldiers and other former rebel fighters, George Weah found himself in the center of that campaign that helped to bring peace to a country that had been bleeding for more than 7 years. Using his image and his international connections, George personally went to various encampments for former child soldiers to help them with their transition to civilian lives by counselling them and encouraging many of them to walk onto the path of peace and normal life. This was a hard thing for George Weah, especially knowing that those were the same child soldiers that were responsible for the murder of some of his family members and friends.

From giving away his own footwear to strangers, to giving out scholarships along with food and monetary assistance to poor people during his glory days in Europe, George Weah has lived far above the natural self-serving tendencies of most well-off Liberians found in and out of the country. His generosity can be spoken of by so many who have encountered him in and out of Liberia. From his humble beginning, he had been an exceptionally free-handed person. As a child, life in Gibraltar and Liberia was not so kind to him as it has been for his children—they were born on the lucky or blessed side of life. Weah and his siblings grew up being poor and seeing poverty robbing potentially wealthy people of their successes. At times, he would go to bed hungry after practice when he had eaten his share of the little rice and sauce provided by Ma Emma B, as he and the children living in the house sometimes called their grand aunty. Being an active child who always played football, George's share of the family's daily meal was always not sufficient for him whenever his young aunt, Rebecca Nagbe ditched out and shared the food. He waited most nights to eat with Ma Emma at the end of evening prayer service or he would eat midnight food with the area boys. As a young kid, family members sometimes called George Oppong Weah a 'Greedy Boy or 'Greedy Gut" because of his constant hunger for food. What helped him to conquer poverty was his determination and his can-do attitude.

Unlike most people that escaped from the strong grips of poverty and became millionaires without looking back to life and people from their bitter past, George Weah did the opposite. He looked back! When he became a semiprofessional or a professional football player, coming back home was one of the most memorable things for George Weah. Like most Liberians living in the Diaspora, Liberia made him experience his true worth and his humanity. People would sometimes line the streets to see him walk or drive by. It was exciting not because he was coming home to Gibraltar or Liberia to boast of his wealth. Rather, he came home to celebrate his success with family and friends. He came home to give back to those who needed it the most—encouragement, help, donation, and giving back to the ghettos that once watched him grow from a boy to a successful man.

As the most successful son of the country, it seemed like he was cursed to blessed others. Giving to others contributed to George Weah being broke the moment he tired from playing professional football and making over 80 million dollars. He was like the godfather of Liberia because he was often seen ditching out money and giving it to anyone who came to him for help. While the Liberia Civil Wars of the 1990s and 2000s raged on, he temporarily relocated his mother and some of his siblings along with scores of relatives and friends in Ghana, Ivory Coast and in Europe. There, he was responsible for providing their every need which included rent, food, clothing, financial assistance for education and medical needs, wedding, and childcare. He assisted strangers who he had never met before. If George Weah knew a fellow Liberian was stranded in a foreign country, he would help that person to get out of that situation. Though this was not the case for hundred percent of Liberians due to his own financial limitations, he extended a helping hand to those he could reach. While little is known about other successful Liberians players' deeds, George Oppong Manneh Weah's humanitarianism is known to many Liberians and the world at large.

Often, George Weah was used and abused by so many of his family, friends, and fellow countrymen because of his kind heart. At the heart of the civil wars in Liberia, several criminal-minded Liberians scammed George out of hundreds of thousands of dollars in the name of philanthropy and other social initiatives that they claimed to be involved with. Many of these crooks would fabricate stories about events and situations in Liberia and elsewhere to get money out of George Weah who was somehow trusting of everyone who came into his life. The scams worked for a long while until Weah caught onto many of their shenanigans. As a cautionary measure, he unfriended many of those who conned him out of money both in and of Liberia. The one thing worth noting of George Weah is his intolerance to criminality—he was taught not to take what does not belong to him. He hates for people to take away from him what is duly his because he grew up watching people in high places, especially in government takeaway funds that were meant for national development and human's capacity building. If Weah realized that a friend of his was involved in any form of thievery or that friend was undermining him, he would cut every relationship with that individual. Being a person in the spotlight, he loves being treated fairly, but that is not what happens in the real world. What Mr. Weah needs to understand was that, how the Bible and Qur'an said people should live is far different from how people live today. Most Liberians and Africans are dishonest to the core. Many of them will flatter a person with flowery words that they do not truly mean from their hearts because they lack the fear of God within their hearts. Most of these people do so to get what they want from the person that is being flattered without holding any loyalty to them. As the nation's most beloved and kindhearted son, George Weah was not shielded from dishonest and criminal minded people—he ate with them, drank with them, slept with them, and took good care of most of them. As a Liberian who loves Liberia, he never stopped looking back at the place he came from. If he becomes president one day, and with Liberians expectations so high and funding for national development very low, he should fight to score the winning goal that would help his desperate people, heal the wounds of the mostly forgotten victims left by the more than 14 years of civil wars, reconcile the country's ethnic division created by years of incubated ethnic tensions that had been fueled by bad governance, fight corruption and cronyism and various forms of favoritisms, and transform Liberia into the vibrant and progressive nation that it should be.

Part III

The Rise to Power

"The first method for estimating the intelligence of a ruler is to look at the men he has around him."

Niccolo` Machiavelli

Chapter 17

Entering Politics: The History of CDC

George Manneh Weah (as he now prefers to be addressed) is not a typical politician. Unlike the many politicians in Liberia and elsewhere in the world who often glamour for great wealth, fame, and other personal rewards and perquisites once elected to public office, George Weah is seen by his supporters as an embodiment of service to country and humanity. He sees his entry into politics as a direct response to serving a Liberian population that had been badly abused and scarred by more than a decade of civil strife and well over a century of one-party rule. Without knowing the complexities of the political game, and driven by the philosophy of service to country, Weah made the decision to transition from an international football star to a politician when he accepted the idea of heading a newly formed political movement as a means of making a greater impact on the lives of millions of Liberians. But what he didn't know was that the first casualty for a political novice is their experience—outside of football, Mr. Weah had no real-world job experience. He didn't know that as a politician, he would have to change his lifestyle and not party like he did when he was a footballer. He didn't know that if he wanted to keep flying Nigerian and Ghanaian actresses into Liberia for sex, he had to do it discretely—this importation of women from across Africa and from the Diaspora angered many of the Monrovia-based women within the CDC. There were internal tensions between him and some of his advisors including George Solo, Geraldine Doe, and other decent founding members of the party. At the time, Mr. Weah didn't understand the magnitude of his decision to lead a political organization. He might have thought that he would continue to be George Weah, the Footballer, and not George Manneh Weah, the man who thousands of Liberians had their hopes in.

Now as a politician, just as the name George Oppong Weah once razzle-dazzled millions of fans all over the football world, the name George Manneh Weah is today the brand upon which the Congress for Democratic (CDC) is built and has had the same effect on millions of the Liberian Civil War generation that are now in their twenties and thirties. The CDC minus George Manneh Weah is bound to trigger hundreds of thousands of supporters walking away and turning their backs on the movement. In short, without the Weah's brand, the CDC may one day cease to exist as a political party, or maybe like some of the many insignificant political parties that are roaming the streets of Monrovia and in towns and villages across the country giving people false hope of a better Liberia if they are voted into the highest political office in the land.

The CDC was an idea born out of frustration and resentment for an established political class that was seen to have been misleading the masses in and out of Liberia for well over three decades. This idea was fueled by some farsighted and passionate Liberians that sought for an alternative to Liberia's kleptocratic political system (a system of government or state in which those in power exploit national resources and steal, or a government ruled by a thief or group of thieves) that often shortchanges and shuts the ordinary Liberian out of any political discussion that determines the future of the country.

As it is always, history is an incomplete written record of past and present events. Hence, the history of the CDC is still being written and rewritten every second, minute, hour, day, week, month, and year. And depending on how progressive the CDC will be within the next 50 years; its history will continually be rewritten using many paradigms or archetypes. The CDC was founded in

2004 by change-minded men and women whose love for country was above self-interests. In 2003, following the cessation of hostilities and the end of the brutal reign of Charles McArthur Taylor and several rebel groups, a few thoughtful Liberians began toying with the idea of organizing a political party. The end of the fighting was followed by the ushering in of a transitional government that was super-saturated with warlords from many warring factions, just as many Liberians were picking up the broken pieces left behind by the civil conflicts. This transitional government, known and styled as the "National Transitional Government of Liberia (NTGL)", was headed by businessman Charles Gyude Bryant. This government offered a glimmer of hope for Liberia's transition to a multiparty democracy which political actors like Baccus Matthew, Amos Sawyer, and so many firebrands political dissidents have been fighting for. Bryant's ascension as transitional leader of Liberia followed the signing of a peace pact—the Comprehensive Peace Agreement (CPA)—in Accra, Ghana in August 2003 by representatives of the NPP government of President Taylor and two main rebel groups, the Movement for Democracy in Liberia (MODEL) and the Liberian United for Reconstruction and Democracy (LURD), which sought to put a permanent end to the mayhems that had been going on in Liberia for little over 14 years. During the CPA, Bryant was elected at the peace conference as transitional leader over former vice President, Dr. Harry F. Moniba, and now former President Ellen Johnson Sirleaf. This transitional government was given the mandate to oversee a free and fair democratic election in Liberia within the period of two years. This mandate given to the NTGL, and Bryant by African leaders and other international partners put a lot of pressure on Bryant and his team in so many ways. They needed to succeed to save their country from taking a further downward spiral—they needed to bring Liberia back into the comity of nations.

With the guns of wars being silenced, feared Charles Taylor in exile, and the transitional government in charge, the ordinary Liberians began openly voicing out their frustrations and misgivings about the Liberian political system. As always, corruption was rampant within the ranks-and-file of the transitional government headed by Mr. Bryant. At the time, most Liberians attributed the suffering of the masses to the meandering and maneuvering of a greedy and selective few, many of these people also expressed their frustration about the failure of leadership of the NTGL to chart a new course of action for the nation after the cessation of the civil war. A reasonable person would think that after 14 plus years of bloodletting, the transitional government would do the right things. Instead, officials of the NTGL were wrapped up in corruption as they were allegedly writing blank checks to themselves and raking the country of whatever was left over after the brutal Charles Taylor's era.

Against this backdrop, several individuals banded together to form a movement that would compete in the impending 2005 general and presidential elections. These individuals agreed that Liberia had been misled and plunged into chaos by a generation of politicians and leaders who placed their individual interests above those of the country and its people. At the initial meeting of the founding members of the movement, some argued that there was a need to change the course of politics in Liberia, but others argued that the political system needed a total overhaul and re-building from the ground up. A change the group believed would bring to the table Liberian citizens of unblemished characters who were passionate about the wellbeing of the Liberian people and the health of the country's economy. The group's members wanted Liberians who were selfless and who above all had no part to play in the atrocities of the Liberian Civil Wars. The latter requirement was very hard to source locally since most Liberians supported the civil wars in one form or another.

During the group's initial meeting and several other meetings that followed, the early founders agreed to what many observers saw as a glaring fact that the failure of leadership in Liberia and the just ended civil wars had greatly impacted the younger generation of Liberians—many of whom fought on either side during the dark days of the civil wars. The group then came to the realization that it was incumbent upon the youths to break out of their accustomed complacency and provide a new sense of direction for

Liberia. These suggestions seemed pretty good on paper but real-izing the dream and vision would take a person of astute character and love for country. As has always been the case, Liberians are lip servants—many do not practice what they preach. Leading a politi-cal organization in postwar Liberia at that time would take a person who commands a youthful following, coupled with international connection and some form of financial thrust. No former warlord that had been bastardized by the international community could pull Liberia out of the abyss of destruction onto a plateau of peace, justice, and radical development.

To formalize the formation of the organization with offi-cials, several eminent Liberians' names were suggested. On the top of the list was George Manneh Weah followed by several other people of interest. After eliminating the names of other prospects from the list, George Weah who happened at the time to be a UNICEF Goodwill Ambassador became the ultimate choice to head the new organization, but there was still a problem. The group had to come to one consensus since there were Diaspora groups involved. At the Monrovia formalization meeting, the members of the group also chose Joshua Sackie as chairman. And using the power vested in him, Mr. Sackie made a radio announcement in which he invited Liberians to meet to discuss the formation of a group to petition Ambassador George Manneh Weah to run for the Liberian presidency. For the men and women of the group, Weah was a better choice found anywhere in or out of Liberia. At the time, their unanimity was based on their perceived unblemished reputation and character of George Manneh Weah, compared to other Liberians who had used their political wits and finances to fan the flame of the war, Weah used his talents, fame, and finances to bring relief to the suffering Liberian people both at home and abroad. The Monrovia group believed that if George Weah could be convinced to accept the petition, it would be phenomenal for the pristine organization. Reflecting on the country's brutal history of the wars, it was believed George was the right person for Liberia. His somehow direct non-involvement in the wars along with his humanitarianism was going to be a rallying point that all parties to the conflict in Liberia could easily accept. At the time, Mr. George

Weah was seen as the embodiment of patriotism, love, hopes and aspirations of the masses—for he had the ability and influence to mobilize Liberians into an institution that would spare the nation from the kind of civil war, destruction, and underdevelopment the country had been known for since its founding.

With a consensus reached in Monrovia, the information soon got to George Weah, who at the time, and still, was Africa's only son to become World Best Football Player, that he was being sought as a leader of a soon-to-be political movement in his native homeland. Meanwhile, as these discussions were taking place in Monrovia, there were momentums building among Liberians in the Diaspora and discussions were taking place about forming a grassroots political movement that would field a solid candidate to contest the 2005 elections in Liberia. With cautions mingled with skepticism, the organizers in Monrovia managed their approach to having the politically novice in the person of George Manneh Weah as their leader. At this time, George Weah was already aware of some of the nefarious shenanigans that were used by some of his fellow Liberians over the years to scam him out of money in the name of philanthropy. Therefore, anyone engaging the World Best Football Player about business or anything concerning money had to do it in a carefully honest and authentic way. For he was no longer the free-handed George Manneh Weah that he had been fourteen years earlier—he had been made smartly aware of the criminal minded behaviors of some Liberians and Africans. Most Liberians shun financial risks but are greedy for power and reward. They will often sit back and reap the fruit of what they did not sow.

During one of his many visits to Liberia, George Weah agreed to meet with Mr. Sackie and other members of the newly formed group. According to inside sources, this first meeting took place at George Weah's residence in Monrovia. Several national and personal issues were discussed at this gathering that would ultimately lead to the formation of an upsetting political movement in the country. Some of the touching issues discussed with Mr. Weah included the failure of past regimes due to selfishness and greed, systemic corruption, tribalism, the culture of impunity, and the lack of a broader vision for the Liberian economy, just to name a few. Since character mattered at that time in Liberia, at least this is how members of the group felt; it was suggested that based on his life and character, it would be an honorable thing if he could accept a petition to be the flag bearer of this newly formed political movement, to send a clear message to the old order that the grassroot Liberians were tired of their misrule. At the meeting, the group formally petitioned Mr. Weah to contest the presidency of Liberia in the upcoming October 11, 2005, general and presidential elections.

George Weah didn't want to make a hasty decision by accepting the petition out of sheer excitement or sympathy for the petitioners. Rather, he wanted to speak to his family, his very close friends, and some stakeholders about the idea of running for the presidency of Liberia. Then, he was still bearing the United Nations Flag as UNICEF Peace Ambassador—this position is only reserved for nonpolitical activists. Weah had to make the wise choice that might lead him into scoring another big goal in his life. Therefore, Weah asked the gathering to give him time to consult with his family and friends, especially one of his mentors, Africa's icon, anti-apartheid activist and former president of South Africa, the late Nelson Mandela. To keep the pressure on George Weah, the organizers selected Sylvester Williams, commonly known as Careca, who happened to also be a senior advisor to George, to serve as chairman of the group. To some extent, his position was strategic because of his proximity to Ambassador George Weah. At that juncture, Sylvester Williams was the man anyone had to go through to see George—their relationship is now soured as George have sidelined the man who once helped to nurture his amateur as well as his professional football and political careers. It was believed that Mr. Williams would have made it very easy by influencing the football legend to enter the inferno game of politics.

It should be noted that Sylvester Williams is not one of the newbies around George Weah. He saw the young George Oppong Weah grow from a teenage boy to a man. Sylvester played a major role in George Weah's growth and development than most people are aware of. As a civil servant of the government of Liberia, working for the Liberia Petroleum Refining Company back in the 1980s, Sylvester rendered financial assistance to the up-and-coming George Weah during his struggling days while living with Ma Emma in Gibraltar, Clara Town, Monrovia, Liberia. George Weah never forgot about Mr. Williams and many of the people who helped meet some of his needs when he could not afford them. Once he became a successful football player, George Weah kept Careca closed to him wherever he went. Weah personally took care of Mr. Williams and some of his family members during the Liberian civil crisis. George is one person who never forgets the bridge that he crossed over when he was in need. The relationship between George Weah and Mr. Williams has remained cozy up to this day.

Following George's first meeting with the petitioners, there were several other consultative meetings between and among numerous youth groups and concerned citizen movements in Monrovia and other parts of Liberia. From these meetings, it became evident that many of these groups had the singular objective of having George Weah to contest the October 11, 2005, presidential race, which was the country's first after years of skirmishes between warring factions. The organizers continuously engaged other like-minded people that would direct the mission of the new movement that was on the horizon. Soon, the acting chairmanship was passed onto Mr. Macdonald Wentoe. He was charged with putting in place a comprehensive working plan of action that would eventually morph into forming a political party once George Weah accepted to run as standard bearer of the movement. Back then, the group believed that the presidency of Liberia was anybody's to win.

All along, the group never had a permanent facility to call its own. Often, meetings were being held at various members' residence around the city of Monrovia. To add some air of professionalism to the movement, two founding members of the group, Orishall Gould and Varflay Dolley, both of whom worked in the transitional government at the National Social Security Corporation, NASSCORP as Managing Director and Deputy Managing Director respectively, agreed to provide the Conference Room at the agency for meetings of the movement. This decision later proved controversial due to conflict of interest because there were many principal actors in the National Transitional Government that were jittery about this new movement. To quiet down the uproar that was billowing about using a government's facility for hosting political meetings for the new movement, Mr. Gould and other members later secured an office space on the 14th Street in Sinkor where the organization's meetings were held. At the new location, the group's members also conducted an election for the leadership of the Organizing Committee.

Officials elected at that meeting included Orishall Gould as Chairman, after defeating Prof. Edward Forh and Jacob Kollie. Mr. Forh would later run and become Representative of Montserrado County District #16 while Mr. Gould would later breakaway to form a parallel organization aptly named "Alternative National Congress (ANC)". Others elected were Jeror Cole Bangalu as Co-Chair for Administration; Geraldine Doe-Sheriff as Co-Chairman for operations; Sam Stevequioh as Secretary General; Mr. Joshua Sackie as Youth Wing Chairman; and Jackie Capehart, Chairperson, Women's Wing. This leadership of the Organizing Committee was tasked with securing a permanent office space, mobilizing membership, soliciting funding, and registering a political party all in anticipation that the most popular son of Liberia, George Manneh Weah, would accept to run as flag bearer for this movement.

After a series of consultations with family members, his close buddies, mentors, and scores of friends, George Manneh Weah finally agreed on November 24, 2004, to be a presidential candidate in the 2005 presidential and general elections. For many of his well-meaning friends, they believe that George made the biggest mistake of his life by entering politics. Many of his good friends believed that politicians were going to use him to accomplish their political dreams and ambition. But what many of these friends forgot to know that George Weah grew up on the street. They forgot that he was street savvy and enigmatically unpredictable. He can be your friend on Monday, and your enemy on Tuesday. He can turn on anyone he feels threatened by in a matter of second. While he may not have had it all together in terms of formal education, but he knows that streets and survival techniques. When one comes to think about it, he outsmarted veteran politicians like, Walter Brumskine, Winston Tubman, Varney Sherman, and lately Ellen Johnson-Sirleaf whom it is believed that he made a backdoor deal with through the help of former Nigerian President Olusegun Obasanjo—George would wait until Ellen serve a two-year term before handing power over to him and not her vice president.

When the announcement was broadcast, the news of Weah's acceptance was welcomed by many youthful citizens both at home and abroad, along with few people in the international community. This pronouncement was made at the Monrovia City Hall in Sinkor amidst cheers from hundreds of thousands of supporters and well-wishers who had paraded from the Roberts International Airport in Margibi County to Monrovia in support of someone they believed to be one of their own—a person rejected by the established political elites, rejected by many in society for his lack of a college education, but connected to the poorest of the poor due to his life experience as an impoverished boy living in the ghetto and for so many other reasons. When George arrived at the RIA from the U.S., Many of his supporters made the 45 miles journey from the airport to Monrovia on foot, something that was unprecedented in Liberian politics at that point in time.

Once the announcement of George Weah's intention was revealed to the Liberian people, the final work of forming a political party got underway by the end of November 2004. Initially, the Organizing Committee (OC) and other stakeholders had agreed to name the new political party, the Liberian National Congress (LNC). But something sinister happened during the formation of the party. The OC could not legalize this name at the Ministry of Foreign Affairs as it was dubiously incorporated by another group of Liberians. For the group of naive political enthusiasts, many of whom didn't understand the cutthroat game of politics, they had to learn the hard way. For the movement and its members, this was just the beginning of a series of political tests the group was to go through before it reached maturity.

In the interim, a committee was set up to come up with alternative names for the new movement—after their first choice was taken away. Astoundingly, there were some 72 names brought forward by members of the committee. Finally, the names were narrowed down to two: The Liberian Grassroots Party (LGP) and the Congress for Democratic Change (CDC). At a general meeting on a somber weekend in Monrovia, the name, 'Congress for Democratic Change, CDC' was endorsed by the entire body. Come to consider the name, it was very appropriate for a grassroots party that was formed on the pillar of effecting change in the lives of the ordinary people that had been abused and assaulted by years of civil strife, political cronyism, and an unrelenting political hegemony that plaque the country for over a hundred years.

On a similar note, as stated earlier, while the CDC was being formed in Liberia, few Liberians living in the Diaspora with a similar vision began discussions of forming a political party that would contest the forthcoming presidential and general elections in 2005. Among some of the Diaspora Liberians involved in the formation of a political movement that was concurrent with CDC's Activities in Liberia were former Liberian student activists Samuel D. Tweah (more of an ideologue than an actor) and James K. Kollie (more moderate in words, but pragmatic in action)—two friends with diverging views took center stage. Both of these young comrades from the walls of the Williams V.S. Tubman High School were then Minnesota residents. A few years following the 2005 elections Kollie would go to work for the Ellen Johnson Sirleaf administration in various capacities while Tweah took assignment with African Development Bank, ADB. Prior to the latter, Tweh and Kollie along with other unnamed members in the Diaspora began meeting with interest groups and interested parties in the U.S., especially in the states of Minnesota and Pennsylvania.

The group in the United States played host to numerous

town hall meetings paralleling the ideologies of the group in Liberia. Tweh and Kollie sought to meet with other like-minded Liberians in the continental U.S. During this exploratory process, a clear mandate evolved from the series of talks. As was done in Liberia by Gould and others, a petition to George Manneh Weah was crafted by the U.S.-based group in close concert with people around him. Once everything was put into place for a visit, Mr. Weah graciously accepted an invite from the group to visit with them in Minnesota after being convinced by a friend named Suku to consider running for president. The U.S. group operating under the name, Friends of George Oppong Weah-USA (FOGOW) was officially formed in Minnesota after their historic meeting with the former football icon. Following its formation, the group's number began to swell, comprising Liberian professionals from all backgrounds, including some longtime acquaintances of George Weah. As consensus was built amongst Weah and the Minnesota's FOGOW group and Weah having accepted the people's petition in Liberia, the groups in the USA and Liberia began the real work of forming a cohesive political alliance—this would eventually lead to the formation of a political party. The confluence of the various groups gave Mr. Weah a platform to project himself as a serious candidate to the Liberian people. The moment seemed like he was what the ordinary citizens were waiting for.

Having petitioned their man and formed a sisterly coalition with the Monrovia group, the name Congress for Democratic Change-United States of America (CDC-USA) was officially adopted for the USA group. A few weeks later, a national leadership team was nominated and put in place to steer the affairs of the US-based organization. Members of the team included Samuel D. Tweah, National Chairman; James K. Kollie, National Secretary General; Harry Gbesi, Co-Chairman for Operations from the state of Delaware; Jonathan Geegbae, National Financial Secretary from the state of Georgia; Alexander Kerkula, National Financial Secretary from the state of Minnesota; and Williametta Peso Saydee-Tarr, National Communications Director from the state of Minnesota. At that point in time for the organization, CDC-USA's mandate was to be a solid supporting partner in the nation building efforts of the home-based group in Liberia. By January 2005, the CDC-USA, under the leadership of Chairman Samuel Tweah, began a statewide CDC-George Weah 'Awareness Tour'.

During these tours, members of the CDC-USA team met stiff resistances from some Liberians to the idea of an ex-footballer with no political experience running for president for a country that had been in turmoil for more than 20 years. A few liberal-minded Liberians in the Diaspora welcomed the idea of Weah's run for the nation's highest office since it didn't need anyone with previous presidential experience. Majority of the youthful Liberian-Americans wholeheartedly embraced the idea of having someone they grew up watching play football to become president of their homeland. On these tours were several members of the newly formed CDC-USA's group. These individuals included Chairpersons of Chapters and Committees, and, some members of already established state Chapters, including Alexander Yonly (MN); Alfred Jardiah (PA); Arthur Katee, Eric Daniels, Onike Sherman (MA); Jerry Barcon, St. Tomalin George, Dave Jackley (RI); Bertrand Kane, Jerome Beysolow (GA); the late Francis Nimene, Rufus Darkotey (OH); Toyuwa Harris, Aaron Davies (NJ); Alexander Nyenkan, Ruthie Deline (NY); to name a few.

The team of enthusiasts traveled to major states throughout the United States including, NY, New Jersey, Pennsylvania, Massachusetts, Rhode Island, Florida, Minnesota, North Carolina, Georgia, bringing the news of this New Generational Call to Action and introducing George Manneh Weah to those who did not already know him as the petitioned flag bearer of the phenomenal grassroots movement called Congress for Democratic Change, CDC. George was ecstatic on his new role and political journey. When he was on these U.S. trips, he eagerly spoke to Liberians and friends of Liberia in each city clearly, articulating his vision for a better Liberia, while Chairman Tweah and other partisans crafted CDC's Platform, Values and Agenda. In May 2005, several members of CDC-USA and FOGOW began returning to Liberia to join hands with their Liberian-based counterparts in ensuring that CDC won a resounding Victory in the General elections of 2005. The biggest problem was that their standard bearer, Mr. Weah, was financially broke after retirement. This later brought disappointment to some of the members in Liberia. For they had the thought that George Weah, having made over 80 million dollars during his professional football career, would have bankrolled the party. Many of the party's stalwarts in Liberia were having a second thought about Mr. Weah due to the financial darkness they found themselves in. By then, it was a little too late as his candidature had gained momentum in Liberia but not so much amongst Liberians in the Diaspora.

While the U.S. group continually built momentum with recruitment and mobilization, the team in Liberia continually swelled its rosters with new members. Many of these members were young, disenfranchised Liberians that willingly came in droves to the organization to be recruited. By the Summer of 2005, CDC's Organizing Committee had secured a lease agreement with the Bernard Family for their property on Tubman Boulevard in Oldest Congo Town opposite the Old Liberia Bank for Development and Investment (LBDI) Complex. Once the lease was signed and payment was made, the Organizing Committee moved into the facility. The location provided enough space that would be used for political gathering, something that was very helpful in the party's mobilization efforts. The Bernard's property would ultimately become the national headquarters for the CDC. For many of the members, the headquarters became a holy shrine where youthful and uneducated members would come to worship their god, George Manneh Weah, a man for whom they are ready to shed blood and even die if it is necessary.

Liberians are a group of peculiar people—they love and gravitate toward new things and ideas many of which they cannot sustain in the long term. Contrary to the latter label, this was not the case with the CDC. Many of the party's grassroots supporters remain loyal to the party up to this day due to the George Weah Factor. For them, George Weah is the only man who can identify with them by giving them a modicum of hope to hold onto when all else is gone, and who they believe can transform their country into what it should be. When words about the new home of the

Congress for Democratic Change went out to the public, people from all walks of life flocked to the party's headquarters like 'white on rice'. Many of these people sought membership to the party. Also, many of them brought their own t-shirts to have the graphic of their savior George Weah printed on them. Many political pundits and fence sitters believe the CDC craze would be short-lived, but that has not been the case as more and more young people have moved to this grassroots movement borne out of deep-seated resentment for the political establishment in Liberia.

Prior to political parties' certification by the National Elections Commission, NEC in 2005, the CDC launched its first nationwide membership drive in its bid for registration at the NEC. Unfortunately, the CDC membership list that was submitted to the NEC was challenged by the election body on two separate occasions. The NEC cited that the names were all made up names. What the NEC didn't know was that CDC had more members in Monrovia and its suburbs than any other political party. Whether they believed it or not, Monrovia back then was CDC's stronghold. With George Manneh Weah as its standard bearer, it was believed that no other political party would ever win her in the nation's capital. After a series of hurdles, the party was finally certified in July 2005 to run in the October general and presidential elections. With the stage set, the real work began. The CDC's biggest problem back then was the lack of funding to power a nationwide political campaign throughout the fifteen political subdivisions of the country. To circumvent this financial hurdle, the party went in house to raise funds by charging those none-core members running on the party's ticket to pay tens of thousands of dollars as their candidature sitting or listing fees on the ballot. This strategy along with raising funds from Weah's deep-pocketed Liberian friends and admirers like Benoni Wilfred Urey, Varney Gboto-Nambi Sherman, and many other sympathizers and fans of George Weah worked. In subsequent elections, the CDC would deploy this technique by charging about $30,000 USD for none-core member representative candidates, and about $50,000 USD for none-core members senatorial candidates. This classic pay-to-play fundraising campaign by the party was unprecedented. It was very much unheard of in

Liberia, but those within the party remain tight lips as it became an internal secret among George Weah and top members of the party's hierarchy. Those who could not afford, paid Mr. Weah later.

As more and more political parties got certified by the NEC and campaign season soon approached. The party had its first National Convention in the port city of Buchanan, Grand Bassa County. To decentralize the process, the Congress for Democratic Change, CDC conducted primaries in the various counties to elect legislative hopefuls on the party's ticket in the impending elections. The party's convention lasted for almost four days, from July 29 to August 1, 2005. This event was highlighted by great speeches which were mostly rhetorical in nature with no specificity. At the end of the convention, members of the party unanimously selected George Manneh Weah as the first standard bearer of the party. In his keynote speech, Mr. Weah promised to improve the lives of all Liberians, and to provide better educational and health opportunities for all. A promise that is core to the CDC's vision as Liberia's most populous and popular grassroots political movement.

Other officials elected at the convention in Buchanan were Cole Bangalu as Chairman; Joshua Sackie as Vice Chairman for Administration; Geraldine Doe-Sheriff as Vice Chairman for Operations; John Youboty as Vice Chairman for Finance; Eugene Nagbe as Secretary General; Acarous Moses Gray as Deputy Secretary General; Sidike Fofana as Youth League Chairman; and Hannah Brent, now deceased, as Women League Chairperson. Louise C. Karmorh was elected as the party's first Chaplain. These officials strategized, planned, and executed the organization's 2005 election bid for the Executive Mansion. At the time some 60% of CDC's elected officials were new to the game of Liberian politics. Few though, had firsthand experience in students' politics from the University of Liberia and from the 1997 elections that brought Charles Taylor to power through a landslide victory in Liberia's first postwar election.

The Congress for Democratic Change ran a good and aggressive campaign to have their candidate George Manneh Weah elected during the 2005 election. If history will be fair to this grassroots movement, it should be said that the CDC participated in the 2005 presidential general elections and achieved greatness beyond the expectations of many political pundits, especially for a young party whose standard bearer was overlooked by the political establishments in and out of Liberia. In the 2005 presidential and general elections, CDC won more legislative seats than any other competing party that year—CDC won the first round of vote with the Unity Party coming on its heels in second place. No political party has ever made the history made by the CDC by emerging with the highest percentage of votes to be the first-round winner in the presidential elections in the history of Liberia. According to some former officials of the party, a run-off game plan was not in the party's playbook—they had come for a first-round victory hoping for Weah's popularity to secure that victory. Unfortunately, the party lost in the second round of the presidential election. Following the second round, George Weah, who was not used to this kind of colossal defeat, was stunned, and surprised at the final result. He and members of the party hierarchy cried fraud and planned a mass demonstration which was later called off by George Weah through the intervention of ECOWAS and then Nigerian President, Obasanjo—Mr. Weah met privately with President Obasanjo and a deal was struck. Immediately thereafter, the party's hierarchy expelled Cole Bangalu from the party for violating a CDC policy statement requiring all partisans not to attend the certification ceremony of Madam Sirleaf as winner of the presidential race, in protest over the party's fraud allegation about the elections. On a similar note, Cole Bangalu and Geraldine Doe-Sheriff were both accused of secretly passing CDC's campaign strategies to their rival Unity Party during the presidential campaign.

It is worth noting, however, that the CDC and other participating political parties considered the presidential runoff victory of the Unity Party as fraudulent due to the allegation of ballot stuffing and multiple voting in some precincts around the country. At the NEC, CDCians believed that the chairman allegedly manipulated the result in favor of Ellen Johnson Sirleaf who was heavily favored by the West, President Obasanjo, and many African leaders as a candidate with stable hands that was more capable of managing a country coming out of a brutal civil war. Many partisans of the CDC viewed this bias as foreign governments meddling in the election of Liberia. Armed with that knowledge, many CDCians (partisans and supporters of the Congress for Democratic Change, CDD) considered President Ellen Johnson-Sirleaf a usurper. Many people within the CDC wanted her illegitimate claim to power and the Executive Mansion halted, but George Manneh Weah seen by many in the international community as a man of peace, decided otherwise after meeting in private with President Obasanjo, other African and Western leaders, or their representatives in Monrovia. While trying to save Liberia from descending into any torrent of violence, George Weah was accused by political critics of receiving a huge payoff from Western and African leaders that favor Ellen Johnson Sirleaf, the newly elected president.

In the summer of 2007, some sixteen months following the 2005 presidential and general elections that ushered in the opposition Unity Party of Ellen Johnson-Sirleaf, and upon receiving an invitation from CDC-USA, several members of the CDC's, including Joshua Sackie, Chairman; Geraldine Doe-Sheriff, Co-Chair for Operations; and Moses Acarous Gray, Deputy Secretary General, traveled to the US to attend a Mini-Convention hosted by CDC-USA. Culminating the Mini-Convention, the CDC-USA group voted in a new corps of leadership team which included Dr. Matthew Nimpson as Chairman; Harrison Sorsor as Co-Chairman for Administration; Jerome Beysolow as Co-Chairman for Operations; Alexander Yonly as National Secretary General; and Alexander Kerkula as the National Treasurer. The leaders of the CDC and some representatives of the NEC also signed a joint resolution that clearly defined the relationship between the two bodies. This new political maneuver between the CDC and NEC was seen by many political parties in Liberia as laughable.

Following the return of CDC's executive members to Liberia after holding a successful meeting with the USA-based counterpart, members of the group went on to hold the party's first Mini-Convention in early 2008. This Mini-Convention was held at

the Thinkers Village resort in Montserrado County located outside of Monrovia. At that convention, Geraldine Doe-Sheriff, now
senator of Montserrado County and Co-Chairman for Operations
was elected as Chairperson of the professed Mighty Congress for
Democratic Change, CDC.

With the much-disputed 2005 elections in their rearview
mirror, CDC stood tall as being the most viable opposition party in
and outside of Liberia. The latter statement was predicated on the
fact that CDC has won various By-Elections and/or Special Elections that have been held in Liberia. The poor majority Liberians
have seen the party as the party of total redemption for their quest
to move from "Mat to the mattress". Many urban dwellers have
also seen CDC as the preferred party of their choice. This perception has been proven to be true because the Liberian people freely
voted CDC over the ruling Unity Party on so many occasions. One
such codification of the people's support for the CDC was most
recently seen in the senatorial elections of Geraldine Doe Sheriff in
2009, and George Manneh Weah in 2014 respectively. These two
candidates won with such a high margin in what many CDCians
referred to as an astounding "tsunami' victory over the incumbent
UP's candidate.

As a party born out of resentments for the political establishment in Liberia, members of the party still believe that the
CDC remains committed to its position and it grassroots philosophy it held sacred at its inception. The CDC has morphed in so
many ways but has always remained open to all Liberians who
seek accountability and the creation of a new system of government and functional institutions that is focused on identifying and
implementing innovative solutions to the problems faced by the
nation and the people for the 170 plus years of its existence.

Having gotten over the 2005 elections fracas that was
marked by claims and counter claims of foul play and election
meddling, the CDC again participated in the General and Presidential Elections in 2011. This time, it was Counselor Winston A.
Tubman as its standard bearer while the party's chief patron and

brand ambassador, George Weah was selected as VP at the Congress for Democratic Change primary that was held that year in Kakata, Margibi County—some forty-five miles from Monrovia. For pundits and some members of the movement, this was the wrong combination, especially running against an incumbent opposition party with a less known candidate as the standard bearer. Political observers and many party members believed that Mr. Tubman bribed Mr. Weah for the number one spot on the party's ticket after Weah's colossal loss to the well-connected Harvard educated politician. Some supporters and some founding members also believed that Winston Tubman was lacking in so many areas. They believe that he did not speak in the voice of the grassrooters (coined), he did not believe in the core value of the movement other than pursuing his own political agenda of becoming president like his uncle, William V.S. Tubman was far removed from the party's core supporters that is mainly made of poor people from the lower realm of society. Seeing all of these warning signs on the wall, the party continued with the former United Nations Diplomat and Harvard University educated lawyer into the presidential and legislative elections. This strategic blunder of fielding Winston Tubman as the head of the movement cost CDC the election that year. Unknown to many CDCians, this was George Weah's strategy of waiting his turn in line for a better opportunity, especially heeding to his prior arrangement with Ellen, Obasanjo and other leaders after the 2005 elections in which he was wildly believed to have won. Also, George Weah knowing how difficult it is in Africa to win an incumbent president, found Mr. Tubman to front the party while he took a backseat. Though the party came second in the first round, members believed that the party was once again the victim of electoral fraud and irregularities orchestrated by the NEC and the ruling party. Contrary to the allegation of fraud, many critics believe that CDC did not have a second-round strategy in its playbook to campaign against an already established president, Ellen Sirleaf who out campaigned, and out spent them by 10 to 1 on the campaign trails. People who witnessed the 2005 elections, knew something was wrong. George Weah was less enthusiastic about the 2011 campaign after throwing the front-row seat to Winston Tubman. He went out to campaign less. He would tell George Solo, Isaac Vah Tukpah, and other within his ranks that he was not going out to campaign due to security concerns. To save face before his supporters, he instructed to Mr. Solo and other to cry fraud.

As is the unfortunate case with claims of election fraud by oppositions in most African countries and in many countries around the world, the NEC and international election monitors did not consider CDC's claims as weighty with a preponderance of violations to nullify the elections' results for the first round. As peaceful in appearance as always, Weah pacified his fellow partisans to accept the result, but the CDC made certain demands (mainly to replace the chairman of the National Election Commission, James Fromoyan) to the Commission for the second round—this demand was never met as the NEC decided to proceed with the second round with Mr. Fromoyan as Chairman. The CDC in collaboration with other political parties urged their members not to participate in the second round, which eventually led to Madam Ellen Johnson Sirleaf winning in a landslide fashion. Without the CDC participation in the 2011 run-off presidential election there were reports of very low turnout at polling places. In hindsight, many critics believe it was wrong for CDC to have boycotted the election, given the fact that it was the most popular political movement within the country. Again, it was believed the organization fielded a less known elitist candidate in that election. Following the announcement, CDC staged a mass demonstration to protest the lopsided election that gave Ellen Johnson-Sirleaf a second term to the Liberian presidency. Like 2005, members of the opposition CDC and other political parties called the president elect a usurper—she was using her local and international connection to rig an election that was badly frauded during the first round.

For a political movement to remain as significant as the CDC has done, it is seen as a very impressive deed in Liberia. While the CDC may have lost two presidential bids, it won the 2017 presidency and consolidated power. The organization has an enormous task of remaining significant after George Manneh Weah term ends in 2029—that is if he wins the 2023 presidential election for a second term. With a party built around a single individual, its survival is never guaranteed after the departure of the one single force of influence. Most critics believe that there is no CDC Without George Weah—a CDC without GMW is a dead CDC. Therefore, pundits think that for CDC to endure, it must institutionalize itself which the organization has refused to do for over a decade. While forward thinking members of the organization often view this assertion of George Weah being the center of gravity for the party as de minimis, the possibility still exists considering the power of "The George Weah's Brand) for the movement to outlive its current political leader. Well-wishers believe that the leadership of CDC needs to rethink and rebrand the party into a political institution if it will remain relevant in Liberian politics. In Africa, a political party is often built around a single individual rather than being institutionalized as it is in the United States and in other western countries. The culture of building a political party around a person is often due to the highest bidder mentality—a more financially potent person is seen as the more capable leader for the group, even if that person has no leadership ability. In Liberia, money buys everything and anything.

None CDCians believe that if the party must remain relevant in Liberia's body politics, the George Weah's effect should be ignored at a point in time and a more prudent and institutional approach should be taken for the survival of the movement. CDC needs to take a cue from their rival, the Unity Party that was recently defeated by them in the second round of voting in 2017. While the party's chief patron is a force of his own, his current influence should be harnessed and built into a lasting institution that will remain long after George Weah has departed the party. Let those who come after George Manneh Weah say, "This is the party of Weah, the pride of Africa. The man who introduced a disruptive political campaign in Liberia that reverberated across Africa and the world." To remain influential in Liberia, Mr. Weah must extend his sphere of influence in other parts of the country where the party is less popular and less important. If the CDC is to remain significant, it must also be built around the philosophy of George Manneh Weah whose love for his people is unsurpassed by another politician of his time. Weah's sympathizers want the CDC to always be a party about the masses that are underrepresented and undereducated. Political scholars believe that if the CDC is to remain vital to the young men and women who will come after the likes of George Manneh Weah, Samuel D. Tweah, Moses Acarous Gray, James Kpadeh Kollie, Geraldine Doe (now deceased), Joshua Sackie, Jeror Cole Bangalu, and so many of its astute leaders, the party should be more committed to the firm foundation of love for country—just like its legendary leader, George Manneh Weah has demonstrated his love for Liberia and its people his entire adult life.

Chapter 18

The 2005 and 2011 Presidential and General Elections

The 2005 election had many firsts for so many reasons. It was Liberia's real free and fair first postwar election after more than 14 years of ruthless civil wars that saw the death of thousands of innocent men, women, and children. It was the country's first election to have a celebrity turned politician as a presidential candidate, as well as corporate lawyers, several graduates of Harvard University, and dozens of female candidates running for various positions. It was Liberia's first postwar election to have more than 1.5 million registered voters. The 2005 presidential and general elections were the first ever election that spurred a lot of interest in many segments of Liberian society, along with a widespread press coverage involving media organizations from all over the world pouring into the small West African country. This election would eventually put the people of Liberia on the map of the world for making history across Africa because it was the first ever election that shattered the invisible glass ceiling of an established patriarchal African political hegemony and brought in the first-ever female to a presidential palace in an African country. The news of Ellen Johnson-Sirleaf's election ushered in a new view and a firm belief around the world and across Africa that females across the continent could change the course of a dying country into a positive new direction. This new belief is yet to be proved, as President Johnson-Sirleaf ended her second six-year term in January 2018 admits mixed reactions from Liberians across the spectrum and other international friends of Liberia. For the very first time, the 2005 elections witnessed the introduction of a disruptive political campaign by a nonpolitician who used his celebratory star-power to come close to winning the highest seat in the land that year.

As the proverbial leader of a populous political movement with only a career experience from the football field, the odds were stacked up against the star. For a political neophyte with hundreds of jeering and rowdy supporters mainly in Monrovia in 2005, a second place in a highly contested election was a signal to his pundits that a real force had arrived on the political scene in Liberia. On the other hand, many of George Manneh Weah's hero-worshipping supporters would not accept anything short of a win for their candidate whom they sometimes referred to as the *"rejected cornerstone that the builder refused."* Like many of them who saw themselves as social rejects due to their poor social statuses, they believed that this cornerstone in the person of George Weah had come back home to become the head cornerstone that would rebuild and strengthen a nation with a broken foundation. Like those that cheered him on, he too dearly believed that God or Allah had brought him home to rescue his people from poverty and marginalization. As Bob Marley sang in one of George Weah's favorite reggae songs, "Ride Natty Ride" in which the hero 'Dready' had to overcome powerful oppositions to achieve his goal by not retreating, but 'de deh' or showed up every time it would seem as if he'd been defeated and would never return. Like Dready who never gave up in the face of powerful defeats and brutal oppositions, George Weah, the people's hero never gave up in the face of difficulties—he kept on showing up (de deh), and he kept on coming through by encouraging his supporters of an impending victory at the end of their journey. As a leader of a hopeless generation, no matter what happens, if the cause that is being pursued is in the best interests of the common majority that will bring equality and justice to a nation, it is something that is worth fighting for. On the other hand, critics and other analysts are unsure if this head cornerstone, George Weah who is still a novelty in Liberian politics, can deliver as promised and not be corrupt like other leaders before him have been.

The October 11, 2005, Election for George Weah and members of his CDC political machine was an election that ushered in a new breed and a new generation of politicians on the political landscape of Liberia. For members of the CDC, it was an experience like never seen before—especially having George Weah as their leader who has a huge following among the young people in and out of Liberia. Mr. Weah was the most popular and globally iconic Liberian among all the presidential candidates that year. Apart from Charles Taylor, former Liberian president who was forced out of power by African and western leaders in 2003, George Weah is the only Liberian most non-Africans would have heard of during the 1990s. This was due to his glorious career as a striker for first class football teams like, AS Monaco, AC Milan, Paris St Germain, Chelsea, and Manchester City. At the time of his golden years and up to now, if a person would ask any fan about George Weah, they will remember his Wonder Goal from 1996 against Verona when he ran the entire length of the field as he dribbled every player and defender that came to tackle him. Prior to that year, he was the greatest football player in the world. Before his "From Weah-to-Weah goal" (as that goal is referred to), he swept every award in football's history as the World's Best Footballer of the Year, the Best African Footballer of the Year, and the Best European Footballer of the Year in 1995. This is a feat no other African player has achieved and may never achieve in a thousand years. But when George Manneh Weah entered the game of politics in 2005, he saw a different breed of players—it was a game with no referee, no lines men, no rule to follow, and no protection from infringement or harm. These were players that didn't follow an established rule—they would chew him up alive and spit him out, so to speak. In this game, George Weah was a complete novice who was flying blind without a structured game plan for himself or the political party he was representing.

What differentiated Weah from the rest of the pact in the

2005 general and presidential elections was the natural love his fans and supporters had for him. He never had the financial means to fund his campaign like Varney Sherman who spent the most money because his campaign was bankrolled by Lebanese businessmen and other foreign interest groups. According to many observers, if money could win an election, Varney Gboto-Nambi Sherman would have won the 2005 presidential and general elections outside of his self-absorbed and arrogant attitudes that he is known for. Sherman would later endorse and finance George Weah during the runoff. For George Weah, having had a blissful football career behind him, many Liberians never saw the legend but only heard of him on the BBC Sports programs and read about him in local newspapers. The power of his legendary status drew tens of thousands of people to his campaign. Many in the throng were young people who were not of voting age, and people who grew up watching him play for their national team, the Lone Star of Liberia. At every campaign stop, tens of thousands of people would turn up to see George Manneh Weah, the footballer turned politician. His persona and energy were infectious—people could not get enough of the football player who wanted to become president in order to save his country from falling into the wrong hands of some cunning politicians. This disruptive campaign sent out a sea of fear into the hearts of the mainstream politicians in Liberia and across the region. While many candidates were paying hundreds of thousands of dollars to buy voters' loyalty, George Weah was using his celebrity status as the greatest African football player to draw people to his campaign. Weah never bribed anyone to vote for him like it was allegedly done by Ellen Johnson-Sirleaf during the runoff—she was accused of buying CDC members voters' registration cards days before the election. In that election, George's message of hope was good enough to convince people to believe in him as a viable candidate. Many of his supporters during the 2005 and 2011 elections willingly made financial contributions to CDC's campaign. Some brought their own white T-shirts to the party's headquarters to have his picture and campaign slogan printed on them.

For many Liberians, the 2005 election was a watershed moment for the country in so many aspects. First, there was a complete absence of most of the rapacious militia or rebel groups that were responsible for the country's destruction of the country during those years of civil wars. Second, no candidate enjoyed the immense powers of incumbency which is normally such a mark of Liberia's political contests. On the other hand, Ellen Johnson-Sirleaf had more international contacts and support than any other contestant. Third, ethnic or entrenched party loyalty played little role in the election that year. Nevertheless, there were few ethnocentric alliances and support coming from the northeast corner of the country for some of the candidates—Gio and Mano voted favorably for Prince Johnson and his choice of presidential candidate. With these established facts, it can be viewed that the 2005 elections were not under the influences of either the settler oligarchy or the successive dictatorships of Samuel Doe who came to power in 1980 by murdering Tolbert, and Charles Taylor who came to be elected in 1997 in fear of him returning the country to another round of civil war. In other words, the 2005 presidential and general elections were the most free and fair election in Liberia's history.

In Liberia and in many African countries, people vote their fears and not their hopes for a better future. The 1997 election was an election in which people voted their fears and anxieties for someone more atrocious. Understandably, the voters' fears of Charles Taylor and his band of rebel fighters wearing civilian clothing were real—they could not afford to choose a more abled and professional candidate in that election knowing the terror that hung over them. Fast forward to 2005, many of the politicians played on the people's fear of the country returning to another round of war if their opponents were elected—the either me or none other syndrome. For many people in the international community and a handful of Liberian political pundits, the 2005 presidential and general elections that ushered in a new politician like George Manneh Weah and many political newcomers along with some old hands in the game of Liberian politics, was a true landmark election. With Liberia making an entry in the Guinness Book of World Record in 1982 for hosting the most fraudulent presidential election in the world back in 1927 in which there were only 15,000 citizens registered, but a vote of 240,000 were cast. According to international election observers, the 2005 election was the first ever free and fair elections in the country's long history since becoming an independent state in 1847. Since independence, Liberia has always had a one-party system in which the presidency was decided by members of the True Whig Party. Those outside of the group trying to organize a political party were often shut out of the electoral process. During many of these elections, the native population were never allowed to vote. But when the ruling True Whig Party wanted the electoral process to have some semblance of democracy by allowing other parties to participate in the election, it was always a sham as the opposition never won. This practice of one party's domination of the political system continued for over 130 years until on the morning of April 12, 1980, with the ouster of President William Richard Tolbert Jr.

The 2005 presidential and general elections in Liberia were a big milestone for the war-torn country. As a post conflict nation, many would think that the expression of views by the ordinary person would have been uncommon like in the past. In 2005, the political and economic views of the ordinary Liberians were heard. People would congregate on street corners and freely express their political views without the fear of retribution from the authority. The young men and women from the lowly ghettos and burrows would call out corrupt government officials from the current and past administration using various mediums. As a political party of the disenfranchised, the CDC became a vehicle for the voiceless to express their views and frustrations. Soon, students turned politicians from the University of Liberia and various universities took center stage on various issues and ultimately made these issues a rhetorically political talking point.

As the 2005 election took off in grand style with festivities, political vitriol of all kinds, and various types of pageantries, there was something lurking in the dark that members of the CDC weren't prepared for. This six-hundred-pound gorilla was the lack of education of their first partisan, George Manneh Weah. When Mr. Weah's education came to be questioned by members of the opposition, members of the CDC and his loyal followers came to his defense. Their point of argument was long made clear to the Liberian people because their candidate, George Weah had admitted to the Liberian people and the world that he has had little schooling due to his football career, but his lack of college education had nothing to do with his patriotism and love for Liberia. While his critics seized on his admission of not having much education and making it a selling point to their supporters and the international community, his loyal supporters in Monrovia and in other places around the country sang and shouted in unison, "Book or no book, we will vote for him." As it had been within the last 14 years up to the 2005 election, it had been a popular belief among the ordinary Liberians, especially those who found themselves at the bottom end of Liberian society believed that "*The Book People*", the educated elite, the politicians, have all failed them in the past. Many of George's supporters were of the view that the past leaders had been using the uneducated people to achieve political power. As is the case with politics all over the world, many politicians played on the uneducated people's low-level of intelligence to get voted into political office. Therefore, with George Weah in the race, the common people wanted to try something new. For many of these destitute and misguided people, George Weah was the new unblemished wine and the best alternative to the corrupt elites that had ruined the country and shortchanged the population for generations. For George Weah, at the time, he believed that college education should not be used as a yardstick to determine who becomes president or who had a better vision for the country and its people. While the pundits made unnecessary noise, the people's love for George Weah grew by the minute, hour, day, week, and month. At many of CDC's campaigns, another popular slogan "Educated People Failed Liberia" became the anthem that reverberated again and again as partisans and supporters danced and cheered their political leader, George Manneh Weah. George also danced to the tone of his supporters. Meanwhile at the time, his mother, Anna was attending adult high school to obtain her General Education Development (GED) certificate in the state of Illinois while living with her elder son, William Tarpeh Weah Jr. A.K.A Junior Boy.

To an extent, these songs or slogans became a liability for

George Weah and the Congress for Democratic Change. The opposition twisted the songs and made them a trap for many of these market women that once believed in Weah as one of them. They made many of the market women to believe that the songs of the CDC were disrespectful and disingenuous to their true efforts. Other than struggling for survival, 90% of these people work day in, and day out to educate their sons and daughters for a better future. The opposition knew that anything that was viewed as bashing educated people would not go down well with the market women and people from the lowest fringes of Liberian society. For some of these people who come from the lowest spheres of Liberian society, many of them asked questions such as, "If education was not important, what in the world they be working so hard to send their children to school if it was a waste of time to do such?" For some of these market women, they came to believe that George Weah and his supporters were accusing them of being stupid for working hard to educate their children like Ma Emma had done for him. At least, this was the message that the opposition political parties and their leaders like Ellen Johnson-Sirleaf, Varney G.N. Sherman, Winston A. Tubman (who in later years would go and run on a CDC ticket as standard bearer), Charles W. Brumskine and others wanted their supporters and many of George Weah's supporters to hear. Often in an election in many African countries, people are more likely to vote against a candidate who would make them feel imprudent; this is exactly what happened with George M. Weah in the 2005 presidential election.

On elections day on October 11, 2005, running against 21 other candidates, subdued by his people's loyalty, and feeling fueled by an impending wind of change, George Weah knew that the CDC had made history as it was leading in preliminary results that were pouring in from different precincts around the country. When the result was announced several days later with CDC winning a first victory with 28.3 percent and the Unity Party of veteran political tactician Ellen Johnson-Sirleaf coming second with 19.8 percent, Mr. Weah and members of the CDC scrambled to the drawing board in an effort to strategize for a second-round campaign. For members of the CDC grassroots movement, a second-round campaign was not in their playbook—they had only anticipated a first-round victory. The political novice and his young team have left everything on the field during the first round of campaign and voting. They were out of strategy, luck, money, and energy that fuels a modern political campaign. They could not continue like the veteran Ellen Johnson-Sirleaf who had suffered several political defeats herself.

With an election in overdrive and an opposition candidate with more than 40 years of corporate and political experience, George Weah and his CDC grassroots movement found themselves sailing against a powerful head wind in a tempest ocean. During a second round of campaign, George had to foot most of the campaign bills from his pocket with the little money he could scrape around—he was a broke man upon his retirement from professional football. By this time, most outsiders and a few core members of the party have realized that George was no longer the freehanded person who he once was. With whatever money he could get from friends, he funded everything and everyone from mobilization to members of the security, transportation, and forming of alliances with other political parties. Opposition politicians like Varney Sherman who was a staunch nemesis of Ellen, came to Weah's aid by infusing a little over half a million United States dollars into his campaign. Varney wanted Ellen defeated at all costs—they had an ingrained hate for each other that no political marriage could ever fix. On the other hand, Ellen Johnson-Sirleaf got help from Nigerian millionaires and billionaires through her longtime friend Dew Tuan-Wleh Mason who had lived and worked in Niger for more than 20 years. Inside sources said Mr. Mason was promised the Minister of Foreign Affair cabinet position when Ellen Johnson-Sirleaf became the president—this of course never happened. Politically savvy Ellen screwed him and stopped answering his phone calls.

Soon, George's credential became a subject of focus in the other camp—the Unity Party began to use his lack of education during the runoff as something that was needed by the person who was to lead postwar Liberia. This strategy worked to some extent from the result of that election. Members of the Unity Party, UP, argued that Weah's education was insufficient to serve as president that year. According to the standard propounded by the UP, the next president needed to know a little bit of everything (economic, history, security, health, education, technology, diplomacy and international protocols, and plethora of other things) to become an effective president at the stage where Liberia was. On the other hand, many Liberians believed that the election was about a candidate's character, commitment and love for country, and patriotism. For the majority of Weah's supporters and many of the victims of the political system, it was not just about education, it was about what the next president could do for a dying country and its destitute population. Liberians wanted someone who could reconcile them, bring economic relief to them, fight institutionalized corruption, bring peace and security in their towns and villages, and rescue their children from the streets out of the strong grips of abuse and drugs. For many of Weah's supporters, it was not how many degrees or experience the president had, it was his heart and love for the country that mattered. Sometimes in a contested election, education and experience can mean everything, and can sometimes mean nothing at all to the voters. It is the voters that decide the fate of their country, but the leader who sits in the captain's chair is the one who steers the country in the direction of progress and prosperity.

At the end of voting during the 2005 runoff, and when all votes were tallied, the Unity Party of Ellen Johnson-Sirleaf won with an overwhelming majority with 59.4% of the votes cast. As it is with most elections conducted in Africa and monitored by international observers, the international community declared the runoff election free and fair. But the Congress for Democratic Change, CDC protested the results and claimed fraud. For so many unknown reasons, there are always hiccups in elections the world over. While there may had been some irregularities during the process (the alleged buying of voters' registration cards by the Unity Party), it was not widespread to be considered a fraud by members of the international community. Therefore, stakeholders from Across Africa, the West African sub region, worked behind the scenes to quiet down tensions that were building up in Monrovia among supporters of George Manneh Weah. Many CDCians believed that the election was rigged in favor of Ellen Johnson-Sirleaf since she was seen as a more viable candidate to lead a post conflict Liberia and not a high school drop out with no experience and international connection. For members of the international community, the ending of the war had not ended the bitterness and soothed the anguish in Liberia. The country needed to be placed into the steadiest hands of someone who could heal the wounds and sooth the bitterness. Though the guns had been silenced for more than two years, a multitude of tendencies had emerged in Liberia because not all the former warlords were supportive of the creation of a sense of normalcy and the development of democratic institutions at that time in the country. For some of them, they wanted to remain relevant in the country, though the people wanted to move on and forget their bitter past. The perfect storm was the absence of the oligarchy, and many of the warlords in the 2005 elections provided opportunities for Liberians to construct a new governing paradigm and to craft a totally new institutional arrangement through the process of constitutional choice free from fear and harassments like were seen in the 1997 presidential and general elections that brought Charles Taylor to power.

Being raised by a God-fearing woman who always preached peace and reconciliation, George Weah agreed to accept the result of the runoff presidential election after intervention from members of the international community and West African leaders led by then Nigerian President Olusegun Obasanjo. With a whirlwind of criticisms behind him from political parties that supported him and members of his own party for selling out, George Weah took note of everything as he allowed peace to prevail. For him, condemning the result and resorting to violence like many African politicians do was not something within his political and personal DNA. He knew that the Liberian people had suffered a great deal in the hands of warlords and bringing people onto the streets to demonstrate was antithesis to his lifelong philosophy of peace. He decided that if the agony of defeat was something he was going to endure for the next six years, so be it. With mounting allegations against him, he completed on leaving the party like he did after the Lone Star football team after their defeat during the team's World Cup Qualifier. But George Weah boldly accepted all the blame for CDC's loss. After internal squabbles, he readied himself for a life after the election knowing that he had age, time, and loyal supporters in his favor.

His decision of conceding the election to Ellen Johnson Sirleaf cost him dearly. He lost many supporters and some loyal friends within his inner circle. George Weah became the subject, predicate, and verb in discussions for being a coward to have caved in to the demands of the international community. He had to deal with a personal depression having come very close to winning an election that was seen as anybody's to win, but only to be defeated at the last minute. Like many of the football matches he had played and lost, this was the only match that had an enormous impact on him and the hundreds of thousands of people that looked up to him for everything. But as a professional football player who had weathered some losses, he did not allow the loss to dimple his faith in the Liberian people because he had the stamina to live and fight another battle. For a while, George Manneh Weah remained quietly effective as he continued to live in Liberia as leader of the country's largest opposition political party while he looked forward to running and win the presidential and general elections in 2017 as arranged by President Obasanjo of Nigeria and other West African leaders. These leaders believed that George was not matured politically to rule Liberia at that critical time.

Soon, the years went by so fast before most people could realize as the 2011 presidential and general elections came rolling around the corner. For the previous several years, the administration of Ellen Johnson-Sirleaf was plagued with allegations of corruption of all types. Corruption within the Unity Party-led government became a rallying cry for CDC and the other political parties during the October 11, 2011, presidential and general elections. While there were huge gains made by the Ellen Johnson-Sirleaf administration within her six years of governance, the administration had been plagued with corruption, nepotism, and other forms of favoritisms. For George Manneh Weah, supporters and members of the CDC, the 2011 presidential and general elections were just as important as the 2005 elections. The party having gone to a convention and elected Ambassador Winston A. Tubman who was a less known member of the organization and George Weah serving as his number two man on the party's ticket, the CDC went back to its 2005 campaign playbook in mobilizing its supporters—only this time with much less enthusiasm being displayed within the party's ranks.

Throughout the 2011 campaigns, something was evident here—the crowd was not as energized as they had been in 2005, but due to George Weah's presence on the ticket, loyal supporters of his showed up at rallies. Some members of the party vehemently opposed the candidacy of Winston Tubman as an elitist who was part of the establishment that was responsible for Liberia's woes. Others within the party accused George Weah of selling the number one spot on the party's ticket at the convention to Mr. Tubman who was somehow kicked out of the National Democratic Party of Liberia (NDPL) of former Liberian dictator, Samuel Kanyon Doe whom Weah used to love and admired like the big brother he never had. But as the brand name that the party was built upon, whatever George Weah agrees on is what stands. When Weah came out to campaign with Winston Tubman, the crowd of supporters willingly followed their proverbial leader on the campaign trails. Every stop was crowded by supporters who came out to meet and cheer in support of Tubman and Weah's ticket. As with the game of politics, there was another six hundred pounds gorilla lurking in the dark for the CDC during the 2011 elections. The opposition Unity Party would launch a negative campaign against Tubman and the CDC that would ultimately tilt the elections in their favor.

As campaigning continued and rhetorical speeches of all sorts were being made throughout the country, members of the international community, including ECOWAS, AU, and the UN that intervened in the bloodletting in the Liberia in 2003 were on edge. For these organizations, the October 2011 elections were very critical for the country's peace and stability. In the unique words of

Liberia's National Elections Commission, *"the elections will test the readiness of our post-war country to inculcate little exogenous elements and increase the endogenous variables."* In ordinary words, the outcome of the elections would determine the level of foreign support to Liberia's peace building process, though it was clear that whatever the outcome of the polls would be, international support to Liberia which had been massive, including thousands of UN troops and civilian personnel costing over $500 million, or about twice Liberia's annual budget, would likely to be seriously downgraded. Therefore, it was their hope for the election to go as peaceful as possible.

At the time in 2011, some people might have quickly forgotten how Liberia got to this point with so many people's hands in her affairs. Liberia is a country that was founded by racist Americans for the banishment of their free blacks after hundreds of years of slavery. Many of these former slavers believed that the two races could not coexist after so many years of their inhumane treatment of black people in the United States of America and the Caribbean. Others racist whites were of the belief that the blacks were of a more inferior race and needed to return to their original land of origin where they could pass on the little knowledge they had acquired during years of slavery to their fellow blacks in Africa. After more than three centuries and a half, the freed blacks returned to Africa and founded Liberia. Contrary to their original mission of coming back home to educate their brothers and sisters in Africa, they instead enslaved those they had come to meet on the land. The former slaves that were referred to as Americo-Liberians ruled the country from 1847 to 1980 when the government was overthrown by U.S-paid mercenaries with the help of native Liberian soldiers of mixed ethnicities sponsored by the United States Central Intelligence Agency, CIA. The coup was front by Master Sergeant Samuel Kanyon Doe. Doe openly admitted to his inner circle that he was a CIA informant and that the Americans had his back—his back they had for a little while at a point in time until he got smart to spot their true intentions for Liberia. When Master Sergeant Doe became a head of state in 1980, Liberia took a downward spiral as the land became polarized with violence coups and counter coups—with the revolution eating up its own babies. Almost every member of the coup was killed by Doe and members of his Krahn inner circle.

With tensions between natives and settlers, and natives versus natives that began more than 100 years before and after independence which eventually festered into a full-blown crisis, Liberians found themselves in the middle of a brutal civil war that was not of their own making. Given the country's ugly history, this was a war that was unequivocally bound to happen no matter who would have been president at the time. To recap the full event, on Christmas Eve in December 1989, Liberia was invaded by National Patriotic Front of Liberia rebel forces with the help of Felix Houphouët-Boigny who was also known by his people as Papa Houphouët and the Ivorian government. Backed by the Burkinabe and Ivorian armies, a few dozen armed insurgents were led by a little known former Liberian government official named Charles Taylor. He and his men crossed the Ivorian and Liberian border into the town of Butuo in Nimba County. The group of Libyan-trained rebels had a mission to overthrow the government of President Samuel Kanyon Doe who happened to have found himself at odds with the government of the United States of America for refusing the US access to Liberia's only international airport, Roberts International Airport in Margibi County, and for leaning closer to the Soviet Bloc countries. Contrary to being a war that was only targeting Samuel Doe and his officials, the war quickly devolved into ethnic factional civil genocidal fighting, with the Gio and Mano tribes that had long been suffering from Samuel Doe's despoliations of the country and of Nimba County, rallied in support of Charles Taylor's National Patriotic Front of Liberia, NPFL. The Krahn tribe from Grand Gedeh County and few from other regions in Cote d'Ivoire, many of whom from Doe's ethnic sect of the Krahn with a few elements of the Mandingo tribe rallied to support Samuel Doe in his fight against the slaughter from NPFL rebels. A war that was widely supported by most Liberians quickly escalated to a full-scale ethnic violence and massacres.

By the mid-1990s, the war had become widespread, subsequently taking the lives of tens of thousands of innocent Liberians. As stated in previous chapters, many of these victims were mostly civilians made of women, children, and the elderly. Many of these victims had been targeted largely because of their perceived association, ethnic backgrounds, and religions. For example, Christian rebels killed Muslims or anyone with a Mandingo name, and Muslim or Mandingo rebels killed anyone with a Christian background or anyone they believed was associated with the NPFL rebels of Charles Taylor. The insane Liberian Civil Wars of the 1990s and 2000s unleashed a humanitarian catastrophe on a massive scale—something more than the nation could bear. This mayhem forced the complacent U.S. government through the CIA along with other western nations and African leaders to initiate talks and direct armed action to end the madness. Their action created ECOMOG and UNMIL in the early and mid-1990s. With the guns being silenced for more than eight years, members of the international community wanted to maintain some level of peace at all costs, even if it meant maintaining the status quo or working with people with tainted characters.

Fearing a flare of an imminent conflict, stakeholders had to delicately manage the election that would solidify the democratic gains that had been made over the past six years. Any turmoil from the contested October 11, 2011, elections would have undermined the fragile peace and reversed the significant gains made. With millions of dollars going into building Liberia's crumbled infrastructures and millions more at stake, the election was closely being watched by both foreign and domestic stakeholders. Though the major players in the Liberian conflict were off the political scene, like in 2005, the major players wanted this election to be as transparent as possible. They could not afford to see Liberia return to war as it did several years after the election of Charles McArthur Ghankay. Taylor. With a strong incumbent who was favored by the United States and other African leaders, winning an election with a less known presidential candidate was impossible for George Manneh Weah and his Mighty Congress for Democratic Change, CDC. Though he had been in politics for a little over five years, Weah was still considered by members of the international community as inexperienced, naive, or worse due to his association at the time. Prior to the 2011 elections, Weah publicly embraced Charles Taylor and other formal warlords to the Liberian conflicts. For his CDC base and certain constituencies, this played very well. But it is very unlikely to win him any favors among Liberia's influential foreign partners, especially the U.S and some of Liberia's neighbors, Sierra Leone and Guinea. In June 2010, George Manneh Weah found himself in the middle of an embarrassing and potentially damaging situation of being linked to an alleged drug dealer and money launderer, James Bestman living in the state of Maryland in the United States of America. James, who was also a member of the Congress for Democratic Change USA Chapter was a close associate of George—George had to publicly disavow James who once bankrolled him. George Weah's association with questionable characters scared, if not, worried members of the international community very much. Therefore, a Tubman and Weah's presidency was not something that was being considered as an alternative to Ellen Johnson-Sirleaf who was more manageable for friends of Liberia and international organizations like the IMF, World Bank, United Nations, the EU and so many international stakeholders in Liberia's postwar reconstruction efforts.

As the October 11, 2011, election campaign got underway with sixteen presidential candidates, George Manneh Weah, and supporters of the CDC were less enthusiastic about their presidential candidate. With the arrangement between he and President Sirleaf burned in his brain, he intentionally made Mr. Tubman to front in that election. In secret, George and many of his supporters knew that Winston Tubman was not like many of them, nor did he understand their struggles. Since core CDCians believed that the primary was rigged in favor of Counselor Winston Tubman, they had dwindling confidence in the man on the top of their party's ticket—a powerplay that would serve George Weah well comes 2017. Ordinary members of the party openly made fun of Counselor Tubman for trying to act out of character or for trying to speak like the little guy from the ghetto. For example, Winston Tubman could not pronounce the party's slogan like 'Muyan or Jai Cha' and other battle cries that rallied the troops. Soon, members of the opposition launched a negative campaign against Counselor Winston Tubman who was 70 years of age at the time of the election for his alleged involvement in the sales of the Liberian Embassy on 8 Rue Jacques, Bingen 75017 France, for allegedly being a Togolese national, for incarcerating and torturing Jackson F. Doe and Edward B. Kesselly during the time he served as the Minister of Justice under President Samuel Kanyon Doe during the 1980s, and for denigrating Ellen Johnson-Sirleaf's achievement after being nominated for a Nobel Peace Prize along with Leymah Gbowee. On the later, most people in the opposition as well as the ordinary Liberians did not think that Ellen Johnson-Sirleaf deserved the prestigious prize after openly admitting her involvement in the Liberian Civil War (she admitted contributing US $10,000.00 to Charles Taylor for the war effort or relief efforts during the fighting) that allegedly took the lives of more than 250,000 women, men, and children.

With an election going into overdrive after candidates of the two leading political parties, Unity Party, and the Congress for Democratic Change, failed to secure a 51% single majority vote, the events of the 2005 runoff came to play out all over again for the CDC. Going into the 2011 election, many Liberian watchers believed that Counselor Winston Tubman and the Congress for Democratic Change did not have a second-round game plan in their playbook, along with the fact that Nimba County Senator who is believed to be a kingmaker (a person who brings leaders to power through the exercise of political influence) threw his support behind Ellen Johnson-Sirleaf—he referred to her as the lesser of two evils. Moreover, Winston Tubman did not have the financial franchise to continue a second-round campaign battle against a more financially potent incumbent that was favored by members of the international community and her fellow partisans. As it was done in the 2005 elections, the CDC cried foul and rejected the final result of the first-round of the October 11, 2011, election, citing several irregularities at the polls and by the election commissioners. But their cry of foul play was never heeded by the NEC or international observers that had monitored the first round of voting that October. A boycott of the second-round was called by the CDC, followed by a mass violent demonstration on the eve of the runoff election on November 8, 2011. This demonstration that was called by the political wing of the CDC was met with brutal force by the Liberian government's security forces which was backed by United Nations Military Mission in Liberia, UNMIL security taskforce. According to the government of the Republic of Liberia, the demonstration led to the death of at least one supporter of the Congress for Democratic Change. On the contrary, the leadership of the CDC movement cited that at least four of its partisans were killed by security forces loyal to the President, Ellen Johnson-Sirleaf. Several other supporters of the CDC were badly injured during the demonstration in which some members of the security force used live ammunition to disperse the unruly supporters of the CDC grassroots movement.

When the election's dust was settled and the result was announced, incumbent president Ellen Johnson-Sirleaf won with a whopping 90.7% vote while Winston A. Tubman got a marginal 9% of the total vote. This low turnout was due to CDC's boycott followed by the violent demonstration that took the life of one or four of its supporters on the eve of Election Day in 2011. Following the announcement of the election's result, international stakeholders began to hold secret and aggressive negotiations with Tubman and Weah in the background—the details of those negotiations remained murky to many core CDCians in and out of Liberia. Like in 2005, George Weah took a softer tone while Counselor Tubman took a more hardline stand with negotiators. He wanted a rerun of the entire election—something the NEC, the Unity Party, international stakeholders, and some Liberians refused to do. Finally, George Manneh Weah prevailed upon Tubman to acquiesce to the demand of the international community in the interest of peace. For George Weah, peace was more important than a person's ambition of acquiring state power—Winston Tubman wanted the presidency at all costs. As leader of a populist political movement, Weah personified this moralist image to many of his fans and supporters. Therefore, George Weah mattered more to his partisans than anyone within the CDC.

Like in 2005, Weah's decision to accept the 2011 election

result, again, brought cynicisms among high-ranking members of the CDC—many of them believed that he had sold out because of self-interest. While other members wanted to continually challenge the National Election Commission's announced result, and others crossed over to the ruling Unity Party, George Weah saw the bigger picture. Though he had prior agreement with Ellen and African leaders about waiting his time in line, but he knew that peace was more important than pursuing Tubman and few of his partisans' agenda or standing with Counselor Winston A. Tubman to give them what the international community would not allow. Again, he knew that with age in his favor, he would be around to put up another fight in his political career. As a former professional football player, he saw a scoring opportunity ahead for himself on the political field. Soon, people within as well as outside of the party, began to call Weah a sellout for his acceptance of the result of the 2011 runoff election. In hindsight, what would George Manneh Weah have done when the election was influenced by so many external factors that favored a Nobel Laureate president who was a darling of the west? Weah and the members of the mighty CDC had to save their energies to fight another political battle that would bring him closer to the corridor of power—into the hall of the Liberian Senate in 2014. Political scholars and academics viewed this political maneuver as unorthodox—moving from being the presidential candidate to vice president, and then down to running to become a senator. This mood was never heard of in Liberian politics, especially coming from someone as popular as he was at the time.

Being a man who is used to winning and having been on the losing end of two elections, George Weah had to get his mojo back and start winning again. If he really, really wanted to win the presidency of Liberia, he had to change course and move in a totally new direction and not make things seem obvious that it was preplanned behind closed doors. He had to adopt or develop a whole new tactic in order to win. To prepare himself for the 2017 presidential and general elections as he was contemplating to do, George Weah threw his hands into the Montserrado County's 2014 senatorial race after consulting with executives and members of the CDC. Undoubtedly, with Montserrado County being his home turf, it was not a difficult task in winning on his own field against any opponent. No wonder he won the race against the Unity Party's fielded candidate, Robert Sirleaf who is the favorite son of then President Ellen Johnson Sirleaf with more than 78% of the votes. Winning any election in Montserrado County for George Weah who is idolized in Monrovia and everywhere in Liberia is a no-brainer. His celebrity star power is particularly strong among hundreds of thousands of young people in Monrovia and all over the country. For Weah and the CDC, it is a political boon in a country where more than half the electorate is under the age of 33. This win became Weah's stab to the presidency. With this victory, he stood a better chance at gaining the political experience for which members of the opposition often criticized him of not having.

Chapter 19

Lessons Learned From the Elections and Weah's Preparation

Liberians are a very peculiar group of people. Many of them are fickle, wicked, liars, and wind-driven. Most Liberians will never keep their promises to a person or hold genuine loyalty to someone other than for the better securing of their daily bread. In Liberia, people will flatter a person with empty praises that they do not truly mean. The virtue in most respects is to gain from the person more than they can give back to the person or their community. By the same token, if a person gains the trust and respect of the poorest of the poor in Liberia as George Manneh Weah had done, that person will forever be in their hearts. No matter what that person does to them or what others tell them of the one they trust, will never be believed by their confidante. If the poorest Liberians give a person their natural loyalty, many of them will fight for that person, talk for that person, or give their lives for that person, even in defeat or at the edge of their personal destruction.

As a man who knows the taste of victory and the agony of defeat, George Manneh Weah has learned a lot about Liberians on his road to become this enigmatic legendary leader of the Congress for Democratic Change, CDC. Along the road leading to the corridor of Liberian politics and power, he had come to meet so many people, and he'd also made so many friends and so many enemies.

Yet, he had never lost the vision of what he wants for the Liberian people and who he is as a person. George Weah has overcome so many objections in his quest to become president of the country he loves so much. If Weah didn't know the behaviors of Liberians after becoming a professional football player and upon retirement, then he learned them after venturing into the unchartered water of Liberian politics that is filled with mudslingers, backstabbers, and shrewed politicians. As a nonpolitician prior to entering politics, his guiding philosophy had caused him to only see vanity in such things as wealth gained without work, pleasure that comes without a person having a conscience, knowledge that is gained without a person having a good character, and trade that is conducted among nations and people without morality being involved. As a matured man, he has confronted some sciences that have come to impact human's civilization without humanity in them, and the worship of God that is conducted in various religions without sacrifice being made to accommodate others that are not like those that practice those religions. Weah has also seen politics being practiced in so many places around Africa and the world without a good moral principle. He has realized that many of these politics do not benefit society and have brought down great men and women all over the world to a miserable end. As a political newbie, he has learned the attributes and fickle characters of his fellow Liberians in so many different ways. To a certain degree, he learned that most Liberians cannot be trusted because they are capricious, if not deceitful—many of them will often not keep their words and promises to their fellow Liberians. To better deal with them, Mr. Weah had learned that one must meet them where they are, and one must be able to feed them with a long cooking spoon.

What needs to be noted here is that George Weah did what a great politician and a patriot like Samuel Kanyon Doe and countless other African politicians have done on their way to the presidency of their country—he fought his way to the top through so many different obstacles. But the problem is that Mr. Weah did everything backward which in and of itself is deemed as a necessary strategy by members of his party and supporters—but political pundits view it as dementedly unnecessary. It is often difficult for people to understand George Weah's moves or state of mind at times. For political critics, it was believed that Mr. Weah was being 'puppeted' by avaricious individuals that may have had their own hidden agendas for his presidency at the time. Maybe his timing for running for the presidency might have been wrong given Liberia's prevailing situations—a country that had just emerged from a brutal civil war and needed a lot of international help, stability, total healing, and national reconciliation. Losing the 2005 election was a bitter lesson learned by the 39-year-old football legend, but he learned well and moved forward without being compulsively attached to the outcome of the election. The loss was mostly felt by some of his senior lieutenants and supporters who wanted George Manneh Weah to continuously fight for a nullification of the election's result that was hailed by members of the international community as being free, fair, and transparent. From a competitor's standpoint, at least he participated and came close to winning, although several external factors or influences might have tilted the election the other way.

Could it be, though, that he was somehow misled by the people that had petitioned him into running for the presidency knowing full well that he had no past political experience? Or could it be that many of those petitioners and supporters pushed him into seeking the nation's highest office for their own selfish interests? Whatever reason it is that can be cited by pundits or supporters of George Manneh Weah for working his way toward the presidency in a backward fashion, it is only time that will judge the many reasons. But these experiences that he had along the way have taught the once skinny poor kid from the ghetto of Gibraltar a lesson or two about Liberian politics and Liberians at large.

The election of 2005 taught George Weah that education mattered most to some Liberians than the love of country that he may have had within his heart which no one could see with the naked eyes. When journalists and leaders of other political parties and their surrogates made Weah's lack of formal education an issue during the campaign, it was the brutal truth that led him to remedying this deficiency years later by obtaining a college education from an American University, though he had obtained his high school GED years earlier. Within himself, there was no denying the fact that education was important to nation building and human capital development. He could not deny the fact that he was among some of the least educated candidates in the election of 2005, but he forged forward with a blind hope that his love for his people would make up for, or trump his lack of education and would eventually help him win Liberia's most important postwar election against a Harvard University educated candidate with a vast international connection, and Liberian government and political experiences.

As a young and new politician on the block, Weah was not prepared for many of the divisiveness that arose during the two presidential and general elections in which he participated, one as a presidential candidate in 2005, and the other as a vice presidential candidate in 2011. So many of the people that he knew were heard calling him unfit for the presidency. As hurtful as that may have been at the time, many people believed they were speaking the brutal truth to power because they believed that at least a college degree would have sufficed for his lack of government and political experiences. Many of his political opponents used surrogates to parrot their talking points in attacking Weah who was and is still a force in Liberia's political domain. While many of these attacks may have been a legitimate political tactic aimed at getting under Weah's skin since he was thin-skinned at the time, George Weah did not take these attacks lightly. He knew there were people that didn't like him as a successful professional football player, and now as a young and powerful political leader of the country's populous political party, coupled with being a man who had the power to rally hundreds of thousands of supporters and fans at any given point in time. Indeed, just as he had put fear in the hearts of dozens of defenders, goal keepers, and fans on the football fields and scored spectacular goals as a professional footballer, George Manneh Weah's presence on the political field in Liberia put a whole lot of fears into the hearts and souls of career Liberian politicians and other established African politicians that were afraid of the Weah celebrity turned politician virus spreading into their own countries and infecting their nations' politics.

Along the road to success, so many things happened to and for Mr. Weah as he climbed higher and higher in his football career and politics in Liberia. George Weah is known generally as a people's person and a peaceful man, but he may have ruffled a few feathers along the way to success, whether unintentionally or intentionally. As a result, not all his friends speak well of him as a football player and now as a politician. But he has learned to keep a level-head as a human being to accept these facts. And, as Mr. Weah would normally say, *"One cannot please everybody all of the time. You may be able to please some people, but not one hundred percent of people can be pleased or happy with you."* Due to tension within the CDC following the 2005 election, George Weah broke pact with staunched CDCians like Samuel D. Tweh, James K. Kollie, and dozens of others who blamed Weah for the loss—some of these members believed he took bribes to concede the election to Ellen. George excommunicated Tweh, James Kollie and those he saw as undermining his legitimacy as absolute leader of the party. It would take the intervention of family and friends including James Bestman, and the party's US Chairman Mr. Isaac Tukpah to mend fences with Weah and many of those individuals who he believed threatened his overarching authority over the party.

During the many elections that George Weah participated in, some of the very people he thought were his friends turned against him—sadly this is politics because it makes a lot of strange bedfellows. In their views, he was not qualified to become president of Liberia or to become a senator of Montserrado County. George who was still a young politician, this was a low blow for Weah who thought he knew his friends well. As the saying goes, "In good times, your friends know you. But in bad times or in a time of need, you know your friends." This was the case when many of Weah's close friends questioned his education, his ability, and his motive of wanting to become president of a war-ravaged country, despite his achievements on the football field. Again, George Weah being the progressive person he is, never faltered.

Like a good striker, he continued to press on toward his goal. While the critics analyzed, critiqued, and sliced and diced his every move, he kept his eyes trained on the mark. He'd earlier learned from the game of football that, if a player kicks a hundred balls at a goal post that is manned by a very good goalie, one of those balls will find its way at the back of the net for a goal. Therefore, he learned to persevere and never gave up or listened to his critics as he neared the finish line.

After losing the 2005 presidential elections, George Manneh Weah decided to put the issue of not being educated to rest. In 2007, George Manneh Weah enrolled at DeVry University in Florida, where he owned a home, to pursue his bachelor's degree in business. Like many educated Liberians that are ardent believers in education, Mr. Weah believes in the continuity of education. Like his mother who obtained her GED years early with her belief that there is no age limit on education, George too held onto the philosophy that, it is never too late to learn. As he was in his 40s, he returned to the classroom to silence his many critics that demeaned and disparaged him for his lack of education and his lack of job experience. With a BSc. in business under his belt, George Manneh Weah knew that he would gain the basic training in managing a business and human resources, especially with him being a businessman apart from being a politician. Indeed, unlike in the past when many Liberian presidents barely possessed a high school education, Mr. Weah was now at a place where he believed his many critics would remain silent, but the criticism only got worse and louder. The critics said he was lacking a real-world job or government experience. Besides working at the Liberia Telecommunications Corporation in the mid-1980s as a switchboard technician, George Weah never had any job experience other than playing professional football in Europe. In reality, it was George Weah's lack of professional or political work experience that was under question for his electability. But the grim reality is that it is very difficult to please Liberians, especially those that are not in favor of the person under scrutiny. One thing George Weah and his supporters learned from the constant barrage of accusation is the insatiable nature of Liberians' thirst for petty things that do not impact national development. George and his fellow CDCians believe that no matter how hard he tries to close or narrow the gap of their demands and criticism, they would always find another area of his life to criticize.

Having participated in several high-profile elections, George Manneh Weah had learned the unstable nature of presidential politics. Mr. Weah has come to the realization that election being a game of numbers, it is never guaranteed to the person who is seen as most favored by his constituents—victory is sometimes incumbent upon external forces such as the election commissioners, foreign bodies, and the voters that decide in secrecy at the polling stations. No matter how hard a candidate campaigns, no matter how many times a candidate is endorsed, the results of an election mostly depend on those latter named factors. To better prepare himself, and with the help of few trusted friends and advisors within the ranks of the CDC, George Weah had to form alliances and forge friendships of all types and in odd places. Weah had to veer from the party's core value of not liaising with key players in the Liberian crisis. He extended an unclenched fist to embrace a warm handshake from former enemies while making new enemies inside and outside of his political party. He had to change his message to appeal to people on the other side of the aisle. Weah had to spend more time within the country, stayed away from attacking the president, and avoided any form of controversy that would give him bad press. If he was to score a final winning goal for his side, he had to be swift on message and play the devil's advocate like many politicians do. These strategies helped him win the senatorial race in Montserrado County, which is his home turf.

In Liberia, association can sometimes mean everything, and or nothing at all. To morph into Liberian politics, George Weah had to unlearn some of the bad things he had learned in the ghetto of Gibraltar about such organizations like the Freemason, Knight of St. John, UBF or Alpha and other fraternities that had been operating within the country for over a hundred years. As a means to an end, Mr. Weah had to seek membership into many of these fraternities for his own development and political network. Sometimes in life a person's network becomes their *"Net Worth"*. To secure his political future in Liberia's body politics, the World and Africa's Best Football Player had to rub shoulders with certain established orders. To maintain a delicate balance with his loyal supporters that view him like a demigod and be accepted into the mainstream, George Weah joined the Monrovia chapter of the Freemason brotherhood. Being a member, he would get an inside working knowledge of government by rubbing shoulders with current and former members of the national government and with people in high places.

As the one and only quintessential leader of the CDC, George Weah learned to rid himself of some of his inherent *"self-mentality"* to be a more effective leader of the CDC and the people of Liberia. Though he had been accused by friends and critics of being intolerant to dissensions, it is believed that Mr. Weah had learned to listen to critics that point him in the right direction, rather than listening to those who tear him down without making genuine suggestions. For some within his inner circle, Weah being able to accept constructive criticisms is a sign of maturity, both socially and politically. As a human being first and being a Liberian who is highly opinionated, he sometimes comes across as being arrogant and thin skinned. These past behaviors and other observable characteristics of Mr. Weah have made political observers and pundits to question his ability as a leader—some see him as a dangerous dictator. From past elections in which he'd been blamed for many of the woes of his party, George Weah managed many of these allegations without faltering or shifting blame on others like other politicians do. For example, when the 2005 presidential and general elections campaign ended, a lot of the campaign incidents were reported by observers alleging that it was members of his party that were serving as officials of civic and community-based organizations, government figures, and media outlets were engaging in partisan activities in favor of the CDC. But Weah being the peaceful person he is, did everything he could do to debunk some of these misconceptions or misinformation by urging his people to abide by the rules of the National Election Commission, NEC.

During the final days of the 2005 and 2011 campaigns, political rhetoric became increasingly inflammatory on both sides of the political aisle with the CDC taking majority of the blame. This raised a lot of concerns among stakeholders in the "Liberian experience" as fear lingered of a possible election-related violence. Again, as Bob Marley said in one of his songs 'Ride Natty Ride', George Manneh Weah 'de deh everyday' (show up every day) at his party headquarters to encourage his fellow partisans to obey the laws of the land and rules of the election as stipulated by the NEC. He showed up to quell down these concerns made by Liberians and many of the international community by managing his supporters well. He urged many of his disenchanted supporters to remain peaceful during the critical period in the country's transitional history. Though he was seen as inexperienced at the time, he was still able to control the hundreds of thousands of supporters from resorting to violence when they had felt that the second round of voting was rigged by the NEC in favor of the Unity Party of Ellen Johnson-Sirleaf. This was a classic example of leadership and maturity on the part of George Weah who many had considered a political novice and for being uneducated, according to their own-established standards.

In all that he had gone through as a person and as a standard bearer of the Congress for Democratic Change, CDC, Mr. Weah has kept on putting one foot in front of the other on his way to the Executive Mansion on Capitol Hill in Monrovia. Whether or not he had a clear shot at the presidency, he sometimes kept leading with confidence while his partisans closely followed him without questioning his leadership. On his presidential quest, George Weah had been viewed through so many lenses and had been considered to be a different person other than what the public sees him to be. He had been considered by some of his beloved friends and political critics as a person who is too intemperate to be president of a fragile nation like Liberia. Many critics have also alleged that George Weah is a person who neither welcomes free thinkers within his entourage, nor does he allow the free flowing of ideas that are contrary to his own to prevail, especially when he disagrees with the person advancing the ideas. Other political critics and pundits are worried that Mr. Weah being a man who is believed to be thinned-skinned and intolerant to criticisms could be a dictator in the making should he become president of Liberia. Those friends that were close to him says that he keeps an enemy list. Many of the former friends fear his unpredictability—he can be very jovial with a person one minute and bitter with them the next; especially when there arises an unfounded rumor about that person. Since coming to fame, George Weah has had too many fake friends around him that try to manipulate him of his loyalty to them. So many of them know that he relishes in rumor, they therefore take rumor to him in order to get an upper hand or get closer to him. Some of Mr. Weah's critics who have been around Liberian politics for a very long time are very worried that if George Weah becomes president, he would fail to make a positive change in the country just like past presidents have failed to do. They believe that his administration would be filled with, criminals, sycophants and brown-nosers who will only sing empty praises to him or dress him up with honors that he does not truly deserve. Whatever the views of these critics are about George Weah, it is no doubt that he has evolved as a person and as a politician over the many years he had been in the game of politics. From afar, his supporters and a few of his critics can now admit that he has learned from some of his shortcomings that have been identified by people who lovingly and sometimes, unfairly criticized him during his quest for state power. Having gone through several election circles and Liberia's divisive politics, one can only say, *"it is now up to Mr. Weah to rise above the many criticisms and do better tomorrow than he is doing today"*.

While Mr. Weah had played his own hands by accepting political arms (money) from every Liberian politician that wanted to use him for their own political gains, he had learned through the process and had become a different political animal in the end. He managed to use his street smartness to outwit ever major politician who wanted to piggyback him to power. While he was not successful in stopping many of them in their tracks, he in return used them for his own political end. While may not be seen as book smart, George is truly a street smart fellow.

Chapter 20

Graduating From University with a BSc. & MPA

For most people, education is a journey that leads a person on a road to success and enlightenment. The road to pursuing an education is an unwinding one. Sometimes it leads the pursuer in paths unknown to the human endeavors—narrow passages, rocky hills, and mountains, through the deepest valleys, through muddy paths and in garbage laden streets, and for George Weah, up on Front Street in the heart of Central Monrovia. As a role model to millions of impoverished youths in the tiny West African nation and in many other places around the world, Mr. Weah obtaining a college degree from an American university meant a lot to him, to his family, and to so many of his fans and supporters worldwide. Though it was a degree that was given to him, but it was a degree he'd earned for the millions of boys and girls who share his story and millions more that look up to him for direction in guiding their own dreams. His degree symbolized hope for many poor young Liberians and millions more across the world. Like Mr. Weah, many of these young men and women from the lowest fringes of society have the firm belief that with education anything is possible.

From birth, young George Weah was set up for failure by the system of government he was born under. From the first day he entered elementary school, up until high school, obtaining an education in Liberia was a rocky road for George. Like George, this is a reality for many people born of lowly birth—they have no future and no hope for a fighting chance. As mentioned in previous chapters, George Weah barely made it through high school had it not been for his skills on the football field and the generosity of kindhearted people that helped secure him a scholarship at Muslim Congress Junior High School and the Wells Hairston High School where he later dropped out during his senior year to pursue semiprofessional football career in Yaounde, Cameroon. As determined as he was, growing up in poverty-stricken Clara Town, young George failed to capitulate to the negative label that the mainstream Liberian society had placed on most people from the slum—uncouth, uneducated, violent by nature, and prone to remain at the bottom of the social ladder. As it is an established fact, Weah's dream of acquiring an American college education would have never become a reality hadn't it been for his success on the football field along with skills he'd developed on the muddy fields in Vai and Clara Towns as well as in many other places around Liberia.

In 2006, he completed high school courses to earn his high school diploma or General Education Development, GED. In furthering his education, he enrolled at DeVry University to pursue his bachelor's degree. Following intensive four years of studies that were marked by homework, essays writing and research paper, and exams, he finally graduated with honors on June 25, 2011, with a Bachelor of Science in Business Management, four months shy of the presidential and general elections in Liberia. Following his graduation, pundits, frenemies, and other political foes attacked his degree—they believed that he never earned it. Rather, they believe that George Weah earned his degree with the help of some paid friends who completed all his academic work while he was having a good time and partying around the world. Many of his critics said he could not have possibly earned a BSc or any kind of degree from an American Diploma Mill University when he George Weah still can not read well, write well, or speak proper grammar. These political foes openly said Mr. Weah was intellectually bankrupt, academically corrupt, and a spineless political neophyte.

But what many of these pundits didn't know was that, George Weah earning a degree after retirement from football, and after being defeated due to his lack of education unleashed a force across African and in many other places around the world. The news of Mr. Weah going back to school encouraged hundred of thousands of illiterate men and women around the world to go back to school and earn a diploma. His educational success became a new benchmark of success for poor illiterate adults who had the heart to improve their lives and society. For George Weah and his supporters, a degree granted, is a degree earned; no matter the circumstances or the tempest around said degree.

At a gathering organized by family and friends of Weah following the graduation commencement programs in Florida, Mr. Weah said that he had gotten a college degree to inspire disadvantaged children so they could see school and education as the way out of poverty. Knowing the daily struggles children in Liberia go through in the pursuit of education, especially having experienced it firsthand, he wanted these poor children and children from different backgrounds to know that it is never too late for education. At the small program organized for him by his friends, he eventually dedicated his degree to all such suffering children and people; just as he had dedicated his politics to freeing them from misery. His statement was poignantly moving words that captured the enduring class and status divisions that had been inherent in Liberian society for decades. If one looks around the country, a significant fraction of the nation's youth is still experiencing a similar squeeze of poverty and deprivation George Manneh Weah experienced in the past. Today in Liberia, very little progress has been made in improving the quality of life for more than 90% of all Liberians.

During the 1940s up until the 1970s, there weren't that many opportunities for many of the indigenous Liberians who had the brain but lacked the financial strength or political will power to obtain a college education in Liberia. In those days, only people from the upper class had the means of going to college as it was believed by many indigenous Liberians as a strategy designed by the central government to continue Americo-Liberians' domination in politics, finance, and everything that would control Liberia. This system also impacted George Weah's father who was only able to obtain some level of high school equivalent education which eventually enabled him to learn a livelihood trade in auto mechanics as a means of feeding himself and his family. Often in many countries, Liberia included, it is a person's connection that unlocks doors for them. If a boy or a girl from the slum or the village works very hard and graduates from high school and does not have funding to further their education, that youth's education would often end with the high school diploma. He or she would be forced to find employment, peddle commodities as a merchant, get married and start having children (if the student is a female), or join the family and make farms (if the student is a male). On the other hand, George Weah found himself lucky with the talent he developed which eventually propelled him to stardom and wealth in Europe and the United States of America where he completed high school and obtained university education.

With a college education now under his belt, especially a degree that came under so many excruciating circumstances since graduation George Weah has been using his education and experience gained in the Liberian Senate to ensure that majority of the country's children do not experience the squeeze of hardship for which he had a front row seat during his early childhood days in the ghetto of Gibraltar in Clara Town. Prior to reaching this level in his educational journey, George was like many children currently in Liberia who do not have a decent shot at education. George Weah faced many challenges during his early upbringing. As mentioned in previous chapters, his chances of being a successful man was very slim. In Liberia and in so many countries around the world, many young men and women from poor backgrounds are currently faced with similar dire and protracted hunger for education and success the World Best and Africa's Best football player, Mr. George Weah faced daily in Gibraltar. During his days of hard ship and a bleak future, the harsh conditions deprived him of his humanity, the energy he needed to perfect his football skills, stamina and motivation that would allow him to master reading fluently, writing and math skills as well as trek to school from Clara Town to Central Monrovia and back. It was only by sheer determination along with the help of so many good-hearted Samaritans like, Sylvester Williams, Carlton A. Karpeh, Samuel N. Burnette, Esther Parker, Barrie the son of the Gambian Consul General in Liberia who use to drive him around Monrovia in this Peugeot 305, Willard Russel, and dozens of others that he was able to overcome many of life's challenging conditions and predisposed life's objections. On the contrary, a person's success often wipes out their days of struggle—success doesn't remember the days of struggles and pains of the past. Rather, a person's success invites strangers and companies of all kinds, and sometimes blinds them of past realities.

More than 40 years ago, it was believed that the Southeastern part of the Republic of Liberia had the most educated people in the country, especially the people from Grand Kru, Sinoe, and Maryland Counties. People in Liberia often referred to the Kru people as the "Book People". Being born in a tribe with that label, most Liberians expected George Weah to be one of the educated people now that he was the most popular Kru man from the region without considering the circumstances of his birth, growth and development, and his family financial circumstances. Sometimes assumption can become the mother of all misinformation and misconceptions. To many of Weah's clansmen and supporters, obtaining a bachelor's and a master's degree was a clear validation and vindication for the Kru people as still being the most educated people in Liberia. Though many critics claim that his output can still not measure up to his education, but his supporters and people that know George Weah say the opposite—he has become more refined, analytical, and shows a flair of leadership than ever before.

Education is the fuel that powers a modern nation and its people because it is not attained by chance but by acute diligence and perseverance. While George Manneh Weah may have gotten a late start in college due to career circumstances, he reached his targeted goal, which has brought him head-to-head with his pundits and with those who seek his downfall. What needs to be noted from Weah's experience in his educational journey is that education is like a veteran football champion which no misfortune can really depress, which no level of crime can never destroy, and which no type of enemy can really alienate or enslave by any level of despotism. In Liberia, there are thousands of educated people masquerading as experts in nothing. Many of these educated people often criticized Mr. Weah for not doing what many of them have never done—so Liberia's plethora of problems. Many of them have not provided any solutions to Liberia's many woes. Now that George Weah has overcome the demon (his lack of education) that bedeviled him during his early political career, now he needs to harness or unleash the full power of his degrees by using it to do good and groom a new generation of leaders within his party and throughout Liberia or across Africa.

As stated earlier in subsequent chapters, education and experience often afford a person to develop functional plasticity which is the ability of a person to change their behavior based on an experience gained through education, job experience, or personal interaction with others. Having obtained a master's degree that requires a person to develop research skills, analytical perspective of things, and a deep-rooted self-derived aptitude, Mr. Weah should be considered an independent thinker who has changed many of his past behaviors. Often in education, learning experience is typically derived from structured learning environments where people develop soft skills. The brain of a person is fluidly expendable because as a person learns, he or she is supposed to become more rational and analytical—i.e., less reactive to both external and internal stimuli, matured in decision making, and selective in making friends in social and political environments as well as letting go of friends that are liabilities. Many of Mr. Weah's critics do not believe that he has grown beyond his former self. This because he has not changed his associates and those within his entourage. While this assertion may be unfounded, many of George Weah's supporters believe that he has evolved 'behaviorally' over the years since he came into politics. Many of his friends think that he has become more expressive—speaking his mind freely and taking position on national issues that may not have necessarily been popular with people within his own party. Education has served George Manneh Weah well. He can no longer fit into the stereotypical perceptions of those who once called him misfit or uneducated. Had he not been married to Clar, he would easily be accepted into any family of Liberia's educated elites that warned their daughter against dating a person like George Weah, the boy who grew up in the ghetto of Gibraltar with no hope, and no chance of becoming successful.

Chapter 21:

Weah's Role in Liberia and the Rebranding of CDC

How could George Weah revamped and rebranded a highly polarized political organization like the Congress for Democratic Change (CDC), which has gained the reputation of being populated with various political dissidents and many types of social agitators? When Weah decided to take centerstage after two failed elections, and after obtaining a highly needed education, the answer was obvious—he needed the right attitude and the right people around him to become a constant pain in the side of the ruling party. This strategy worked to the advantage of George Weah and the CDC that many citizens were now referring to as *"Children Destroying the Country, CDC"*. After losing two presidential elections over the past seven years in two election cycles, many political observers thought that the CDC would have lost its saltiness and disappeared into the dustbowl of political oblivion. But the party kept making itself relevant by engaging the governing Unity Party of Ellen Johnson-Sirleaf. While other political parties went silenced after the 2005 and 2011 elections, few well-known CDC's political agitators and social advocates like Moses Acarous Gray, George Solo, Isaac Vah Tukpah, Mulbah Morlu, and Isaac Saye Zawolo, a one-time instructor at the University of Liberia, along with many others from the party's ranks, actively engaged the ruling UP on many national governance issues. As a result, members of the CDC were viewed by members of the international community both internally and externally as provocateurs and political dissidents.

With Government's scrutiny and constant social engagement being part of the party's overall strategies, the CDC stalwarts
kept engaging the government through public demonstrations,
radio talk shows, and claims of all types against the Ellen Johnson-Sirleaf administration. While this tactic worked for the party as
a means of staying relevant after the elections, it sometimes back-
fired and sent the organization into a freefall. Often, the party's
prime stalwart, George Weah was blamed for many of the blow-
backs that evolved from many of his men's claims and allegations
against the government. In as much as many of these activists'
claims of corruption against the government of Ellen Johnson
Sirleaf were well based, the opposition put a spin on them and
made them political talking points and traps for many of the young
men and women of the CDC. On a similar note, then CDC's USA
Chairman, Isaac Vah Tukpah once compared the living conditions
of poor Liberians under the reign of the Unity Party as being way
below the living conditions of dogs in the United States and in
many Western countries. A statement though true at the time, came
under a stern criticism from members of the Ellen Johnson-Sirleaf's administration and other political parties that have been
silenced on such social, political, and moral issues since UP came
to power. For CDC to remain a check and balance force for the
Johnson-Sirleaf's governing party, its leader had to take the moral
high ground, or the movement would have died under its own dys-
functional political weight. To achieve the latter, Mr. Weah had to
become more of a leader and a national healer by remaining quietly effective as he continuously led the party from behind. George
Weah's proclivity of steering his party in a brand-new direction by
making it a pressure group within the country propelled the CDC
to several senatorial and representative elections victories, one of
which Mr. Weah himself was a senatorial candidate.

Having established himself as a serious political leader for
the soi-disant (French word for 'self-styled') Mighty Congress for
Democratic Change in the mid-2000s following a near successful
run for the Executive Mansion on Capitol Hill in Monrovia, and

with a back door deal between he and Ellen Sirleaf under his belt, George Manneh Weah was now being viewed by many critics and pundits as a political force to be reckoned with in the country. While many of his supporters hold him in a messianic status, the establishment viewed him as a threat to their way of life—for he had come to disrupt the normal way of doing things in Liberia and in many countries across Africa. Many of them felt that if he becomes president, it might send the wrong signal across Liberia and around Africa and the world—a celebrity too can become president in any country. Many African politicians and world leaders wanted to stop this George Weah Virus from spreading and infecting the political atmosphere within their own country. Whether the people of Liberia are aware of this fact or not, Mr. Weah has done more than well in changing the political dynamic in Africa and in Liberia and within his own organization, the CDC. He assumed a political movement that was built to replace a dying methuselah political generation that included Baccus Matthews, Togba Nah Tipoteh, Amos C. Sawyer, Ellen Johnson-Sirleaf, Dew Tuan-Wleh Mason, and dozen others vanguard political agitators that brought down a futuristic president, William R. Tolbert as well as dictators like Samuel Kanyon Doe and Charles McArthur Ghankay Taylor. With Weah holding the mantle of power for his CDC in Liberia, he had placed himself at the upper echelon of power and leadership in a country of four plus million people that are never satisfied. Now that George Weah has neared the steps of the Executive Mansion almost becoming president of Liberia, Liberians will still complain about his leadership the day he takes power and become the first football player to win the presidency of a country.

Since he came to political prominence in the post-war election of 2005, and with the   CDC losing two successive presidential elections that Liberia has had, the party has been fortunate to dominate the Legislature in both the Senate and the House of Representatives. George Weah's loss in the presidential election in 2005 was predicated upon the fact given by critics and many Liberia watchers that he was an inexperienced politician with low level of education and political intelligence. Now that he had the chance to mystify his critics by acquiring a master's degree at his alma mater DeVry University, he is closely being watched to do what has never been done by many people of his stature. Knowing these facts, he and members of his party veered on a new mission in revamping the organization into something more attractive to the disenchanted professional and a younger generation of leaders that have broken a pact with the ruling Unity Party.

From its inception, the CDC had been viewed by many as the party of children, hooligans, and societal rejects—no wonder it was called *"Children Destroying the Country"*. To change this negative stereotype about the party, the executive had to do a lot of house cleaning and confidence building among professionals living both in Liberia and the Diaspora. Between 2007 and 2014, CDC USA recruited many disenfranchised professional Liberians living in various states across the U.S. into the full force of the policy and political ranks of the party. During the outreach period, professionals like Isaac Saye Zawolo Jr., George Solo, AB. Massaley (he didn't go too far with the group due to ideological differences), Massa Washington (like other professionals that folded and exited the party, she didn't go too far with the group due to personal reasons), Moses Watson, and so many other well-meaning Liberians that saw the Unity Party led government of President Ellen Johnson-Sirleaf as a corrupt and criminal enterprise that needed to be pushed out of power through the ballot box. Using a similar approach in Liberia, former members of the Ellen administration along with members of past regimes were recruited as part of the rebranding effort. The CDC that was previously viewed by many Liberians as a party that was crowded with kids was now being populated by old hands in the Liberian political games. This strategy was a massive departure from the party's early philosophy and doctrine of not accepting people with shady character into the CDC.

While welcoming people with questionable characters into the party was seen by some party's members as a violation of party's core principle, other members believed it was the most politically expedient thing to do—though politics make a lot of strange bedfellows. At the time of reaching out to every Liberian to join the rebranded CDC, Mr. Weah and his team believed that sometimes in politics, it is never too late to do the right thing, or too wrong to do the right thing. As humans, people sometimes allow fear to keep them focused on the past by making them worry about the future that is never guaranteed from a political standpoint, especially when it comes to dealing with fickle people like Liberians that often vote their fears and emotions, rather than voting for their political and economic futures. While Acrous Gray, George Solo, Nathaniel McGill, Jefferson Koijee, Mulbah Molu and other CDC operatives and agitators may have gotten under the skins of so many people by virtue of their comments, allegations, and writings, George Weah, and a few smart thinking CDCians acknowledged many of their past controversies during the rebranding process and went ahead to do what they felt was right for their party. They did not allow fear of past grievances committed by few of their low-level firebrand members from impeding their progress. While the CDC executives may not have openly apologized to victims of members' political attacks and rhetoric, they may have acknowledged said behaviors behind closed doors. Sometimes if a leader can only and sincerely acknowledge his fear of wrong that he or his partisans have done to others, it can make a big difference because things will turn out to be so much better for him and those who he is leading. Contrarily, a public acknowledgement of wrong is a sign of political weakness.

When the CDC was being rebranded and repositioned, George Manneh Weah remained quietly effective behind the scenes. Being a man with limited media engagement, lacking in baseless meandering of words like many showboating Liberian politicians, he kept a low profile while his surrogates did many of the talking and political grandstanding. Often, he was accused of leading from behind by a few members within the party as well as some of his political critics. Understandably, it was one of the best things he did, especially the party having lost two presidential elections to a more powerful and a more preferred candidate in the person of Ellen Johnson-Sirleaf. Analysts believe that sometime in politics, a political party and its candidates must be managed and marketed like a product and services that once had the people's craving after. For George Weah and his CDC political movement to win the presidency, they had to breakaway from their past ideologies and core principles of non-inclusion of bad apples. As a means to an end, according to many of his critics, Weah had to reach out to the incumbent, Ellen Johnson Sirleaf, who he once bastardized and criticized as a failed and corrupt leader of Liberia. This political move proved useful, as the relationship would put George Manneh Weah in a better electable position for the 2017 general and presidential elections.

One thing that stood out to everyone during the rebranding of the CDC was the "George Weah effect". In Liberia's body politics, Weah remains a force of its own. He has the ability to call crowds wherever he goes—Weah is like a sweet-smelling flower that attracts honey making bees and so many hummingbirds. He has the admiration of the young people within the country. Like a magnet, he attracts everyone's attention by his mere presence everywhere he goes. His celebratory status was gained because of playing football as legendary as has never been seen in Liberia or Africa. As a result of his star power, more and more young people moved toward the CDC when they felt disenchanted by media reports of corruption within the Unity Party government.

Knowing elections to be a game of deception and numbers, Weah and members of the CDC kept shedding lights on many of the corrupt practices of the government and many of its officials that were siphoning public funds into foreign bank accounts. As it is with politics, if the ills or corrupt acts of the incumbent continuously become a topic of daily media discussions, the public which is the biggest stakeholder within the nation's politics often sides with the opposition that has brought the issues to light. This strategy of continuously attacking the Unity Party of wrongdoing by members of the CDC worked like a charm! Soon, more than 60% of people living in the country began to blame the Ellen Johnson-Sirleaf administration for such things as hikes in the price of petroleum, rice and other basic commodities that were being imported by Lebanese and Indian merchants. To add insult to injury, President Sirleaf intimated that her government does not have control over the price of the various commodities—this brought a loss of confidence in her administration. The CDC was being viewed as a possible replacement of the Unity Party that had ruled the country for more than a decade.

What must be noted, however, is that Liberia is a very tough country to govern—the citizens are mostly spoiled people. Many Liberians have the syndrome or suffer from a severe form of dependency disease. Having been founded to be the home for used and abused former and freed men and women of color in the United States, the settlers that governed the country didn't do justice to the country and its native population. After arriving in Liberia and forming the country, the settlers continually depended on handouts from the United States of America through the American Colonization Society, ACS. These former slaves received almost everything from their former slave masters, some of whom were still living in the United States of America and occupying powerful positions within the U.S. Government. The former slave generation received such things as salt, oil, soap, rice, onions, potatoes, clothes, just to name a few. With the constant supply of food and basic needs flowing, the settlers became very lazy and showy. Many of them only knew how to dress up in fancy clothes while they forced the natives to work for them as domestic servants and unpaid farm workers. They did not industrialize the country like they should have because food, and other supplies continuously came by boatloads to the new settlements in Liberia. This dependency syndrome was passed unto the aboriginal population the former slaves generation met on the land. Apart from the sugar industry that once thrived in Liberia for over sixty years, food crops production was lacking. While the former slaves depended on U.S. imports and handout, it was the natives that continuously practiced subsistence farming—a practice that still exists in today's Liberia. Unfortunately, since the end of the civil wars, there are fewer people engaged in subsistence farming or rice production in Liberia. The country still relies on foreign importation of rice, which is the national staple.

While trying to reestablish the CDC brand with a professional touch, Weah who had obtained a college education had to endure years of verbal and emotional insults from political enemies and some ordinary citizens, including insults to his mother's womanhood and his family. As a senator, his credibility was questioned by the press for not being too visible within the chambers of the senator. While he may have worked with other senators to put forth legislation, he was still being viewed by critics and many political pundits as a mum (deaf and dumb) senator who did not contribute to laws that were being passed or for not representing his constituents like they expected him to have. With all that was being alleged, he kept a leveled head while reviving his spirit with positive hypnotic thoughts like, *"I will make it. We will win national power one day. I am different from other politicians. I will become president one day with the help of God."* Mr. Weah has much more work to be done, especially being the name brand of the party that is poised to be around for a long while. He needs to be the bigger person within his CDC by remaining above the fray that often consumed and jittered politicians in Liberia. Being the brand name behind the party, George Manneh Weah has tried to stay away from many of the petty things he was once accused of. Often with age comes maturity and wisdom. Therefore, George Weah is more open to new ideas than he ever was. After losing the 2011 presidential election to Ellen Johnson-Sirleaf, he began to turn a listening ear to the use of Facebook as recruitment platform, Twitter for following other leaders and speaking out on political and social issues. Weah's embracement of these communication platforms have made a big difference within the party's membership numbers. Personally, Mr. Weah has hundreds of followers on Twitter and thousands more on Facebook. The adaptation of technology has made a big difference for both the CDC and Weah.

As part of his re-branding and re-imaging strategy, Mr. Weah took the moral high ground as a means to an end. George Weah, having endured more than ten years of personal and verbal insults to his intelligence and character from opposition politicians and ordinary people, learned to accept the views of others without insulting those on the attacking front. Though he was betrayed by dozens of close friends and associates, but he welcomed them back to the flock without being vindictive as he has been seen by those who do not truly know him. As a newbie, he accepted the under-hand views of so many political vultures without knowing he was being set up by those with hidden self-serving agenda. To put the latter experience behind him, he learned from many of the mistakes of the past and has tried to become once again, 'the lord of the poor' and the arbiter of goodness for both the 'Haves' and the 'Have Nots' in Liberian society. To better prepare for future leadership, he learned from the pattern of failures of past governments in the country. Whatever George Manneh Weah has done for the CDC and the Liberian people, it is only time that will be his judge.

Chapter 22

Liberia: A Beautiful Country With Much Potential

As hurtful as this statement may sound to some Liberians, many Liberian observers believe that Liberia is a country where anything is possible, and everything is acceptable. In its current state, it has become a country that needs a leader who will nurture its growth and development and teach its people how to walk again the second time. A country with a considerable potential, Liberia is a land that holds so much promise for its children and those who enter her gates. Her warm Mona Lisa-like welcoming smile puts everyone at ease. The beautiful smiles that are plastered across the faces of her citizens serve as a beacon of hope for so many persecuted people across the world. Liberia is a beautiful country that is rich in natural resources and blessed with a youthful population— some of whom could one day turn their country's failing destiny in a positive new direction. As an old nation whose strength lies within its youthful population, Liberia is a success to be had. Liberia is a success story waiting to happen if the leadership changes priority and adopts a human center development that is fueled by technology and honesty.

While many people may be unaware of its unique position in the world, Liberia is a country that has so much to offer its people and to the outside world. Liberia is the 12th cleanest country in the world (America is at number 27) in terms of air quality. And, with more than 60 percent of its citizens speaking good English, Liberia can be a pure haven for ships and companies looking for employment laws that are less stringent. This small West African country has more than fifty thousand international companies registered there, but none of these companies have a physical presence within the country—this is an opportunity for the creation of a totally new industry. With low corporate tax laws, Liberia can serve as the hub or headquarters for international companies looking to take advantage of its young and professional workforce and friendly culture. Currently, Liberia owns 12 percent of the world's entire maritime fleet, including the world's largest cruise ship which is owned by Royal Caribbean International. Liberia's 'Flag of Convenience' offers a greater opportunity for vessels' owners around the world. Liberia, being a founding member of the 'Intergovernmental Consultative Organization, IGCO' which was later changed to 'International Maritime Organization, IMO', plays a pivotal role in shaping policy at the organizational level—though the country has no vessel of its own. Being in this strategic position, the government of Liberia needs to harness its status as the largest virtual owner of the international maritime fleet by ensuring that Liberians are gainfully employed on vessels flying her flag on the high seas. The climate and air quality in Liberian is far better than Ghana, Nigeria, or Kenya because the average temperature is around 76^0-degree Fahrenheit with less air pollution.

The strength of any country lies within its population. Liberia is a nation that is swimming in vast wealth because it has plenty of youthful human resources, many of whom are enrolled at various institutions of learning across the country. With a population that is progressively pursuing higher education, it will make a good partner for any international organizations in search of a young, progressive, educated, and smart population—Liberia has a pool of professionals that can meet the needs of any organization from around the world. While many countries in Sub-Saharan Africa and in other places across the African Continent are rapidly losing their ecosystem, Liberia has a huge forest reserve which offers the potential for ecotourism. Indeed, Liberia has a lot to offer people, organizations, and institutions that are willing to make foreign direct investment, FDI, in the country. The most admirable thing about Liberians is their ability to bounce back after a catastrophic event—the scars of war are slowly disappearing. Liberia is a resilient nation with a people that exhibit a diehard attitude. Often, after every devastating event, be it a military coup, civil war, deadly plague, flood, or landslide, the people always bounced back, picking up their broken pieces, and rebuilding their lives and their community. In Liberia, whenever the wind of devastation passes, many of the people in the country wear a beautiful smile on their faces and have moved on with their individual lives. This resilient character found in every Liberian makes the people of the country unique in a very special way. For example, following the advent of a war or disaster, a Liberian man or woman does not dwell on their losses. Rather, they will try to rebuild their lives with worn out tools if one exists. Unlike people in the Western World that have means of rebuilding their lives in the aftermath of a catastrophic event, many Liberians do not have that luxury, even if the government says it has the capacity to do so. George Weah is a witness to this. He was part of a relief effort initiated by public school students in 1982 to raise funds for victims of a landslide incident that took the lives of over 200 people in No-way Camp, Grand Cape Mount County.

Liberia, which was once a vibrant tourist destination in the 1960s and 70s, plunged into a torrent of unrest, has come roaring back like a sleeping giant that had been awakened after years of long slumber. Liberia's golden shimmering shores have a lot to offer visitors. From roaring surf spots along the stretch of the Atlantic coast, to pristine forests and jungles found deep in the interior of the country, the various counties can serve as a habitat for biodiversity by providing homes for various plants and animals species. While it remains an unknown fact to many, Liberia's most famous national park is the Sapo National Park in Southeastern Liberia. This Park sits on more than 1,800 square kilometers of land in the Upper Guinean Rainforest. The Sapo National Park contains the highest mammal biodiversity counts anywhere in the world. Many of the species in this park have never been discovered. In fact, the park is home to the world's only pygmy hippopotami,

West Africa's only white-crested Diana monkeys, various types of crocodiles, leopards, speckle-throated otters, and different types of chimpanzees. Yes indeed, Liberia has so much to offer its visitors in terms of ecotourism and sightseeing. Besides the Sapo National Park in Sinoe, there also exists the Lofa-Mano National Park which has been renamed the Gola National Forest in northwestern Liberia. Like its compatriot, the Gola National Forest is home to a plethora of plants and animal species. Most prominent within this biodiversity are numbers of verdant canopies and seemingly endless stretches of colossal tree trunks and boughs with hidden fern fields and exotic dragonflies that flit between different species of flowers in the dense forest. The forest also contains many chimpanzee species and Liberia's famous rare pygmy hippopotamus and listless of other plants and animal species.

This small West African country with a glittering shoreline is a surfer paradise. Robertsport, which is about an hour and a few minutes-drive from the capital city of Monrovia, is a destination for both local and international surfers. The waves and tides are among the biggest that can be found in places like Oahu, Hawaii, Jeffery's Bay, South Africa, Maverick's California, and in many other surfing spots. Since the war ended, Liberia's surfing sport has been gradually developing. Aside from Robertsport, there are dozens of other surfing locations along the coast of Liberia. Since its discovery as a surfers' paradise, surf schools are also popping up that are giving beginner surfers the basic training on the out and onto the waves' techniques. In Robertsport, some visitors only come to hike the beautiful coastal stretches to see the pretty reaches of the famous Cape Mount Bay and see the trademark timber and stone churches that are found on the shore. Liberia is a beautiful place and sight to behold. Over 98 percent of the beaches in Liberia remain underdeveloped. With the right investment, many of these untouched beaches could be developed into beautiful tourists' destinations.

No matter what the country and its people go through, the spirit of the people can never be broken. The people of Liberia love life and pleasure more than the civil wars they were known for all over the world. In fact, during the years of the civil wars, the various warring factions would take a fighting break to celebrate Christmas and New Year holidays. This beautiful country is filled with friendly and giddy people—no matter the impoverished conditions of some of her citizens, Liberians will always smile. Often, Liberians will find reasons to celebrate and party, be it the country's famous National County Meet Football Competition, the funeral of a loved one or the birth of a newborn baby. Having gone to hell and back during the dark days of the civil wars which have long been forgotten by the younger generation, those that experienced the wars believe that one day Liberia will rise like a phoenix from its ashes and soar to an unbelievable height. This can only happen when Liberians begin to look under their feet and around them. The reason being, what it takes to develop Liberia and its human resources is right under the ground and not in Washington DC or London, Paris, and Berlin. A country such as Liberia with such a great promise, all it takes is a patriotic and nationalistic leader like George Weah who have sold himself to the Liberian people and the world to be the one who can break the cycle of poverty and develop the country using its vast natural resources.

Chapter 23

Changing Liberia to What It Should Be

Liberia, having been assaulted and plundered by Samuel K. Doe, Overrun, and destroyed by Charles Taylor, used, and abused by Ellen Johnson-Sirleaf, and has now fallen into the inexperienced arms of George Manneh Weah like a new lover filled with venoms of the past, should never remain what it is. It should be transformed into what it ought to be. As a nation, Liberia has never had the chance to live out its full potential due to how it had been managed by past leaders. George Weah and the next generation of Liberian leaders should never allow Liberia to remain what it was when they assumed state power. Rather, they should build and make it into what it ought to be as the oldest independent country on the African Continent. Being the oldest free nation and free of European colonialism and European exploitations, Liberia has remained underdeveloped and mired by corrupt leaders that have badly managed it. Sometimes the ordinary Liberians are tempted to ask this hard question, "What are the causes of poverty in Liberia which is the oldest independent country in Sub-Saharan Africa?" The answer may somehow be multifaceted, but many academics believe that some of the main reasons are, corruption, government conflict, laziness on the part of the ordinary citizens, lack of vision and innovation, and the lack of patriotism. The new leader of Liberia should try to rid itself of governmental corruption that has been the major epidemic infiltrating many of the other sectors of Liberian society. A recent report by Transparency International, cited that the low public sector salaries and a lack of decent training have created the incentive for corruption in Liberia.

Many Liberians believe that George Weah and the CDC have a perfect storm on their backs to move Liberia into a positively new direction. Many think that Mr. Weah and the CDC have the opportunity to restore citizens' faith in their government and rescue the country's young men and women from the streets and out of the strong grips of poverty. With the right partners and associates, George Weah and his CDC coalition can put Liberia on a better path to prosperity, only if they want to. Past leaders have mostly failed to cleanse themselves of corruption—they have used revenue generated from the country's natural resources for themselves and their inner cycle. These previous unpatriotic leaders failed to utilize the country's natural resources in a productive way. For Liberia to thrive, George Weah needs to be more patriotic in his deeds rather than words—he needs to be tough on corruption, even if it is committed by his own family or one of his best friends. As a leader for a struggling economy, the world is watching him. In retrospect, Liberia is not a poor country. Rather, it has only been poorly managed by its leaders, many of whom do not have love for the country. What the people of Liberia know is that the country is rich with mineral wealth including iron ore, timber, diamonds, rubber, and gold, just to name a few, but the wealth from these natural resources of the country have never been used to the maximum benefit of all its citizens. Liberia's natural resource management has continually dealt with a high level of corruption and governance issues. Liberians can only enjoy their country's wealth if the natural resource management can remain uncorrupted. If this can happen, the country can use these mineral resources in a way to bring in legitimate funding that will change the living conditions of the ordinary citizens. Liberians should never be allowed to suffer in this day and age, especially given the fact that the country has vast human and natural resources available.

The young men and women should never be used to as war machines and killers like they had been used by former warlords. George Weah and the next generation of Liberian leaders should protect the precious jewels of the country from being used to destroy their own country and people. According to the United Nations and the IMF, the cause of poverty in Liberia is that during the wars, more than 250,000 people lost their lives in a conflict that was not their own making. Many Liberian children were forced to fight in these wars and have had few opportunities to adjust back to a normal civilian life. This then results in them turning to crimes and a life of perpetual poverty without the necessary intervention. If one goes into the ghettos and boroughs around Monrovia and in other places around the country, there are males and females Zokos and Zokas (names for drug users and or addict) that are bent on abusing drugs and other controlled substances daily. The fact of the matter is that Liberia was never like this, and it should never remain this way.

Following the end of the civil wars in Liberia, the country has become Africa's biggest transit point for drugs being transported to Europe and the Americas. Every year in Liberia, tons of illicit drugs, mostly Cocaine from Nigerian and South America are brought into the country at an alarming rate. Hundreds of youths are recruited daily nationwide by illicit drug dealers in ghettos and on street corners in Monrovia and in other places around the country. Many of these recruits come from ghettos and slums all over the country as they are moved toward the disorderly use of illicit drugs in Liberia. Many of the illicit drugs come from more developed countries like Mexico, Colombia, the United States of America, Nigeria, India and a few other countries from Eastern Europe and Asia. Unfortunately, the drugs are impacting many of the youths who are supposed to be the nation's builder. The sad story is that Liberia's development and progress rests on the shoulders of these teens, and young men as well as young women. George Manneh Weah and the Congress for Democratic Change need to do more than their predecessor in combating the drug epidemic that is ravaging the country's youth. Liberia needs an educated and professional youthful population that will compete in the 21st Century Economy. According to UNESCO, many of the youth living in the ghettos in Liberia are referred to as children from a country of 3Ls or Low, Level Literacy income inhabitants. Many of these poor young men, women and children trying to survive, have been exposed to drugs, crimes of varying levels, and are vulnerable to hardened substances that are coming into the country. This problem needs to be fixed so the youth can stop using their leisure time negatively. The harmful abuse of illicit drugs by young people in Liberia has a very serious long term mental health implication. The result can be seen by the number of mentally ill young people that roam the streets of Monrovia daily, and in other cities and towns across the country.

An estimated 64 percent of Liberians live below the poverty line and 1.3 million live in extreme poverty, out of a population of 4.6 million, according to World Food Programme (WFP) and the International Monetary Fund (IMF) reports on Liberia. What makes the situation bad in Liberia is the country's dependency on imports, which does not help with its agricultural markets already being integrated poorly by the government. There are inadequate rural road infrastructures, limited smallholder participation in value chains and restrained institutional capacity of farmers' organizations. According to the WFP, Food security is also affecting 41 percent of the population, making chronic malnutrition very high in remote towns and villages all over Liberia. The long fought civil wars played a negative part in destroying the subsistence farming system that existed in the country since its independence in 1847. George Weah and the CDC should never forget to zoom-in on agriculture, especially mechanized-farming as a way of combating hunger, which is a catalyst to so many of Liberia's instabilities. Liberia's watchers hope that whenever he acquires power, he should strive to fix hunger, support innovation and creativity, and encourage investing in regional railroad project that will increase trade and other forms of commerce among the people of Sierra Leone, Guinea, and Cote d'Ivoire, and then fight the incurable disease called 'CORRUPTION' wherever it shows up.

When he assumes power, it will only be prudent for George Manneh Weah to surround himself with the rightful people that will help him achieve his dreams when he becomes president of

Liberia. Anything short of that will lead to his political demise. When he's lucky enough to become president, which is inevitable, he should make Liberians become more self-reliant and less dependent on foreign aids and the trapdoor of Chinese, US, and IMF's loans. Currently in Liberia, the people are still benefiting from the work of some organizations like Mercy Corps, which is bringing aid to those in poverty. The fact is that these aids from NGOs are not helping the people to become creative. Instead, it creates the cycle of dependability on outside sources for very basic things like salt, soap, and safe drinking water. Some of these organizations are providing water, food, and teaching locals how to provide for themselves in a developing economy. Many of these organizations believe that they are helping to fix Liberia's market gaps as well as helping its economy recover. While many of these assertions might be true, some of the results are not sustainable. Pundits want Mr. Weah and his party to Liberianize some of these initiatives that are often headed by international NGOs. Though Liberia is slowly on track of overcoming poverty, Liberians need to ultimately get involved in this recovery process because more help is needed than ever before. With financial assistance from other countries including the United States of America, when corruption is stopped, Liberia and Liberians can emerge out of the powerful clutches of poverty.

No matter how one frames the current situation in Liberia, be it good or bad, George Manneh Weah and future political leaders should remake Liberia into what it should be for generations to come. Political 'Fat Cats and Vultures' should be destroyed in whatever form they exist. For Liberia to become what it ought to be, economic equality should be championed, social equality for women should become the law, young boys and girls should be rescued from the streets and those that are exploiting them should be sought for and prosecuted to the fullest. Mr. Weah as a future leader of Liberia should learn to put his hand on the arc of Liberian ugly and backward history and bend it toward a brighter day and justice.

Chapter 24

George Weah's Rise to Power

This six-foot two-inch gentle, amazing football legend called George Oppong Forky Klon Jlaleh Gbakugbeh Tarpeh Tanyonoh Manneh Weah, who is believed to be an adversary to cruelty and a lover of justice with eyes that have never forgotten how to cry; and a heart that was once filled with loving disciplines from a God-fearing grand aunty, Emma Brown, is a very happy soul today. Having scored some of the most brilliant goals during his football career, he has finally scored the most important goal of his political career—winning the presidency of Liberia. Still, many of his critics and a few political pundits think that the voters may have emotionally made the biggest mistake of their lives by electing George Manneh Weah as president for a country that is still trying to heal itself of a devastating and brutal civil war, bounce back from the economic devastation of the Ebola Virus Disease, and recover from the bad governance of the previous administration. But for George Weah and his CDC political movement, their rise to power had been a long time coming.

It all started with a dream from a boy born in Ganta, Nimba County and raised by a loving woman in the slums of Clara Town. His rise to power was a dream born in the ghetto of Gibraltar, that he harnessed on street corners of Liberia, in cook shops, and at drinking stalls in Monrovia, and channeled on various football fields around the world. George's dream has come true!

George Manneh Weah's life is a true embodiment of the larger Liberian story which encapsulates the harsh reality of poverty, and a life that he made better for himself than the one he was given at birth. His rise to fame, wealth and state power have been phenomenal in a sociopolitical sense—he defied all the odds that were lined up against him. It can almost be seen as a miracle or a sort of Cinderella Story—coming from nothing to something at the dying moment when others have given up on him. What started as a mere thought from a few friends and political speculators has now turned into reality to the dismay of critics, experts, intellectuals, and Liberia's international partners that once viewed George Weah and the Congress for Democratic Change as a big political risk in the country. For George Weah, he played the game well.

Many outsiders still believe that George Weah is not prepared for the presidency of Liberia. These critics believe that having the weight of a nation on his shoulder is far different from carrying a football team on his shoulder as a team's captain. Yet, his supporters, mainly the young people of Liberia, think he can do better than his predecessors, and that he should be given the chance to do what others haven't done for Liberia. During his struggles for the Executive Mansion, many of George Weah's young supporters never hid their admiration and affinity for him. They have placed their faith in a man who they only know from a distance. Mr. Weah now has the burden to prove his critics wrong in the political arena as he has done on the football field time and time again. But being the captain of a football team or its most talented player pales in comparison to the presidency of a nation like Liberia. Pundits and members of the international community believe that while he may be the best football legend in Africa and was good at leading football clubs to victory in Europe and in other places, many of them believe that he is unable to run a country as good as he does with the football on the pitches. Many people still view him as naïve, unpolished, and lacking gravitas to lead a country like Liberia with a hard-won fragile peace. Whether he knows it or not, George Weah ran a better campaign and made a good alliance in 2017.

The dream of George Weah, the greatest living African football legend who might have been the most unlikely person to become Liberia's president, occupying the Executive Mansion on Capitol Hill in Monrovia, finally came true following the December 26, 2017, presidential runoff election between Joseph N. Boakai of the Unity Party. President Elect George Manneh Weah's journey to the Executive Mansion has been a bumpy one—he made many friends, lost many friends, and made countless enemies along the way. His friends and inner circle have grown and shrunk on many occasions; yet George Weah popularity has sustained. Though Weah was used to winning on the football field, the presidency of Liberia had eluded him ever since he started striking towards the goalpost of the presidency. His steady and persistent stride and efforts came to a happy ending when he finally scored the biggest winning goal of his life on Thursday December 28, 2017, when the NEC of Liberia announced 98% of the results from the runoff election. That day, George Weah's title changed from Mr. Senator to Mr. President. Since the day he was announced as the winner of the presidency, his life has never been the same and it may never be the same going forth. Other than running an excellent campaign and hatching a deal with Ellen, many analysts believe that the Jewel Howard or NPP factor also played a major role in George Weah winning the presidency in 2017.

After the December 28 announcement of the final results of the runoff election, the city of Monrovia erupted with joy and was set ablaze in a frenzy of jubilation by Weah's supporters. The announcement seemed to many of them like they were dreaming because it was what they had been fighting for. There were thousands and thousands of supporters of George Weah dancing, drinking, crying, singing, and shouting battle cries of all kinds in a hysterical cacophony of youthful exuberance to celebrate their hero's victory. For many of them, this was the moment they had all been waiting for the past 12 years. For some of them, he was their savior who had come to save them from the venom of poverty and institutional neglect. But for George Manneh Weah, this was the victory that had eluded him as the Standard Bearer of Liberia's leading opposition political party. Many of his young supporters held him in a god-like status. And for many of the disadvantaged people in the ghetto, most of whom did not have a chance to participate in the affairs of their country, they expected that a George Weah's government would solve their economic, unemployment, healthcare, education, and social problems. Many of them also believed that he would employ them or create jobs that will enable them to change their families' lives.

By winning the election, George Weah created another precedent just as he did in 1995 when he became the first and only African football player to win the African Player of the Year, Ballon d'Or, and the World Best Football Player titles all at once. A trifecta never repeated since and probably will never be duplicated by any other African football super star. On the day of the announcement, Weah became the first World Best athlete to become a president. Using Weah's behemoth achievements as a yardstick, many sports stars and celebrities are going to flood into the arena of politics across Africa and around the world. Many of these celebrities will conjure up the attitude and belief of, "if George Weah can do it, so can I".

Now that he has risen like a phoenix from the ashes of poverty to state power, George Weah has a herculean task ahead of him. He has a country filled with used and abused people that he needs to reconcile and heal of their various maladies and deep wounds. While the excitement and honeymoon are still ongoing, President Weah and the Coalition for Democratic Change government need to come to grips with reality and never make the same mistakes as their predecessors. As would any new administration, there will be false starts in many areas when he gets into office. Hopeful Liberians and many of Liberia's international partners expect Mr. Weah and his new administration to be very swift in turning the corner and breakaway from the past if they are going to be different to fulfill their Change for Hope mantra. In Liberia, the citizens are fickle. Today, they might sing your praises and lift you high in the air, but tomorrow, they will insult, denigrate, and condemn you to hell if you do not live up to their expectations. Still as a young kid on the presidential block, and as a person who has experienced the scorn and disdain of the political establishment, George Manneh Weah needs to govern in a cautiously prudent manner, knowing that it is not every campaign promise that can be fulfilled by a politician.

While Liberia has been stuck at a crossroad since the death of President William R. Tolbert, many of the ordinary citizens are hopeful that maybe a George Manneh Weah administration can move the country past its current dilemma; that is, if he surrounds himself with the right people and the best minds in and out of Liberia. Liberia which is the oldest independent country in Africa is among the least developed countries in Africa and in the world. According to one former interim president of Liberia, Dr. Amos C. Sawyer, there are so many reasons for Liberia's backward state. With mismanagement being on the top of the failure list, lack of patriotism and the country's struggles for sustenance during the scramble for Africa (a time when European powers like Great Britain, France, German, Belgium, Germany, Italy, Spain, Portugal, and other European powers forcefully took ownership of Africans' land for exploitation of their natural and human resources) and colonialism are also contributing factors. Now that it has been more than 40 years since Tolbert's death and the last European direct rule ended in Rhodesia which is now Zimbabwe, Liberia has not made significant progress in terms of infrastructure development like many of the countries across the African Continent that obtained independence from the 1960s through the 1980s. Maybe, just maybe, George Weah presidency can perform one of his Black Magics or Vodoos at the dying moment to save his country from failure just like he did many times over on the football field for the European football clubs he played for. But again, during his professional football career he was surrounded by great players on many of his teams. To replicate some of those magnificent plays he made on the football fields, he must have the best players on his governance team as a way of assuring victory. The question his pundits are now asking is, "Are the members of his leadership team great governance players?"

Now that he had been elected and there exists a popular

belief among many of his supporters and partisans that the United States and other western countries are responsible for many of Liberia's woes, is President Weah going to turn his eyes up Benson Street and Mamba Point where the world's political center of gravity resides, or is he going to look eastward? The election fanfare can only last for so long, but the real work of international diplomacy can define a president's administration and presidency—especially when the country cannot sustain itself with its own undeveloped resources. Many analysts hope that George Weah will meticulously turn his head and eyes toward Benson Street, but he should do it with vigilance.

George Weah getting elected by more than 50% of the Liberian population democratically qualifies him to become president of Liberia. However, being president requires geopolitical understanding and governance maturity to steer the diplomatic high waters and many domestic storms that need to be navigated. It will be wise for the Weah administration to make every effort to be plugged into 1600 Pennsylvania Avenue and other decision-making enclaves in Washington DC and in other countries in Europe and elsewhere around the world. Similarly, effort should be made towards building relationships with any occupant of 10 Downing Street in the United Kingdom. This can only be done with a great team and savvy people that have the right connections in those hard-to-reach places. Many observers hope George Weah will build an integrated advisory team that will be composed of independents and opposition politicians while developing an ear that is willing to hear criticism rather than supplications and empty praises which are not prerequisites to success. The president is president for all of Liberia, and not only for his close friends or family, or those that supported him during his 12-year of struggles in which he endured insults and personal attacks, political backstabbing and ship-jumping by close friends and associates.

George Manneh Weah is a people's magnet—he intrigues people from across generations and from different nationalities. As the president of a divided nation, he can use that personality and his magnetic charisma to reconcile his people and get them on the same national page. Many observers wish for his first term in office to be a priority that is centered around working very hard to reconcile and unify the Liberian people. While he has made a plethora of promises to his support once he becomes president, many analysts know that living up to those promises will be impossible for President Elect George Weah. Experts believe that for Mr. Weah to achieve great things in his presidency, he ought not live by his campaign promises. The reason being, how to achieve those campaign promises is far different from the reality he now finds himself in—a divided country, a broken economy, a sagging global commodities price, and many other problems. As it is with the previous government's failure to unify the country due to former President Sirleaf's involvement in the civil wars, Liberia is dying for a leader who will unite the people and heal their deep wounds. George Weah needs to do better because the people are still bitter with one another due to the history of Americo-Liberian domination, the 1980 coup and horrific acts that ensued, and the 14 years long civil conflict that nearly destroyed the country. While at it, he should never forget about enforcing justice and rule of law. Many Liberians in the Diaspora and Liberia's international partners believe that implementation of the Truth and Reconciliation Commission's recommendations will also be an important testament to his fortitude as president. Everyone considers the TRC recommendations to be a thorny issue to deal with, but there is no wrong way to righting a wrong than doing the right thing.

The fact of the matter is that justice and reconciliation are like two twin-brothers from the same parents; one looks backward while the other looks forward. It can be very difficult to achieve reconciliation in the absence of justice, especially when heinous crimes have been committed. The new President needs to incrementally address these two sensitive issues without putting the already achieved fragile peace at risk. From afar, the task may seem impossible, but the solution may be simpler than what is seen with the eyes. One key school of thought would urge the President to first take the approach that the Chinese use to resolve a problem within a Chinese village or town. With the Chinese village approach, whenever there is a problem between two warring Chinese clans or villages, the elders do not try to resolve the problem between the two conflicting parties. Rather, they first try to repair the broken relationship between the parties. Once the relationship is repaired, the solution sometimes works itself out. On the other hand, in the west, it is the problem that is solved rather than repairing the relationship between the parties. With the latter approach, the problem will generally show up again whenever a newer or later generation emerges. It is the relationship between tribes and ethnic groups in Liberia that needs to be repaired because many Liberians are directly or indirectly related either by birth, marriage, association or by their allegiance to the Red, White, and Blue—the flag that every Liberian pledge allegiance to.

Pundits believe that for President George Manneh Weah to become an effective president, he must come with a heart cleansed of all forms of corruption, past grievances, vengeance, malice, grudge, and every past hurt and pain that others may have caused him. A leader should rise above the fray and embrace his or her enemies while looking straight in their eyes and saying, "I have forgiven you. Now let us join hands and rebuild our country for the next generation." As president, George Weah doesn't have to be everyone's friend, but preferably be a friend with those who will tell him the truth, even if he disagrees with that person. As the leader of a traumatized nation, there are several fundamental things that can inspire success and make a lasting change and impact on the lives of the people. Prominent among them are the appropriate use of power and authority for the betterment of his people. Many Liberia's observers want George Weah to stick to the developmental game plan that he has for the country—that is if he has one. But how a president should rule, and how a president rules is far different when it comes to reality. Power is like a young and beautiful woman who loves adventurous young men. It is like a voluptuous young woman living on a street filled with lonely and horny young men looking for sexual action—she may do some of the most unorthodox things for self-gratification or survival. Power must be used to the best of the president's full discretion, but not loosely. While he may have had a good upbringing, as president analysts think that he needs to unlearn some of those good mores instilled in him by his loving and God-fearing grand aunty, Ma Emma. To get Liberia to a place only he envisions, Political analyst think that George Weah needs to learn how to be able not to be good, or kind to his friends, political allies, supporters, and the scores of opportunists who will break the laws of the land. If he wants his hard-earned legacy to live forever, he should be a fair implementer of justice and the rule of law. As a seemingly principled man who has espoused peace and shown love and care for the Liberian people over the years, the rule of law should be his guiding principles of engagement in his presidency rather than the mother Teresa's principles of Ma Emma. As president, if one of his family members or a close friend commits a crime, he needs to allow the law to take its course, even if his emotions will be broken for a time. Being a person who is viewed by many as an enemy of cruelty and a lover of justice, he needs to allow justice to give an unjust person the taste of their own bitter medicine that he or she has given society or others to swallow. Liberia, being the small country it is, everyone is somehow related or at least knows one another in some degree of separation. Opposition politicians and members within the CDC want President George Weah to focus his efforts on giving Liberia a fresh start in the comity of nations by making the country a hub of commerce and industry, and a safe and secured place to live. Pundits want the President's constitutional responsibility to be for the ensuring of justice prevails and to take its course in every aspect of Liberian society. Breaking down the long held patriarchal barriers or strongholds that allows most men to discriminate against women, subject them to second class citizenship, or treat them unequal should be a goal of his. In this 21st Century, men and women are equal.

Many of George Manneh Weah's supporters believe that his rise to power may have been ordained by God. If that is the case, then he needs to learn from his predecessors. Some of these past leaders did great things. Some had positive leadership characteristics, though most left a bitter taste in the mouths of the ordinary Liberians. Supporters of the African football legend want him to become several Liberian leaders in one. They want Mr. Weah to learn and adopt the patriotic characters of Samuel Kanyon Doe who wanted Liberia to be one of the best countries in Africa that could be compared to any European nation. Under Doe's administration, there was rapid development of the nation in a very short period. But Doe's ethnocentric approach to governing and his murderous dictatorial behavior caused thirteen of the fifteen tribes to hate him and the Krahn people of Grand Gedeh County. Doe finally died a horrendous death at the hands of Prince Y. Johnson after he was encouraged by the United States of America Central Intelligence Agency local operative and leaders within the Economic Community of West African States Monitoring Group, ECOMOG to leave his fortress at the Barclay Training Center (BTC) for a meeting at the Freeport of Monrovia with ECOMOG military officials. The meeting was meant for Doe to get on a boat that was secretly sent at the port by the U.S. government after the country's airports had been captured by Charles Taylor's rebel forces. The boat was to take Doe to Guinea where it would later be taken to Togo to seek political asylum. At the Freeport, he was captured by the Independent National Patriotic Front of Liberia, INPFL, rebels of Mr. Johnson who is now a Senator from Nimba County. George Weah's supporters are urging him to learn and assume the tactics of Charles Ghankay Taylor who possessed the characters of strength and fear as a rebel leader and later, as president of the republic of Liberia. With a Taylor personality, George Manneh Weah will be a strongman, feared like a lion by both friends and enemies alike, but resorting to the dictatorial tendencies of Taylor could spell the early demise of his administration like Taylor who did not complete his first tenure in office. They believe that if George Weah will draw investors into the country and make members of the international community take him seriously, he needs to emulate the charming, cunning, articulate, and sweet-talking qualities of Ellen Johnson-Sirleaf, while eschewing her willful permission of a corrupt culture. With an embodiment of the positive characteristics of these three leaders of Liberia, he might be one of the greatest presidents in the history of Liberia. Without some of these good characters, they believe that he would be one of the worst ever.

For most leaders in Africa, political contamination has always been a big problem. Sometimes it is not done by choice;

rather, it is sometimes done inevitably due to a rotten political system that exists within many of these countries. While it can be conjectured that George Manneh Weah wants to do the best for his country, just wanting is not enough. Many analysts believe that if Weah avoids getting contaminated by old corrupt and Machiavellian politicians and an extractive political economy will be very helpful to him as a first term president. Progressive CDCians want President Weah to only liaise with members of the old order who can help open international doors for him in the west, far and near east, and in African countries like Nigeria, South Africa, Ghana, and many others. The reason is simple. Many old politicians may want to relive their past glories without considering the change in times and the current state of their country. But for those that are patriotic enough and want the best for their country, they will strive so very hard to support the current leadership for their country to succeed in this modern era by helping the leader to navigate international politics. Sometimes with the involvement of the old guard comes the running of a shadow government (which is a government-in-waiting that is prepared to take control of a nation in response to certain events. Or it can be a quasi-government that operates behind the scenes with impunity, and its decisions often undermine the legitimate government in power). George Manneh Weah's supporters are urging him to never allow anyone to undermine his presidency with the running of such a shadow state. These supporters that have been in the political trenches with him, want him to use the power of the presidency to the fullest, especially for the benefits of the Liberian people.

The presidency is huge and bigger than anything George Manneh Weah had previously thought it was. Therefore, he needs to see a reason to reprogram himself into thinking as a president and behave like the great person others perceive him to be. As it has proven time and again, Liberia is a very tough country to govern, given its bitter and unstable history. The people need to sometimes be pampered and massaged with velvet gloves around steel fists. If a Liberian is given authority over others as a minister or managing director of a government's agency, historically, abuse of power and corruption are two things that typically become the end results of that individual's leadership, especially if he or she is not result of closely monitored by the president or the law. As a populist politician, analysts want Mr. Weah to secure the interests of the common majority rather than his own interests should be a huge priority. The focus cannot be on seeking praise or commendation from brown nosers and ass-kissers. It should be on finding solutions to the bread-and-butter issues facing the country and the common people, especially the unemployed and uneducated youth.

While pundits and many of his critics vehemently believe that Weah is a complete chicken who is unable to stand up to a few individuals within his own party for so many unknown reasons, Mr. Weah needs to look some of his hardcore CDCians in the eyes and speak truth to them. Since he has gained the confidence of more than 61.5% of the population during the second-round of voting, he needs to now begin working hard on earning the respect of the rest of the Liberian people and the leaders of the world. The sixty-four dollars question many outsiders will ask as he has now achieved his dream of the presidency is, "How will he gain the respect of the world when he is surrounded by so many loyal and self-serving friends?" Foreign analysts, friends of Liberia, and non CDCians are now urging President George Manneh Weah to take a centrist approach to governing Liberia. They want him to recognize his actions, and whether good or bad, execute them to benefit most of the population. As stated earlier, as a leader of an illiterate society like Liberia whose citizens' loyalty is never guaranteed, Mr. Weah needs to unlearn some of his good upbringings, and learn how not to personalize rigid governance. To appear smart and progressive, President Weah needs to build on the success of his predecessors through the adaptation of robust economic and social agenda while at the same time harshly reprimanding those loyal friends and appointees of his that will be involved in ignoble activities such as corruption, favoritism, cronyism, political pay-to-play schemes, brown nosing, backstabbing, and any form or act that will put an ugly dimple into his future records as president of Liberia. Well meaning critics and ardent supporters of Mr. Weah are wishing him success on his new victory that many see as a new beginning for the younger generation of Liberians that have chosen to part take in their country's politics. These supporters and other well wishers want George to play the political game right if he wants to strike the right political tone. They're urging him to hold the value of the Coalition of Democratic Change that helped to win him the election.

On the other hand pundits and many scholars on Liberia believe that Mr. Weah is still not prepared to be president given his lack of policymaking and visibility as a senator of Montserrado County along with his lack of real world work or business experience. They believe that as a man with limited experience and without political maturity, he is going to be used and manipulated by silver-tongue and underhand politicians for their own political end. But whether George Weah is ill-prepared for the office of president, his supporter and those who helped him win the critical election in Liberia believe that he should be given the chance to prove himself. While it is a fair statement for George to be given a chance to lead Liberia, it is not fair to the Liberia people to have their future to be experimented with by someone without the foresight nor the hindsight as their leader. Whether critics are quick to write him off, it is only a matter of time that President Weah's records will vindicate him or prove his critics right. As always, time is humanity's greatest asset and its unbiased judge. Only time will tell!

WEAH'S PHOTO BURSTS

(*above left*) George Weah as a preteen. Various images of George's childhood home in the ghetto of Gibraltar on Bushrod Island.

(*top left*) Entrance to George Weah's childhood home in Gibraltar. Areal views of Gibraltar and the Samuel K. Doe Community.

Pictorial collage of George Weah. (*From top-to-bottom*), Debah and Weah, Weah in IE jersey, George and friends, Weah in Wells Hairston, Weah in Cameroon in Tonnerre Kalara Club jersey.

Pictorial collage of George and Clar. (*abover left*) on their wedding day i 1993, and various pictures at in their home.

George Weah and Family. (*Left to Right*) *Teta, George Weah Sr.*
George Weah Jr. (AKA Champ), Clar Weah, Timothy (Tim).

Pictorial collage of George Weah and Family.

Pictorial collage of George Weah's professional football career in Europe.

Pictorial collage of George Weah's professional football career in Europe
Bottom two images show George during a Lone Star game and IE USA.

Pictorial collage showcasing George Weah's awards and honors.

Pictorial collage showcasing George Weah's golden years. In this picture w
see African football legends, King Pele, Denzel, Cedric, George and Taylo

Pictorial collage showcasing George Weah's entry into the unchartered water of presidential politics in Liberia.

Pictorial collage showcasing George Weah's 2005 presidential campaign.

Pictorial collage showcasing George Weah's 2005 presidential campaign.

Pictorial collage showcasing George Weah's 2005 presidential campaign and other activities in Liberia.

Pictorial collage showcasing George Weah's graduation from college with a master's degree.

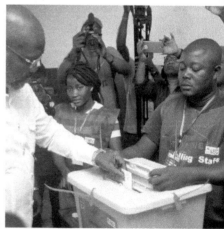

Pictorial collage showcasing George Weah's 2011 presidential campaign with Winston Tubman as lead candidate, and other activities in Liberia.

Pictorial collage showcasing George Weah's 2017 election victory.

PHOTO CREDITS

Organization or Person	Link or Name	Comment
Life Blogger	https://lifebogger.com/george-weah-childhood-story-plus-untold-biography-facts/	George and Clar
Life Blogger	https://lifebogger.com/george-weah-childhood-story-plus-untold-biography-facts/	George and Family
Life Blogger	https://lifebogger.com/george-weah-childhood-story-plus-untold-biography-facts/	Angry George
Life Blogger	https://lifebogger.com/george-weah-childhood-story-plus-untold-biography-facts/	George and TB Joshua
Nigerian Monitor	https://lifebogger.com/george-weah-childhood-story-plus-untold-biography-facts/	Weah and Family 2
Getty Images	https://www.gettyimages.com/detail/news-photo/liberian-soc-cer-player-george-weah-af-rican-gold-bal-lon-1995-news-pho-to/905587996?adppopup=true	George and Ballon d'Or
Getty Images	https://www.gettyimages.com/detail/news-photo/liberian-soccer-player-george-weah-and-his-wife-clar-news-pho-to/905587924?adppopup=true	Weah at Home with Wife
Getty Images	https://www.gettyimages.com/detail/news-photo/liberian-soccer-playr-george-weah-with-coach-arsene-wenger-news-pho-to/905588016?adppopup=true	George and Coach

Getty Images	https://www.gettyimages.com/detail/news-photo/liberian-soccer-player-george-weah-his-wife-clar-and-his-news-photo/905587852?adppopup=true	Weah and Family 3
Getty Images	https://www.gettyimages.com/detail/news-photo/liberian-soccer-playr-george-weah-at-home-news-photo/905587942?adppopup=true	Weah Posing 1
Getty Images	https://www.gettyimages.com/detail/news-photo/liberias-president-elect-and-former-football-star-george-news-photo/908789834?adppopup=true	Weah and Ellen Sirleaf
Getty Images	https://www.gettyimages.com/detail/news-photo/liberian-soccer-player-george-weah-news-photo/905587990?adppopup=true	Weah Posing 2
Getty Images	https://www.gettyimages.com/detail/news-photo/liberian-soccer-player-george-weah-and-his-wife-clar-news-photo/905587930?adppopup=true	Weah and Clar
Getty Images	https://www.gettyimages.com/detail/news-photo/liberian-soccer-player-george-weah-and-his-wife-clar-news-photo/905587932?adppopup=true	Weah and Clar 2

Getty Images	https://www.gettyimages. com/detail/news-photo/ george-weah-of-libe- ria-meets-south-african-pres- ident-nelson-news-pho- to/1243073?adppopup=true	George and Mendella
Getty Images	https://www.gettyimages.com/ detail/news-photo/george- weah-and-roberto-baggio- of-ac-milan-poses-for-photo- news-photo/1216995352?adp- popup=true	George and Baggio
Getty Images	https://www.gettyimages.com/ detail/news-photo/presidential- candidate-george-weah-walks- through-a-crowd-news-pho- to/56118505?adppopup=true	George 2005 Runoff
Getty Images	https://www.getty- images.com/detail/ news-photo/liberian-pres- idential-candidate-and-in- ternational-soccer-news-pho- to/55895645?adppopup=true	George 2005 Election Campaign
Getty Images	https://www.gettyimages. com/detail/news-photo/ soccer-athlete-george- weah-and-guests-speak- on-stage-at-the-news-pho- to/51073510?adppopup=true	George at Epsy Award
Getty Images	https://www.gettyimages. com/detail/news-photo/ george-weah-trophee- onze-mondial-photo-alain- gadoffre-icon-news-pho- to/644841276?adppopup=true	George With Onze Award

Getty Images	https://www.gettyimages. com/detail/news-photo/ george-weah-report- age-magazine-liberia-pho- to-alain-gadoffre-news-pho- to/644841696?adppopup=true	George and Diadora
Getty Images	https://www.getty- images.com/detail/ news-photo/liberian-pres- idential-candidate-and-in- ternational-soccer-news-pho- to/55884639?adppopup=true	George in Church
Getty Images	https://www.gettyimages. com/detail/news-photo/ cape-town-south-afri- ca-liberian-football-play- er-and-former-news-pho- to/75550645?adppopup=true	George Weah in Robin Is- land, South Africa
Getty Images	https://www.gettyimages. com/detail/news-photo/ george-weah-magazine- ac-milan-photo-alain- gadoffre-icon-news-pho- to/644856240?adppopup=true	George Alone at Home in Milan Italy
Getting Images	https://www.gettyimages. com/detail/news-photo/ george-weah-magazine- ac-milan-photo-alain- gadoffre-icon-news-pho- to/644856266?adppopup=true	George Play- ing Pool
Getty Images	https://www.gettyimages. com/detail/news-photo/ african-legends-south-afri- ca-2010-bid-ambassadors-abe- de-news-photo/2697565?adp- popup=true	George and African Players

Photo Credits

Getty Images	https://www.gettyimages.com/detail/news-photo/george-weah-the-liberia-and-ac-milan-player-relaxes-in-news-photo/1236054?adppopup=true	George 1996 African Cup of Nations in South Africa
Getty Images	https://www.gettyimages.com/detail/news-photo/cedric-the-entertainer-and-george-weah-during-2004-espy-news-photo/117889785?adppopup=true	George and Cedric
Getty Images	https://www.gettyimages.com/detail/news-photo/denzel-washingon-and-george-weah-winner-of-the-arthur-ashe-news-photo/117888561?adppopup=true	George and Denzel
Getty Images	https://www.gettyimages.com/detail/news-photo/former-french-football-players-and-coaches-claude-leroy-and-news-photo/1022603806?adppopup=true	George and Former Coach
Getty Images	https://www.gettyimages.com/detail/news-photo/george-weah-magazine-ac-milan-photo-alain-gadoffre-icon-news-photo/644856278?adppopup=true	George At Home
Getty Images	https://www.gettyimages.com/detail/news-photo/george-weah-report-age-magazine-liberia-photo-alain-gadoffre-news-photo/644841216?adppopup=true	George Riding Bicycle

Getty Images	https://www.gettyimages.com/detail/news-photo/african-soccer-legends-and-sa-2010-bid-ambassadors-roger-news-photo/2697170?adppopup=true	George and African Players
Getty Images	https://www.gettyimages.com/detail/news-photo/george-weah-and-guest-during-2004-espy-awards-backstage-and-news-photo/117891765?adppopup=true	George Weah and His Guest at The Epsy Award
Getty Images	https://www.gettyimages.com/detail/news-photo/denzel-washingn-with-george-weah-news-photo/117924138?adppopup=true	George and Denzel
Getty Images	https://www.gettyimages.com/detail/news-photo/george-weah-of-liberia-argues-with-the-referee-during-the-news-photo/1620442?adppopup=true	George Weah Argues With Referee During 1997 World Cup Qualifier
Getty Images	https://www.gettyimages.com/detail/news-photo/george-weah-of-ac-milan-scores-a-goal-during-the-serie-a-news-photo/1552308?adppopup=true	George Scores Against Juventus
Getty Images	https://www.gettyimages.com/detail/news-photo/george-weah-of-chelsea-poses-in-the-dressing-room-area-news-photo/102975893?adppopup=true	George at Chelsea

Getty Images	https://www.gettyimages.com/detail/news-photo/georges-weah-magazine-marseille-news-photo/819923178?adppopup=true	George in Marseille France
Getty Images	https://www.gettyimages.com/detail/news-photo/an-unconscious-woman-is-carried-by-supporters-of-liberian-news-photo/55881509?adppopup=true	Weah's Supporters During a Rally
Getty Images	https://www.gettyimages.com/detail/news-photo/casual-portrait-of-george-weah-with-school-children-news-photo/81446640?adppopup=true	George at a School
Getty Images	https://www.gettyimages.com/detail/news-photo/charles-taylor-georges-weah-magazine-milan-ac-photo-alain-news-photo/644788710?adppopup=true	George and Clar Visit Charles Taylor
Getty Images	https://www.gettyimages.com/detail/news-photo/former-liberian-football-player-george-weah-president-of-news-photo/454956824?adppopup=true	George Donates to ELWA
Getty Images	https://www.gettyimages.com/detail/news-photo/pele-falcao-and-george-weah-at-the-fifa-100-best-players-news-photo/50809080?adppopup=true	George and Pele at FIFA 100 Best Player Award

Getty Images	https://www.gettyimages.com/detail/news-photo/george-weah-of-paris-st-germain-gets-to-grips-with-sergi-of-news-photo/1204465?adp-popup=true	George Chocks Another Player
WTFoot	https://www.wtfoot.com/legend/george-weah/	George and Sons
Blakk Pepper	https://blakkpepper.com/2018/01/who-will-george-weah-settle-on-as-first-lady-clar-or-mamie-doe/	George Breakfast in Bed
Front Page Africa	https://frontpageafricaonline.com/obituary/liberia-family-of-late-senator-doe-sheriff-hails-president-weah-legislature-for-befitting-burial/	George and Geraldine Doe
Getty Images	George Weah and Jean Pierre Papin	George Weah and Jean Pierre Papin
Getty Images	https://www.gettyimages.com/detail/news-photo/charles-taylor-georges-weah-magazine-milan-ac-photo-alain-news-photo/644788692?adppopup=true	Charles Taylor and George Weah
Getty Images	https://www.gettyimages.com/detail/news-photo/georges-weah-mona-co-juventus-turin-1-2fina-le-champions-news-photo/644841516?adppopup=true	George Wea Profile Picture

Getty Images	https://www.gettyimages.com/detail/news-photo/liberian-presidential-contender-george-weah-gets-input-from-news-photo/56141256?adppopup=true	George Weah and Cole Bangalu Reject Election Results
Getty Images	https://www.gettyimages.com/detail/news-photo/liberian-hero-star-and-presidential-candidate-george-weah-news-photo/56118167?adppopup=true	George and His Mother
Getty Images	https://www.gettyimages.com/detail/news-photo/former-football-star-george-weah-candidate-in-the-liberian-news-photo/55884045?adppopup=true	George Weah and His Mother Anna
Getty Images	https://www.gettyimages.com/detail/news-photo/former-football-star-george-weah-candidate-in-the-liberian-news-photo/55884056?adppopup=true	George and His Mother Hannah
Getty Images	https://www.gettyimages.com/detail/news-photo/weakened-woman-is-held-on-stage-by-a-supporter-of-liberian-news-photo/55881471?adppopup=true	Weah and Supporters
Getty Images	https://www.gettyimages.com/detail/news-photo/liberian-opposition-presidential-candidate-winston-tubman-news-photo/131545750?adppopup=true	Solo, Weah, and Tubman

Photo Credits

Getty Images	https://www.gettyimages.com/detail/news-photo/liberian-presidential-candidate-winston-tubman-and-his-news-photo/129359566?adppopup=true	Weah and Tubman
Getty Images	https://www.gettyimages.com/detail/news-photo/liberias-main-opposition-congress-for-democratic-changes-news-photo/128782601?adppopup=true	Tubman and Weah
Getty Images	https://www.gettyimages.com/detail/news-photo/liberian-soccer-player-george-weah-with-his-son-george-jr-p-news-photo/905588020	George and His Son Champ
Four Four Two	https://www.fourfourtwo.com/us/news/wenger-responds-invite-george-weahs-inauguration-liberia-president	George and Wenger
Life Blogger	https://lifebogger.com/george-weah-childhood-story-plus-untold-biography-facts/	Weah As a Teen
Reuters	https://www.reuters.com/article/uk-soccer-africa-liberia-weah-idUKKBN0OP1A320150609	George Weah and Clar in Liberia
Ameyaw Debrah	https://ameyawdebrah.com/photos-liberian-president-george-weah-celebrates-27th-marriage-anniversary-with-wife/	George and Clar Wedding

PHOTO CREDITS

Ameyaw Debrah	https://ameyawdebrah.com/photos-liberian-president-george-weah-celebrates-27th-marriage-anniversary-with-wife/	George and Clar Wedding Dance
IE MSA Liberia	IE Facebook page	George Weah
Tonnerre KC	https://daydaynews.cc/en/sports/291057.html	George at TKC
WSJ	https://www.wsj.com/articles/george-weah-former-soccer-star-wins-liberian-presidential-election-1514496422	George Weah at CDC Headquarters
Black Star News	https://www.blackstarnews.com/global-politics/africa/how-george-weah-went-back-to-school-and-won-liberias	George Weah and Jacob Zuma
Moses Saygbe Jr.	https://www.facebook.com/moses.saygbe.9	George with teammates

BIBLIOGRAPHY

NEWSPAPERS

Daily Observers Newspaper, various date (Liberia).
FIFA Magazine, various publications and dates (Europe).
Front Page Africa, various dates (Liberia).
News Newspaper, various dates (Liberia)
Inquirer Newspaper, various dates (Liberia)
Daily Mail, various dates (UK)
The Guardian, various dates (UK)
The New York Times, various (USA)

WEBSITES & DATABASES

Youtube, https://www.youtube.com/results?search_query=george+op-pong+weah
PSD Database, https://pesstatsdatabase.com/PSD/PlayerClassic. php?Id=234&Era=2
FBREF, https://fbref.com/en/players/186014ec/George-Weah
DBpedia, https://dbpedia.org/page/George Weah
WEFUT, https://wefut.com/player/15/2504/george-weah
GSA, https://globalsportsarchive.com/people/soccer/george-weah/109805/
Shick, Tom W. "Emigrants to Liberia, 1820-1843," www.disc.wisc.edu/liberia/ pdfs/alphalist.html.

BIBLIOGRAPHY

van der Kraaij, Fred P. M. "Liberia: Past and Present of Africa's Oldest Republic," www.liberiapastandpresent.org.

BOOKS AND JOURNALS

Hahn, Niels. *Two Centuries of US Military Operations in Liberia: Challenges of Resistance and Compliance.* Air University Press, Maxwell Air Force Base, Alabama, 2020
Yancy, Ernest. *Historical Lights of Liberia's Yesterday and Today.* Aldine Publishing Company, 1985
Guannu, Joseph. *Liberian History Up to 1847.* Sabanoh Printing Press, 1983

INDEX

CREDITS

Design by Xzibit Art Inc.
Jacket design by Xzibit Art Inc.
Jacket photograph © Getty Images

CPSIA information can be obtained
at www.ICGtesting.com
Printed in the USA
BVHW040947070222
628285BV00011B/401

9 780989 804295